Cover illustration of the Annie Cade
courtesy K. C. Native Sons Collection
Western Historical Manuscripts, UMKC

Published by Indian Creek Books
Kansas City, Missouri

Printed in the United States of America

For additional copies, write to

Indian Creek Books

P.O. Box 8731, Kansas City, Missouri 64114-0731

ISBN 0-9670316-2-1
Library of Congress Catalog Card No.00-190032

Early Days
On The
MISSOURI
RIVER

JOHN EDWARD HICKS

Steamer Sioux City on Her Last Voyage, 1864

Indian Creek Books
P.O. Box 8731
Kansas City, MO   64114-0731

Forward

The effort here has been to tell the story of the Missouri River as it was from the time of Lewis and Clark ascending the river until the steamboats went off the stream approximately a century later. The story is of a time when life was lived upon the wharves and packet boats and in the river towns from St. Louis to Fort Benton; of the picturesque activities along the river when anything not close to its tawny flood was lost in the obscurity of the hinterland.

The story of the river then was the story of the land through which it flowed. Forts were built and cities founded with an eye to the effect upon them of the great waterway. The river was the essence of virtually all history made within its valley and was not without its influence on much history made beyond its reaches, when it was the great highway to the West.

Old riverains said of a skillful pilot that "he kept his steamboat in the river," meaning the most navigable part of the stream, not necessarily the deepest nor the swiftest part, but certainly not the shoal waters. This narrative ascends the river leisurely, but strives at all times to "keep in the river" even on those occasions when, lured by the story of some sleepy old river town, it "goes up the hill," it endeavors to stay within sound of the steamboat's whistle.

A deep and abiding interest still is attached to the experiences of persons who lived on and by the river. There are also wayside gleanings as the story of the river unfolds at once pleasing and instructive, which tend to give its history a patina of charm.

This, then, is the story of the people whose lives were touched by the river, who traveled over or along its waters; or who lived, worked, played, adventured, and sometimes died along the muddy stream.

JOHN EDWARD HICKS
Kansas City, Missouri

Contents

Chapter One

St. Louis Under the Hill

The little French village of St. Louis lay snuggled against the bold shore of limestone rocks that formed the west bank of the Mississippi River. The simple cabins gleamed white in the sun, and the old martello tower and white-washed stone forts atop the hill formed the background of the village, giving it a quaint, medieval look, an air of romance. Only here and there more pretentious homes prophesied the greatness that lay in the future. At the turn of the century, St. Louis was all under the hill. Here the gregarious French lived simply and happily in their village and cultivated their common field, danced and sang, played their violins and enjoyed life with relatives and friends, and asked the Virgin for nothing more.

But the tempo of life was quickening, the atmosphere becoming more boisterous, vigorous, and lusty. All of Louisiana had been sold to the United States, that new nation whence came the Americans. It might be expected they would now be coming across the river in ever-greater numbers, having no longer the necessity even of obtaining a permit from the governor of Louisiana. Already such foreign names as Calvin Adams and William Sullivan had been added to the roster of local tavern keepers.

Captain Meriwether Lewis had come and haggled with old Robidoux about supplies for his party, waiting with Captain William Clark near the mouth of the Missouri to ascend that stream. Two years later they returned from their journey to the Pacific, bringing stories that amazed the citizens.

When in 1808, Joseph Charles as printer, editor, and publisher of the Missouri Gazette, set up a creaking little press in a rude shack at Elm and Main streets and turned out the first edition of that newspaper, the town felt it was indeed approaching metropolitan proportions.

Most merchandise was brought to town by boat, and always, in season, there were a score or more of keelboats, Mackinaws and dugouts moored along the wharves under the hill. There to guard the boats and their cargoes usually were a number of boatmen in red shirts, blue jackets, coarse butternut linsey-woolsey trousers, Suwarrow boots and tanned leather caps, the typical outfit of the riverain. There, or in the doggeries up the hill, would be found boatmen from Pittsburgh, Olean or Redstone on the Ohio; or down from a trapper's trip on the Big Muddy, or from Prairie du Chien or Millimichillmackinac, upriver, or up from New Orleans or Natchez. They would spend the time singing, fiddling, and drinking, being always ready for a jig or a knockdown.

Madame Chouteau, dowager of the little city from its veriest beginning, passed away in the long low house at Chestnut and Main, where she had lived and ruled so long. Her son, Auguste, "the colonel," was the town's rich man and leader of the powerful Chouteau clan.

One Sunday night, Thomas Hart Benton, with four hundred dollars in his pocket, came across the Mississippi River, a fugitive, he said, from the persecution of the Andrew Jackson clique in Tennessee. As a United States senator from Missouri, he was to be for many years the most powerful figure in the Trans-Mississippi West.

The death of Madame Chouteau and the arrival of Thomas Hart Benton were as symbolical as any two events could be of the passing of the old French period and the rise of the American regime. Her demise marked the end of an era; his arrival spelled the beginning of an epoch.

Fine gentlemen and blanketed savages, land speculators and Negro slaves, touring foreigners and free trappers, backwoodsmen, voyageurs, explorers, hunters, half-breeds, settlers, scientists, soldiers, Indian traders, boatmen, and politicians jostled each other on the dusty narrow streets of St. Louis. The city was now becoming the metropolis of the frontier and the fur trade, as well as outfitting point for the settlements that were beginning to dot the country along the lower reaches of the Missouri River. Parties of Indians from every part of the western country promenaded the streets, with occasionally one of their chiefs garbed in the coat of a United States army officer, despite his bare legs, making a vain show of golden epaulettes, military hat and plume. The braves, even in summer, sweltered under their Mackinaw blankets, a scarlet umbrella in one hand and a palm leaf fan in the other. Many of them were beggars, singing or reciting for tobacco, whisky, food or other alms.

The far-sighted founders of the city had selected a site which would not only command the upper basin of the Mississippi, but being so close to the mouth of the Missouri, would dominate the resources of that stream as well. Already headquarters for the fur trade with the Indians of the upper Missouri, getting its substance from the pelts that poured in from the north and west, the city was becoming the market place and importing center of the surrounding country.

In 1817 the first steamboat nosed up to the levee at St. Louis, named for Zebulon M. Pike, that "gay, swashbuckling soldier." The coming of the steamboat, many felt would mean an acceleration of trade, because it would enable boatmen to bring cargoes upstream with the same ease that formerly had characterized down-river shipments. And the little boat was a harbinger of the tremendous steamboat traffic that would in a few years be on the Missouri River.

The little French village was slipping into the background and the American city was coming to the fore. The new century's first quarter had seen the village burst its chrysalis to become the bustling small city – social, financial, political and commercial capital of all that vast territo-

hat adumbrate empire, whose waters paid tribute to the Missouri River. The first town was St. Charles.

When Blanchette Le Chasseur, "mighty hunter, veritable Nimrod of the valley," first looked upon the site of St. Charles, on the north bank of the river, he considered it good. Within a few years, 1769 to be exact, he returned at the head of a group of French-Canadians to effect a permanent settlement and to establish a trading post. He carried in his pocket a document issued by the Spanish government investing in him the powers of commandment of the Territory of St. Charles. This was an area beginning at the west bank of the Mississippi and running west to the Pacific Ocean, at the north bank of the Missouri River thence to the Great Lakes. Here at the mouth of the little creek, which perpetuates his name, he founded his city and called it Les Petites Cotes – "the little hills."

St. Charles was first of all a French town and was laid out as were other French towns, in the Continental style, a square village flanked by common fields of long narrow farms and an outlying commons for farming. In the fields, poppies and cornflowers vied with the growing crops, the flowers being not altogether the result of indolence, for the French pioneers in Missouri loved beauty. They cultivated a flair that was reflected in their music and their song, in the very color of their clothing, and most of all in their simple places of abode. It was present in the whitewashed fences that surrounded their house-lots, one hundred twenty by one hundred fifty feet, the trees and bushes about their porches, the beauty of it all enhanced by flower beds bordered with carnations, and by arbors fragrant with acacia, rose and honeysuckle.

At the turn of the century, there were as yet only a few cabins and several tents along Main Street, a thoroughfare, which then appeared to be "but a path between two large forests." It was only on this street, running parallel with the river, that there was any activity. For here, a little later, were the stores, taverns and groceries, the mart and gathering spot of the town. The town stretched along a narrow plateau for more than a mile and up the hillside of the sloping bluffs for several hundred feet to the round martello tower. The tower, which had been a mill, became the old circular stone fort that was to serve the villagers as a place of refuge when an Indian attack appeared imminent and one day was to become a landmark of the city.

The founding of St. Charles had given impetus to the fur trade on the Missouri River, a trade still growing and destined to reach enormous proportions. For many years it would continue to be the principal, almost the sole, trade on the river, carried on with such primitive craft as the canoe, the pirogue, the bullboat, the Mackinac boat and the keelboat. St. Charles, logically, became the home of many of the voyageurs whose job it was to get these boats up the river and to bring them down again with their loads of fur. The Indians, too, came down the river at times, their boats loaded with peltries and then "one could not see the water, so full was the river of canoes."

Being "under the eaves" of St. Louis, only twenty-three miles northwest by land from the larger city and thirty-four by river, the new village could not hope for trade from the south. To the west, there was only Charette, a miserable little upriver hamlet of half a dozen houses. To the east, only the tiny village of Portage des Sioux, established only recently on the west bank of the Mississippi, six miles above the Missouri. To the north, there was nothing at all. It was fortunate, then, that Captain William Clark, with his one hundred "robust, healthy, hardy young men," was camped opposite the mouth of the Missouri River waiting for the arrival of spring and Captain Meriwether Lewis to begin that magnificent adventure. This trip, which was to take them beyond the great shining mountains and on to the Pacific, thereby opening trade routes through the Northwest would redound to the benefit not only of St. Charles, but also to Missouri, the nation, and the entire world.

The Lewis and Clark expedition was focusing attention on the Missouri River and it was in recognition of the growing importance of that waterway that Governor Wilkinson in 1805 established Fort Bellefontaine on the south bank of the river, fourteen miles north of St. Louis. The place was named for a beautiful spring, source of Cold Water Creek, sometimes called St. Ferdinand River, which flowed to the Missouri at the foot of Charbonnier Bluffs.

The flow of immigration making its way west from St. Louis, Bellefontaine and St. Charles was at first but a mere trickle of hunters, trappers and scouts, that ascended the Missouri where they made camps to carry on trade with the Indians. It was a trickle that was augmented and accelerated by the purchase of the Louisiana territory, when great waves of families came seeking new homes in the wilderness. One such family at St. Charles after 1817 was that of Philip Allen Sublette, late of Kentucky, whose sons were to become famous in the mountain fur trade. The brothers were William Lewis, Andrew Whitley, Milton Green, and Solomon Perry Sublette.

Robert McCloud, son-in-law of Charless, the fighting editor of St. Louis, came in 1820 and set up his hand press upon which he printed the Missourian, the first newspaper of St. Charles. Later, Calvin Gunn founded the Jeffersonian, transferring it to Jefferson City in 1826 when the state capital was moved to that upriver town.

For a brief five years preceding the removal, St. Charles had been the capital city of the newly erected state, the general assembly meeting in a two-story building on Main Street. Behind which was a large enclosure to care for the horses and rigs of the early-day legislators, most of whom arrived on horseback or in horse-drawn vehicles. A few came down the river by boat.

Members of the first legislature all dressed in primitive style, either in homespun and home made clothes, or in buckskin leggings and hunting shirts. Incidentally, these garments could be obtained locally from Squire Colgan, tailor, justice of the peace, who sewed buckskin and dispensed philosophy and kept a pet bear in his house. Some of the lawmakers wore rough shoes of their own manufacture, while others encased their feet in buckskin moccasins. Some had slouch hats, but the greater portion wore caps made of the skins of wildcats or raccoons. Governor

Alexander McNair wore a beaver hat, and was the only man who had a fine cloth coat, but even that was cut in the old "pigeon tail" style.

Since 1804 a steady stream of immigrants had been coming into the country, and within a decade the westering tide of empire was sweeping through the city. At the Mamelle ferry a dozen wagons would be waiting, each with its team of four or six horses, and the procession would include slaves, horses, hogs and sheep. In fact, every ferry on the river seemed daily occupied in passing families, carriages, wagons and carts. The dust of the town's streets was never settled, as the caravans of immigrants, mostly from Tennessee and Kentucky, flowed in and through it.

The Boone's Lick country up the river was becoming settled, having a few hamlets, most notable of which was Franklin, opposite the present site of Boonville.

In the summer of 1819, Captain John Nelson passed St. Charles with the Independence, first steamboat to venture into the uncharted waters of the Missouri River. His destination was Chariton, a new town near the site of present Glasgow, with important stops at Franklin and Cote sans Dessein.

Chapter Two

Along the Missouri Rhine

Femme Osage had been the first objective of Daniel Boone. Charette, forty miles above St. Charles, had been the end of the journey for him. But in 1799, bitterly disappointed by the workings of the law, which deprived him of his lands in Kentucky, he followed his son, Daniel Morgan Boone, into the wilds of Louisiana territory, there to be granted lands by the Spanish government. Here he had spent the time acting as justice, loafing and hunting.

Charette was the last settlement passed by Lewis and Clark as they ascended the river in 1804. Geographically, however, none could have been ahead of the City of Missouri, at the junction of the Missouri and Mississippi rivers, where town lots were advertised in January 1818. Marthasville, sprawling on the river bluffs, a halfmile north of the site of Charette, was established in 1817.

In February 1818, the Boones, father and son, were advertising lots for sale in "the town of Missouri," twenty-five miles above St. Charles.

Ten miles above Marthasville, Pinckney came into existence and near above it was Smith's Landing, which in time grew into the village of St. Aubert. Still on the north bank, just below the point where the Missouri received the waters of the Osage, was the French hamlet of Cote sans Dessein, where the French had settled as early as 1801. William Clark, traveling downstream in 1808, after having built Fort Osage, noted, "some houses on the north side about a halfmile below the Osage. This place is increasing and not with the best characters." Across the river from Cote sans Dessein, a small cluster of houses was designated the French Village.

Still on the south bank, a few miles above this, the little town of Jefferson was honored in 1826 when the state capital was brought there from St. Charles, probably because of the large volume of settlers who lately came to the Boone's Lick country. It was described by a visitor as "a rough looking city, indeed, and one who does not bid fair to become of much importance...about thirty houses and three hundred inhabitants."

In 1819 the town of Nashville was laid out on the Missouri River above Cote sans Dessein and below Franklin, at the mouth of the Little Bonne Femme, giving it "a landing at all seasons of the year superior to most other places." It promised to become one of the principal shipping points on the river, but was swept away by the flood of 1844. The present town of Providence is just above its site.

Across the river, approximately halfway between Nashville and Jefferson City, the village of Marion had been established, and later, in the days of steamboating, became an important shipping point. The last place on the river, before reaching Franklin, was the warehouse at Arnold's Landing, a rocky port at the mouth of the Moniteau, which became Rocheport.

At Franklin, on the north bank of the Missouri, opposite the present Boonville, two streams of emigration met, the one coming up the Boone's Lick Trail, the other by way of the river. This first American town on the river had been the outgrowth of activities at and around the lick, two miles northwest, where Nathan and Daniel Morgan Boone had come in 1807 with the Morrison brothers of St. Charles to produce salt on a commercial basis. Families of settlers came from a distance every summer and camped while getting their year's supply of salt. This saline rendezvous became the forerunner of Franklin.

Franklin was laid out in 1816 and by 1820 it had a fire

department, a post office, thirteen shops for the sale of merchandise, four taverns, a library, two large steam mills, two billiard rooms, a barber shop, and a jail made of logs. Henry M. Bingham, whose son, George Caleb Bingham, became a noted Missouri artist, ran the hotel. The land office was in the charge of General William A. Smith, whose name has been perpetuated by Fort Smith, Arkansas. The town's newspaper, the Missouri Intelligencer and Boone's Lick Advertiser, had been founded by Benjamin Holladay and his brother Stephen, a printer, they having brought a Ramage press from Louisville. Nathan Patten, a printer, small and sickly, bought a third interest and became editor, his name becoming much more identified with the paper than that of either the Holladays. The Intelligencer, in its columns, mentioned the types of various mechanics needed in the Boone's Lick country.

On May 28, 1819, the Independence, first steamer to thread its way up the dangerous Big Muddy, arrived laden with passengers, and a cargo of flour, whisky, sugar and iron castings. In command was Captain John Nelson. Editor Patten was never more truly prophetic than when in the next issue of the Intelligencer, he said: "Missourians may hail the era, from which to date the growing importance of this section of the country; when they view with what facility (by the aid of steam) boats may ascend the turbulent waters of the Missouri to bring to this part of the country the articles requisite to its supply, and return laden with the products of this fertile region."

This was not to be for Franklin. Though it then was the metropolis of central Missouri, the river engulfed the town a decade later, on the very eve of practical steamboating on the Missouri. Early though its demise had been, Old Franklin had lived to catch a foreglimpse of the first offshoots of that continued westward expansion that was to carry the slender line of little river settlements to the westernmost part of the state.

Gottfried Duden settled in the valley of the Missouri in 1824 and found, in three years' residence, much that he could report favorably to his countrymen back in Germany.

He found sufficient to fill a book, generally referred to as "Duden's Letters." The book, which was printed in 1828, had a wide circulation in Germany by the following year. After its release, men of substantial wealth as well as peasants, artisans, tillers of the soil and day laborers, began answering the call of the philosophical dreamer, coming in ever-greater numbers to the Missouri River valley, and augmented still further a few years later by the political refugees of "forty-eight."

The movement of Germans to this country and to Missouri largely was under the auspices of the Philadelphia German Emigrant Society. An organization which helped the emigrants in making the trip from Philadelphia, by steamboat from Pittsburgh, some being chartered all the way through, while in other instances a change of boats was made at St. Louis.

Along the lower reaches of the Missouri, between its mouth and its junction with the Osage River in midstate, the emigrants found, in its beautifully rugged banks, sloping abruptly down to the river, a countryside that reminded them of their native Rhine lands. Being of a practical turn, they noted, too, that those terraced hills were ideally suited to grape culture. Eventually that part of the valley became noted for its fine wines. As the vineyards grew in scope and importance there was a change in population. The French, first to settle at St. Charles, Charette, French Village and Cote sans Dessein, along with their immediate successors, the Americans, with their Marthasville, Pinckney, New Port and Mount Vernon, almost were crowded out by the Germans, coming to settle their Augusta, Hermann, and Washington. Here the Germans predominated, retaining their customs from the old country, and their language. German was taught in the public schools, and English was learned, if at all, as a foreign language.

Duden, in the role of amateur colonist, was only one of the several forces operating to bring settlers to the valley of the Missouri. First of all, there was that seemingly natural urge of expansion toward the west, the significance and ramifications of which has been the subject of many books. There also was the fur trade and the trade with Santa Fe, and latterly, the Oregon and California movements, all serving to draw people into and through the valley, some of whom remained and some of whom returned. An important factor was the growth of the steamboat traffic, which seemed to induce hardy investors to venture ever a little farther upstream in the knowledge that the steamboats would follow. As a matter of fact, the steamboats in a number of instances led the way. Many of the river towns owed their prominence and prosperity to the presence of the steamboats on the river. On the other hand, the boats could not live and prosper without the tonnage which was furnished by the towns. When the boats went off the river many of the towns declined.

Dortmund, only a mile above Mount Pleasant, was founded in 1837 by Julius Mallinckrodt and named in honor of his native city in Germany, but never had more than the founder's house, due to a shift in the river's course. Mount Vernon, two miles above Washington, disappeared when Washington Landing began to take on the characteristics of a village. Murpheysville was twenty miles above Washington. William Hensley was authorized in 1821 to keep a ferry across the Missouri River at his landing opposite Pinckney. Sixteen years later this became the site of Griswold City, perhaps named for Frederick Griswold, who was postmaster at Pinckney at that time. Its shore was rocky, and its waters deep, so steamboats usually stopped there.

With two exceptions, all other towns in the sixty three-mile sectors between Augusta and Cote sans Dessein sank into a state of desuetude, particularly after the decline in the steamboat trade. The two exceptions were Washington and Hermann. In the first class would have been Augusta, Labadie, St. Albans, South Point, Marthasville, New Haven, Portland, Chamois, St. Aubert and Bonnot's Mill.

Leonard Harold laid out Mount Pleasant in 1836, but soon changed the name to Augusta in honor of his wife. St.

Albans was an important town in the beginning days of steamboating. Labadie or Labadie Point as it was know to the steamboatmen, was of some importance as a river port. Its next neighbor on the west, South Point, two miles below Washington, sought with some degree of success to supersede the latter place as the landing point for the Union, being two miles near to that inland town. However, its importance declined when Washington forged ahead, not only of South Point, but of Union as well, as a shipping and commercial center. Marthasville, across and five miles up the river, which for a time laid claim to being a rival of Washington, also was outdistanced in the commercial race. Washington itself grew from a steamboat landing, first know as Washington Landing, later Owens Ferry Landing and Owensville.

In the forties, Washington was still a sprawling little village that had grown up around the steamboat landing. A building boom preceded the coming of the Missouri Pacific railway in 1855.

German emigrants who hoped to make of it a second Leipsic settled Hermann, twenty-six miles above Washington, in 1837, but its population never has exceeded two thousand. Here, more than in any other town on the river, the German spirit continued to live — the language, the customs, such as the Maifest, and even the quaint one of printing black-bordered funeral circulars, which were posted on poles, fence posts, and other public places. With its many vineyards, it became a leading wine mart, shipping as much as a hundred thousand dollars worth of wine annually.

More of the smaller boats on the river were said to have had their ownership in Hermann than in any other town in the valley and some citizens made fortunes in the river trade. One of the princes of rivermen came from the vicinity of Hermann. The widowed mother of the boy who became Captain William Rodney Massie kept a wood yard five miles below Hermann, supplying wood for the Missouri steamers. It was inevitable that the boy would go on the river. He made his first trip to the mountains in 1844 with Captain Matt Morrison on the Bertrand, which belonged to the fur company of Harvey, Primeau, Bonies & Company in St. Louis.

Portland was established in 1833, and because of its excellent landing it soon became a considerable place of business. The nearby Smith's Landing eventually became St. Aubert, now a tiny cluster of houses on a hill. In 1846, Shipley's Landing was between St. Aubert and Isbell, one of the newer towns. Miller's Landing in 1856 became New Haven, Bonnot's Mill was laid out close to the mouth of the Osage in 1852 by Felix Bonnot. For a year or two it had been known as Dauphine, which in turn was a continuation of the old French Village, thus making the present tiny village of Bonnot's Mill the oldest town on the river west of St. Charles. In its heyday, steamboating was a great part of the life and activity of the town, many of its citizens being investors and promoters of steamboat transportation, as well as furnishing many skilled pilots for the river trade.

The French influence in the lower Missouri River valley was yielding to the German, but in the commonwealth as a whole, the dominant tone was being set by the Anglo-Saxon strain of immigrants. There was a coalescing of the two forces in the state's new capital on the Missouri River.

Chapter Three

Dawn of the Steamboat Era

Steam boating on the Missouri River became a matter of ever-increasing interest after that hot day in August 1817, when the Zebulon M. Pike, "the little boat with the big name," was nosed up to the wharf in St. Louis. Captain Jacob Reed charged the gawking natives a dollar a head for permission to go aboard and "see what makes the wheels go 'round." Although it was the first to land at St. Louis, it did not become the first steamboat to enter the Missouri, the astute captain not caring to risk his flimsy craft among the snags and other dangerous obstacles he would have met in that stream. It is probable, too, that he did not ascend the Missouri for the very sound business reason that there virtually was no place to go, except St. Charles, which his potential customers could have reached more expeditiously by land.

But in the next two years the situation had changed. When Captain John Nelson headed the first boat, the Independence, into the dangerous river, there was more reason for making the trip. Franklin had become a booming frontier town, and forty miles beyond that, even, Duff Green and others had established the flourishing town of Chariton, two miles from the present town of Glasgow. This was the destination on that initial trip of the Independence. Then, too, by 1819, the river towns of Boonville, French Village, Cote sans Dessein, Nashville, Pinckney, and Missouri, had become of more importance, some, if not all, of those landings serving an augmented hinterland population.

In that same summer of 1819, there was a splurge in steamboat traffic on the Missouri. This was occasioned by the launching of the so-called Yellowstone expedition, a pet project of John Calhoun, secretary of war, who was roundly criticized for entrusting that important mission to such an untried and dangerous medium as the steamboat. The expedition was under command of Major Stephen H. Long, and for that reason sometimes is called Long's expedition. Some authorities insist it should have been named the Missouri expedition because its work almost wholly referred to the Missouri River.

In reality, the expedition had more than one mission to accomplish. Among them being "to awe the Indians and British traders; to explore the Missouri and the country to the (Yellowstone) falls; to fix upon a suitable location for a military establishment near the Yellowstone River. It is also suspected that the mission was to sound out the potentialities of the steamboat as an instrument of warfare.

As advance guard of the expedition, Colonel Talbot Chambers left Fort Bellefontaine in the summer of 1818 with about three hundred and fifty men. Force wintered them at Cow Island, near the site of the present Fort Leavenworth, setting up Martin Cantonment, first military post west of Fort Osage, as a supply base for the expedition. In the next summer, Colonel Chambers again set out, this time in advance of the five steamboats, which were to comprise the expedition, taking two hundred and sixty men on five keelboats. In September, the steamboat Expedition, with Captain Craig in charge, reached Cow Island. The R.M. Johnson, under Captain Colfax, developed engine trouble and spent the winter at the site of present-day Kansas City. The boat was named for the owner's brother, Richard Mentor Johnson, famed Kentuckian, credited with having personally slain Tecumseh at the Battle of the Thames. The Western Engineer went on as far as Manuel Lisa's fort, five miles below the Council Bluffs, just above the present Omaha. The Calhoun turned back at the start of the trip. The Thomas Jefferson, in command of Captain H.J. Offut, developed trouble at the mouth of the Petit Bonne Femme, about thirty miles below Old Franklin. It was compelled to transfer its cargo and passengers to flatboats to be taken on up the river, the Jefferson itself eventually returning to Shippingport, near Louisville. Some historians are in error in stating that it sank. It was at Shippingport as late as 1823.

So it will be seen that mechanical troubles kept three of the five boats from reaching Cow Island. The steamers had been blowing out pistons, springing leaks, and running on to sand bars, but more dangerous than any of these were the snags, which were trees lying fixed upon the shoals of the river. Planters were upright trees attached to the bottom of the river, embedded in sediment; sawyers were similar to snags, but not fixed, appearing and reappearing on the surface of the stream, and were dangerous in the extreme.

The Expedition and the R. M. Johnson stopped at Franklin in April of the following spring, bound for the mouth of the Missouri, where they were to take on provisions and stores for the troops and proceed immediately to the Council Bluffs. Arriving there, it was decided, due to the lowness of the waters and the loss of two anchors, to leave the Expedition at the Council Bluffs that winter, according to Captain Craig, who passed Franklin on his way to St. Louis.

The story of steam boating during its first decade on the Missouri is sketchy, the flitting of the boats shadowy and furtive. It has been stated that, "Between 1820-25, a boat made regular trips between Old Franklin and St. Louis, stopping at all principal landings," and that, "By 1826 steamboat traffic up the Missouri began to assume regularity." In the first instance, the steamboat is not identified, and neither statement seems to be supported by further references. There is a vague reference, again unsupported, to the Independence having again been on the river between 1825 and 1830. At Fort Atkinson, located at the Council Bluffs, it was noted in 1821 that "steamboats came at rare intervals," indicating the presence of one or more boats at approximately that time. There is some reason for believing that the Exchange, the Post Boy, the Tuscumbia, and the Dolphin shortly followed the R. M. Johnson, the Expedition, the Western Engineer and the Independence on the river.

The Missouri Packet is known to have ascended the Missouri River in 1820, arriving at Franklin May 5, bound for the Council Bluffs, laden principally with flour and provisions for the troops at that place. A few hours after leaving Franklin, she ran against a snag with such force that she sank, but being near the shore in low water, it was expected a considerable portion of the cargo would be saved, and the boat raised and repaired as to proceed to her destination.

The "large and elegant" steamboat Pittsburgh and St. Louis Packet, with Captain Alexander Scott in command, arrived at St. Louis in March, 1823, ten days from Pittsburgh and left for Franklin, "holding her own against the rapid current of the Missouri," and arrived safely at Franklin a few days later. In June 1823, the Cincinnati arrived at Franklin from Louisville, under command of Captain Embree, laden with flour and whisky and one hundred and three thousand dollars in specie for the military and Indian departments. The steamer Magnet, with troops destined for the upper Missouri, arrived at St. Louis from Baton Rouge in September 1823. It was on the river the following year under Captain W. McKnight.

In 1824 the Plough Boy, Captain Burnett, was on the river, while the Mandan, Captain William Linn, and the General Neville, under Captain Crawford, made more than one trip to the Council Bluffs. The General Neville was named for the lieutenant colonel that was commandant at Fort Pitt in the early part of the Revolutionary War, and later assigned to General Washington's army. His estate on Montour's Island near Pittsburgh was a notable place.

James Kennerly, who was sutler at Fort Atkinson in 1824, mentioned in his diary "a man named Barber, who had been cutting wood for the steamboats," and noted again on May 25 of that year that "The S. Boat arrived." Though he recorded with fidelity the minutiae of camp life, he failed to mention the name of the "S. Boat." However, it is known that it was the General Neville, which started downriver May 27, having on board several gentlemen and their ladies from the fort. It arrived at St. Louis June 6, a down journey of ten days, as against some three months in getting upriver.

Captain Mirabeau arrived at Franklin on April 14, 1826, with the steamboat Muskingum from Pittsburgh and departed for New Orleans. This may have been the only boat on the river that year, as a Jefferson City paper in 1839 said, "It was only thirteen years ago that we had but one steamboat arrival during the whole year."

The new steamboat Maryland was reported in January of 1827, as on her way from Pittsburgh to enter the Missouri River trade, while in April of that year, the steamboat Oregon, Captain Green, was reported "now on her passage to Franklin," being followed immediately by the Pilot.

In April of the following year, the steamboats Missouri and Illinois left Jefferson Barracks, just below St. Louis, for the upper Missouri. Both were carrying troops, Colonel Leavenworth being on the Illinois bound for Cantonment Leavenworth. In August, Franklin merchants advertised goods as having been received "per steamboat Illinois." The Shoal Water was on the river in 1828, but went down when it struck a snag at the Brick House Bend, near the mouth of the river.

The first advertised regular packet between St. Louis and Franklin was in April, 1829, when the William D. Duncan, under Captain Crooks, made the run several times, even going as far as Cantonment Leavenworth when the business warranted it. That same summer, the steamboat Crusader proceeded upriver to the Boone's Lick country, carrying troops to quell an Indian uprising. Later that fall, the steamboat Native was reported as having arrived at Franklin. And that year, too, the Plough Boy, "small and much crowded," was on the river, with Captain Rider in command, and the Mountaineer under J. R. Spriggs as master. That year an observer at Jefferson City wrote: "A steamboat has just passed! What a cheerful sight. The trade on the Missouri River is as yet very limited."

The following year, the traffic set in earnest, witnessing the arrival of such boats as the Talleyrand and the John Hancock, both of which ran the river ten years. Other boats that year were the Car of Commerce, under Captain Read; the General William H. Ashley, under Captain James Sweeney, owner and master; the Liberty, Captain Bennett, master, under Captain J.B. Bonsett, the Otoe, with Captain James B. Hill; the Globe, John Clark, master, with Captain Andrew Wineland, making a trip to Fort Leavenworth for the government; and the Missouri Belle, built by Captain William Littleton, said to have been the first steamer on the river to use a steam whistle.

The steamboat had supplemented, but still was far from taking the place of the keelboat, particularly so with reference to the fur trade. Many were the trappers still using the keelboat. General William H. Ashley had gone up the river with his expedition, recruited for the most part from the taverns and dives of St. Louis. Mike Fink was one of the engaged, reverting to his early-day occupation as hunter and trapper after a lengthy interval on the rivers of the west in which time his name had become a household word as "king of the keelboatmen." His youthful partner, Bill Carpenter, accompanied him, but it is probable they were compelled to leave behind their companion of the St. Louis doggeries, the abandoned woman known as "Pittsburgh Blue," who had been the third of an unholy trio. She might have been the reason for Mike's aiming a bit low, when, on the far reaches of the Big Muddy he played at the game they had so often played, that of shooting the tin whisky cup off his comrade's head. Accidental or not, Mike, a dead shot, killed Carpenter and shortly afterwards was slain by "a man named Talbott," who fell into the river and was drowned. The steamboat first became an active competitor of the keelboat in the fur-carrying trade, when Pierre Chouteau, Jr., of the American Fur Company, decided to use a steamboat in carrying peltries and had the Yellowstone built at Louisville at a cost of seven thousand dollars. In the spring of 1831 it started on its maiden voyage up the Missouri under Captain B. Young. It went as far as Fort Tecumseh, at the mouth of the Little Missouri, twelve hundred miles above St. Louis, six hundred miles higher than any steamboat had hitherto navigated.

In 1831, too, the Don Juan, J. Swager, master put up its sign for Leavenworth, which also was the destination of the new steamboat Union, under Captain W. Bennett. When Captain W.B. Culver lost the steamboat Missouri near Fort Osage in May, he was able to salvage the engine and the furniture before the boat sank. In June, he was again on the river with the Walter Scott, which announced for Franklin. The Chieftain, under the veteran Captain John Shallcross, announced for the Missouri River trade, but burst a boiler about eighty miles above St. Louis and was compelled to return to that port. The Talisman, J.W. Pollock, master, began running to Franklin and the new town of Independence.

The Argus, Crooks, master, went up to the mouth of the Kansas River in April 1831, with merchandise for Francois Chouteau, who had a trading post there.

Thus within a dozen years, the business of steamboating on the Missouri River had become firmly established.

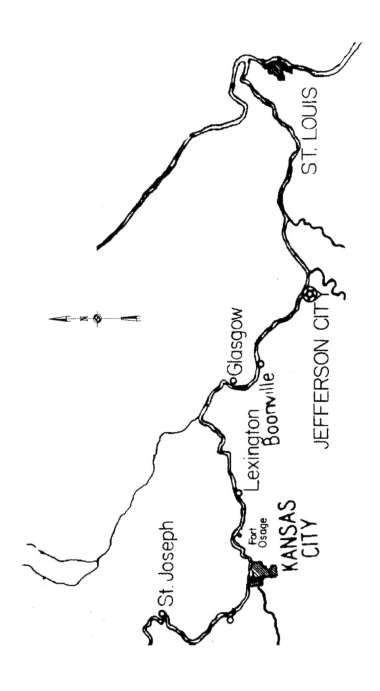

ST. LOUIS

JEFFERSON CITY

Glasgow

Lexington

Boonville

St. Joseph

Fort Osage

KANSAS CITY

Chapter Four

Jefferson City and the Osage

The passing years have demonstrated the wisdom of those men who chose Howard's Bluff on the Missouri River as the site of the permanent home of government to succeed the temporary state capital which had been located at St. Charles.

The site was well within the forty-mile limit prescribed with reference to the mouth of the Osage River, being but ten miles from the mouth of that stream. In time Jefferson City came nearest to fulfilling the claims that had been put forth on behalf of the proposed city of Osage – that it would become a city of first importance to both the Missouri and the Osage rivers. This was particularly true in the heyday of steamboating when both rivers, as the state's principal highways of commerce, teemed with steamboats, and Jefferson City sat proudly on her hill near the junction of those highways.

No Brangwyn could depict the view that met the eye of those early-day legislators who climbed to the gallery of the little two-story building which served to house not only both branches of the legislature, but the governor and his household as well. Here a most beautiful prospect could be had for many miles up and down the river, as well as each way over the rugged hills of the surrounding country. None yet can explain the spell of enchantment that holds one who, from the hilltop that is Jefferson City, gazes across the river toward the far limestone cliffs that lie in the Kingdom of Callaway. That note, more than any other, is struck in the reminiscences of those ladies who have at some time occupied the governor's mansion; "Our favorite spot was in the garden at the north of the mansion, where we had a view of the river."

Jefferson City grew by what seemed inevitable accretion: One dwelling followed another; one by one the business houses came to be added to those already in existence. The town never knew decadence, but surely, slowly, has built and grown until it has far outstripped all the river towns between St. Louis and Kansas City, seeing many of its erstwhile rivals stop growing when they had reached the status of lively villages and seeing others sink into oblivion.

Catering to an out-of-town clientele, as it did, Jefferson City was a place of taverns, "groceries," as the grog shops of those days were called, hotels and places of entertainment. In anticipation of the capitol yet to be built, John C. Gorgon established the Rising Sun Hotel on the Madison Street Hill, opposite the site of the proposed capitol. William Jones, Ralph Briscoe, Job Goodall, and Josiah Ramsey, Jr. soon opened other places.

By 1826, the original habitations of Jefferson City, "made of logs, mostly hewed, giving comfort without much cost," to quote editor Calvin Gunn, were being superseded, or at least augmented, by six brick and two stone buildings. Gunn had brought his newspaper up from St. Charles and renamed it the Jeffersonian Republican. By 1840, the Inquirer was able to report that Jefferson City "contains over one hundred buildings, many of which are of brick of very respectable dimensions and appearance."

The little capital resounded, on the eighth day of January, each year, to the celebration of the anniversary date of General Andrew Jackson's victory over Pakenham's redcoats at the battle of New Orleans. This crowning victory of the War of 1812 was near and dear to Missourians because of the personnel of Jackson's army had been those "half-horse, half-alligators" of the vicinity of Kentucky and Tennessee whence had come a preponderance of Missouri's population. There were some men along the Missouri River who had participated in the battle; there were many more who boasted of relatives who had "fit with Andy Jackson."

In 1837 steamboating began on the Osage River with the ascension of North St. Louis, which became stranded on the river. The next year the Adventure made the trip ascending the Osage one hundred and sixty-eight miles. It had the previous year been in the Galena trade on the upper Mississippi. In 1840, the Osage Packet, operated by Benjamin B. Bryan, went up the river, followed in 1841 by the Leander and in 1843 by the Maid of the Osage, owned and operated by Captain Nansen Bennett of Cote sans Dessein. The year 1844 saw the Huntsville, Captain William Miller, the Warsaw and the Agatha enter the Osage River trade. In 1846 the Otter and the Cora came in. Abram Shinkle was captain of the Otter and Charles E. Pancoast, clerk. Before being purchased by them, it had been in the Galena trade. Pancoast gives an entertaining description of his misadventures on the Otter and the St. Louis Oak, which he and Shinkle later purchased, including being frozen in all winter on the Osage, in his book, Quaker Forty-Niner. The Cora was under Captain Joseph Throckmorton and went on the upper Mississippi the following year, being the first boat at Fort Snelling.

In 1847, the St. Louis Oak and the Wave made their appearance. The latter, owned by Captain William Waldo of Osceola, ran only to the mouth of the Osage. The St. Louis Oak, said to have been the first steamboat built entirely in St. Louis, was partly owned by Captain James Dozier of that city, his son Frank acting as second pilot.

The Lightfoot, Lake of the Woods and the Haidee came on the river in 1848, captained by William Phelps, Jacob Tice, and Joseph Bordeau, respectively. The following year saw the Eliza Stewart, the Martha and the Pearl No. 2 in the Osage River trade, the first under Captain William Edds, the second under Captain Joseph La Barge.

The Fayaway, Captain Robert M. Barclay, was among the boats in the early 1850's, named for a character in Herman Melville's novel, Typee, which had been published in 1846 and was enjoying a considerable vogue.

The decade preceding the Civil War saw steamboating on the Osage River reach its height, and with the coming of the railroad and imminence of civil strife, saw it die. In May 1849, the James Monroe, and old sidewheeler, came up the Missouri, loaded with men bound for the gold fields of California. Cholera broke out on the boat with great loss of life and an attempt was made to land at Jefferson City to put ashore the sick and dying before proceeding to the boat's destination, St. Joseph. However, a thoroughly apprehensive citizenry brought a cannon to the landing and threatened to blow the James Monroe into fragments if a landing were attempted. The boat went a mile downstream and dropped the gangplank, permitting the passengers to crawl ashore. Then the citizens had a change of heart, or perhaps another group entirely took charge of affairs, for the town's churches were turned into hospitals and the homes of the citizens opened to the misfortunate Argonauts. Several months later the ill-fated steamboat was taken back to St. Louis.

The upstream traffic on the Osage consisted principally of salt, groceries, nails and iron, while downstream were sent pork, furs, peltries, grain, apples, bee cords, dried beef, tallow, tobacco, venison hams, wagon spokes, wax and whisky.

All this traffic, going up and down the Osage, in addition to the augmented volume on the Missouri River, was reflected in the steady growth of Jefferson City. And no institution in that city was more closely identified with the industry of shipping by river than the huge store of Charles F. Lohman, strategically located at Lohman's Landing at the foot of Jefferson Street.

It was known far and wide by travelers, to many of whom it spelled the end of a journey; to others, only the beginning, while to still others it was a pleasant way-stop, an important situation on the highway of water across the state. This building, cut from the hillside where it sat, was built of cheap marble and used as an inn, a store and a shipping center, as well as a home for its owner. Teams and wagons milled about in front of this place or congregated on the river front while awaiting their turn to haul away the shipments of commodities that had come in by steamboat and had been stored in the spacious Lohman warehouse.

Owners of numerous steamboats plying the Missouri and the Osage rivers looked to Lohman's store as their agent in Jefferson City.

This old building, with its wide gallery, spelled romance to the early-day swains and belles of the city and was the social center of the community. Here, along the levee, "down under the hill" at the foot of Jefferson, the fashionable vehicles of the day brought the young people for an evening at Lohman's or perchance for an excursion on one of the many steamboats that landed there.

The amiable Captain Ben Glime of the F.X. Aubrey, a young bachelor himself, was only one of the many captains to take parties up or down the river. On one occasion when he was host, the Aubrey left the Lohman Landing at eight in the evening, ran downstream as far as St. Aubert and returned with its load of tired but happy young people at four in the morning.

The old white stone building that once echoed the gaiety of Jefferson City's youth, still stands, its romantic gallery ripped away, looking out across the dark and smooth flowing waters of the Missouri as if reminiscing of the old days that have flown forever.

One of the earliest towns on the river to bear the unmistakable print of Americanism was Marion, founded in 1820 fifteen miles above the site of Jefferson City and proposed as the new capital of Missouri to succeed St. Charles. It lost not only the race for the capital, but eventually lost the county seat to Jefferson City. There was a period when Marion was of considerable importance as a steamboat town. Then, with hands folded, it sank into a state of apathy which deepened with the years.

A dozen miles above Marion, steamboats landed at Old Commerce and Iuka, the two landings finally producing one village, Wolfe's Point, still doing business as Lupus.

Across the river from Marion, an ambitious man, Asa Stone, along with Peter Wright and William Ramsey, laid out in 1836 the town of Stonesport. Stonesport flourished and was considered another rival for Jefferson City until, after the big flood of 1844, a sand bar formed and the citizens moved to higher ground a mile south to establish the present Claysville.

Above the site of Claysville on the north bank of the river, halfway between Cote sans Dessein and Franklin, the wealthy and eccentric genius, Ira P. Nash, established Nashville in 1819. The flood of 1844, too, ruined this town, and the citizens moved to higher ground, marking the death of Nashville and the beginning of Providence. The latter was considered a boom town in its day, much of its commerce consisting of goods unloaded by steamboats to be taken into the hinterland, particularly Columbia, which was connected with this river port by a plank road.

The next important town above Providence was Rocheport, at the mouth of the Moniteau, from which stream settlers of the vicinity began about 1818 to launch their flatboats, loaded with farm products bound for downstream markets, the principal one being St. Louis.

With the coming of the steamboats in 1819, it was inevitable that this site would become an important place in the itinerary of the boatmen, because of its harbor facilities, its densely wooded points, furnishing fuel for the boats, and because of the increasing number of its hinterland population.

It is legendary that a band of river pirates operated there in its early days, seizing barrels of sorghum, boxes of provisions and other commodities from the wharves and storing them in nearby caves. A posse of enraged boatmen finally caught up with and gave battle to the marauders at the mouth of one of the caves, several of the pirates being killed, so that thereafter there was no further trouble from that quarter.

If in after years, following the thread of the legend, horse thieves made good use of the many chambers and winding tunnels of the caves, that would have been no concern of the boatmen. This legend, with its sanguinary implications, furnishes a key to the appreciation of the rough-and-tumble character of early day denizens of Rocheport.

Chapter Five

On the River in Crinoline Days

No backwoods road was so difficult as to deter the Yankee peddler who came with his wagon loaded with "calicoes, cotton checks, gingham, tin cups, iron spoons, coffee pots, spools of thread, papers and pins, cards of horn buttons, cakes of shaving soap, bolts of ribbon, pepper boxes, sausage stuffers, tablecloths, tin plates, knives and forks, razors, neckcloths, handkerchiefs, hose, Jew's harps, wax dolls, clocks and nutmeg."

And the Yankee peddler had his counterpart on the river in those itinerant merchants who loafed down the waterways dealing in "dry goods, cheap jewelry, and catch-penny trinkets." Such artisans as blacksmiths, tinners, tinkers, cobblers and tailors worked the river, tying up their boats wherever there would be little or no competition and exchanging their services for food and a little money. Later, according to Herbert Quick, in his "Steamboating on the Mississippi," came the traveling photographers and medicine men, and there are vague hints of boats equipped with gambling paraphernalia, saloon equipment, and a few women from the vice districts of the big cities.

When Old Franklin, spreading over the rich bottom land of the Missouri River, was the bustling metropolis of the West, the little huddle of huts called Boonville, perched on the rocky bluff opposite, was a despised poor relation. It was called Boonville as early as 1816 when it had only a store and a tavern, the one kept by "a man named Robidoux," and the other by a man named Reames. A young man in Old Franklin wrote; "They have laid out a town opposite here on the river, called Boonville, which they expect will eclipse this place, but the traders think Franklin will eclipse any town in the West. I think it likely will if the river will let it alone." But the river didn't let it alone.

Santa Fe traders packed their wagons at Old Franklin, ferried them over to Boonville, toiled up the long Main Street hill, and encamped for the fist night on the outskirts of Boonville. Perhaps they began asking themselves if it would not be more practical to have the boats land their goods on the south bank of the river. As if to remove any doubts, the capricious river ate away the site of Old Franklin and Boonville perforce became the initial point of the Santa Fe Trail. It also became the trade center of a large territory south of the river.

Boonville did not long continue as the first town of the Santa Fe Trail, for it was the beginning of the ship-by-water era, and goods that could be sent by steamboat were not relegated to the more cumbersome and more expensive overland cartage. Accordingly, as time went on, goods intended for the Santa Fe trade were unloaded ever farther up the river. But Boonville continued to expand because of its growing importance as a steamboat town. More and more its citizens became interested in building, owning, and running steamboats. Its capital was largely invested in steamboats, it offered more boats than any other town on the river, and up to the time of the Civil War it probably was the greatest steamboat town on the Missouri River.

One of its earliest steamboat captains was Justinian Williams, a Methodist preacher, who, in April 1835, took the Far West out of the near-by Bonne Femme where it had been built and set out on its maiden voyage to New Orleans. Captain David Keiser, Kentuckian, lived six miles south of Boonville, and for many years engaged in steamboating on the Missouri River. Captain Joseph Kinney, most famous of Boonville's river men, had been a pioneer steamboat man on the Mississippi River before going to

Boonville in 1844. Twelve years later he built the big steam-boat W.H. Russell, named for his friend, the senior member of the freighting firm of Russell, Majors & Waddell. Kinney had in his day worked as teacher, surveyor, pork packer and shoe merchant, but with the advent of the W. H. Russell fortune began to smile on him. Russell and other Lexingtonians were interested with Kinney, the boat hav-ing been built at Lexington. The steamboat burned at St. Louis with fourteen others.

Across the river from Boonville, Kinney built Riverscene, a fabulously expensive mansion, sometimes called "Kinney's Folly." This home for his eleven children still stands and is a showplace and museum of Boonville.

Other steamboat men of Boonville were McKee, Gaunt, Spahr, Hilliard, Chester H. Brewster, Captain John Porter and his boys, Jim, John and Cook; George, Ferry and Zade Hanna; and James B., Jesse and George Homan.

The levee became a lively place as the steamboats unloaded goods, including supplies for the new mines at Osceola and Sarcoxie in southwest Missouri, whence came lead, hauled in prairie schooners drawn by many yoke of oxen, for shipment to the East. The "mud clerks" of the boats, the receivers of goods, the deckhands and the roustabouts, the mate swearing and shouting gruff orders, the captains giving their commands, constituted a colorful scene. The wharf was piled high with merchandise, all but covered sometimes by huge hogsheads of sugar, surround-ed by bees and small boys, the latter having contrived ingenuous reed scoops for removing sugar form the trian-gular holes in the ends of the hogsheads.

Boonville continued to grow in commercial impor-tance and the heart of it was the old City Hotel, where guests frequently wrote on the register beside their names short observations on any topic from politics to steam-boats, sometimes a commendatory note on the steamboat from which they had just landed. One enthusiastic guest wrote; "The St. Louis is the boat to take – lots of gals." The skipper of that boat, Captain George Taylor, was well known in Boonville, a very large man with a voice like a

Beautifully restored, the grand mansion is once again the pride of the Missouri River and the Boone's Lick region. You can take a walk back in time and stay with Ron and Jody Lenz, the hosts/owners of *Riverscene Bed and Breakfast.*

foghorn who could be heard for miles up and down the river when he was bellowing orders.

The City Hotel register for 1843 showed more than three hundred steamboat arrivals at Boonville.

Occasionally the advertisement of some newcomer to Boonville would throw light on the customs of the time. Such was the notice of John Casey, who, in 1844, announced that he had "located himself in the city of Boonville, two doors east of E. Hart's bookstore, where he will manufacture and keep on hand a general assortment of hats, beaver and otter, nutria, Russia, silk, brush, broad-brimmed rabbit, and wool. For cash or peltries such as beaver, otter, raccoon, mink, wildcat, muskrat or rabbit. Better work than any other in this far western country."

The town was moving toward romance and culture when Miss Mary Hansen, a beautiful belle of Boonville, was married in 1848 to Captain Isaac McKee, skipper of the Clara. The brass band, which was the pride of Boonville, was on the boat that night. Steamboat weddings and honeymoons were not uncommon in those rosy, sentimental days before the war, when the river was alive with steamboats, the large side-wheelers crowded with people, and mirth and music and dancing never seemed to end. It was the Clara, incidentally, which in October, 1851, picked up a party of Sioux, Cheyenne, Arapahos, Crows and Snake Indians at Westport Landing, headed by Tom Fitzpatrick on their way to Washington to visit President Fillmore.

At mid-century, Boonville had become a prosperous shipping point—the most important town on the Missouri River, enjoying a large and profitable wagon trade with the Southwest, while north of the river were rich hemp and tobacco districts with many slaves to tend them. But within a few years thereafter, three things happened definitely affecting the future of the town. First, the railroads came and began hauling through the town formerly discharged at that point for transshipment, thus seriously curtailing the extent and volume of trade. Next, the Civil War enveloped the town, bringing tragic dislocation of even the circumscribed commerce and a plague of local prejudices and hatreds to form obstacles in the development of the city. These animosities became dim with time, but not before the steamboats had begun going off the river in ever-increasing numbers, yielding to the railroads the river traffic that had grown as Boonville grew and that made it the foremost steamboat town on the Missouri River. The story of the rise of Boonville was almost a duplication of the story of the expansion of river trade.

With the second trip of the Yellowstone in 1832, under the command of Captain A.G. Bennett, the onetime storekeeper at French Village there began that era of growth and expansion in steamboating that well might have been described as the burgeoning of the river trade. The epoch-making character of the Yellowstone's trip is hinted at in a St. Louis newspaper, the Missouri Republican, which said; "The steamboat Yellowstone, A.G. Bennett, master, arrived here after a voyage of three months, to the mouth of the Yellowstone, distant two thousand miles up the Missouri, carrying the goods to the traders employed by the American Fur Company and bringing back a rich and full cargo of furs, peltries, and buffalo robes. Many of the Indians declared that the Hudson's Bay Company could no longer compete with the Americans, that the dogs and sledges of the British would no longer be useful while the fire boat walked on the waters."

The Yellowstone was joined on the river that year by the Chian (Cheyenne), which also was a fur boat. The Trenton, the Halcyon under Captain Shepherd, and the Warrior under Captain Joseph W. Throckmorton, continued on the river for nearly thirty years. Captain Throckmorton was described as "a short, heavily built man, considered one of the best navigators on the river. He never used profane language and did not countenance it on his boats," according to Philip Edward Chappell in his History of the Missouri River. That same year the Warrior carried government supplies to Prairie du Chien on the Mississippi and took part in the Battle of Bad Axe, firing on Black Hawk's forces, as they were withdrawing across the river.

Early in the year, the Car of Commerce, "all-locust

steamboat," set up its sign for Franklin and Chariton with J. Penrod as master. Other boats on the Missouri that year were the Union, Symes, master; and the Globe, under Captain J. Gunsollis. Mrs. George C. Sibley had made a "tedious passage" to Fort Osage from St. Charles on the Globe in the year preceding this, probably then under command of Captain Andy Wineland.

In 1833, the Yellowstone again made the long trip to the upper reaches of the river, having as a companion the Asssiniboine. A passenger on the Yellowstone was Maximilian, Prince of Wied. He was described as "a thin, worn man of fifty, sans teeth, excitable, choleric." He had fought in the Prussian army against Napoleon, was made a prisoner of war, had been decorated with the Iron Cross, and as a major general had ridden at the head of his division when the Allies entered Paris.

Bernard Pratte, junior, was captain of the Assiniboine, which two years later was wrecked and burned at the mouth of the Heart River, eleven thousand buffalo robes being part of the cargo lost.

Other passengers included Carl Bodmer, artist, who was accompanying the prince; Kenneth McKenzie, whose headquarters were at Fort Union; and John F.A. Sanford, agent to the Mandan Indians. McKenzie, a native of Scotland, was known as "king of the Missouri," and it was by his insistence that the Yellowstone had been built despite the vigorous opposition of Pratte and Cabanne, two of the most influential members of the firm of Pierre Chouteau, Junior & Company. Sanford later was owner of Dred Scott, named after the central figure in the celebrated slave case.

In November of 1833 the John Nelson, built at Louisville came up the Missouri, carrying goods from Pierre Chouteau for Francis Chouteau's trading post at the mouth of the Kansas River. This boat had been named in honor of the aging Captain Nelson who had brought the Independence to Franklin. He died at Louisville, Kentucky, in 1850, full of years and full of honors. Captain John Shallcross, master of the John Nelson, was even then a veteran of the river, having been operating the Chieftain of the Missouri and the Mississippi. In the latter connection, he took four companies of the Third Regiment under Major S.W. Kearney to Prairie du Chien in June 1830. In 1831 he had taken the Chieftain, laden with goods for the Chouteaus, to the mouth of the Kansas River.

The Diana succeeded the Yellowstone the following year as the American Fur Company boat, and the Boonslick was another boat to come on the river. A year later the Boonslick collided with the Missouri Belle just above New Orleans, sinking the latter. The Boonslick rescued its passengers.

It was in 1834 that Captain Shallcross commanded the Iowa and one of his passengers noted that, "The boats that ply the Missouri River do not leave St. Louis until they are fully laden, which is some days or even weeks after they have been advertised to leave." From another source: "The steamboat Iowa carried about two hundred passengers, mostly poor adventurers engaged for a year by the Missouri Fur Company to man its posts in the West: bearded Parisians, Danes, Germans, Spaniards, English, Negroes, mulattos, Indians and half-breeds. Mostly Canadians, accustomed to hardships and dangers, skilled hunters and tireless explorers."

These steamboats were not the first trickles of traffic on the Missouri, but rather rivulets presaging the flood that soon would be coming up that stream.

Chapter Six

Burgeoning of the River Trade

Captain James B. Hill of the Otoe was the subject of some withering sarcasm in the spring of 1834 when a Columbia newspaper said; "In consequence of the neglect of the captain of the steamboat Otto (sic) to land at Nashville a quantity of paper shipped to us, we have been compelled to issue this number on paper a size smaller than usual. The above boat arrived at Nashville ten days ago and from thence departed for Liberty. When it returns, the captain may possibly find it convenient to land it."

The Otoe was named for an Indian tribe of southeastern Nebraska, but frequently is referred to as the Otto in literature of the river. It was in the service of Sublette & Campbell, competitors of the American Fur Company, who in 1833 had brought sixty-eight Pottawatomie Indians from Alton to Fort Leavenworth. They had come from Indiana, the first of their tribe to emigrate. In 1832 the Otoe had as passengers the party of Nathaniel J. Wyeth, from the Boston-Baltimore area, ostensibly bound for the Columbia River country "to operate a fur trade." The Otoe took the group to Independence where it joined the wagon train of William L. Sublette, first to cross the Rockies.

The Columbia newspaper that was so put out with the forgetfulness of Captain Hill took belated notice of the shipbuilding activities going on virtually under its nose.

They added, "We have heretofore neglected to mention, that a steamboat is now building at Franklin, Missouri, and another at Boonville, intended for the Missouri River trade. The commerce of the upper Missouri now keeps several steamboats constantly employed." The first-mentioned boat was the Far West. The second is not identified.

The Iowa struck a snag and sank, and Captain Shallcross was probably in charge of the Diana in 1835 when a missionary, traveling on that boat to Bellevue, Nebraska, wrote: "The captain, when troubled was very passionate and profane." Captain Shallcross was in charge of the Diana when it sank in 1836 at the Diana Bend, below Rocheport.

The Aull brothers, merchant princes of the western Missouri, had a small interest in the Otoe, but sold it and had the Chariton built, to be run under the command of Captain M. Littleton, who held one share. The boat made money despite its various mishaps. She sunk at the mouth of the Gasconade, but was raised and sank a second time at Wayne City, near Independence. In July 1837, she exploded her boiler at the levee in St. Louis, killing ten persons, and finally sank for keeps in Euphrasie Bend below Glasgow October 12, 1837.

After eighteen months the group that had owned the Chariton sold out to Captain Littleton and bought the Siam, which lost money. A tribute to the ability and popularity of Captain Littleton, no less!

Dr. Marcus Whitman and his wife, the beloved Narcissa, left Pittsburgh March 15, 1836, on the Siam, bound for Lapwai and Fort Vancouver to do missionary work in the Columbia River country. At Marietta, they stopped to pick up the Rev. Henry H. Spaulding and his wife, who had been appointed missionaries to the Osage Indians of western Missouri. They finished their trip down the Ohio on the Junius and took the Majestic to St. Louis. Arrangements had been made for them to travel with a fur caravan under Tom Fitzpatrick that would leave Bellevue, near the mouth of the Platte River. They were to take the Diane to Bellevue.

At St. Louis they learned the Spauldings were to go with them and a group of workers to the Columbia River. They also learned the Diane had departed without them.

They took the Chariton as far as Liberty, reaching there April 7, and expecting the Diane to return for them there. The St. Charles, which was to have brought their goods from St. Louis, came up without them, saying they had not been ready. The Diane came down, went on to St. Louis for the goods, but when it came back upriver it failed or refused to stop for the missionaries. This conduct of the part of the captain has never been explained. It probably was Captain Shallcross, "very passionate and profane."

The missionaries by frantic overland travel covered the two hundred fifty miles to Bellevue only to learn the caravan had left without them. They pursued along the North Platte and overtook the caravan seventy-five miles away.

The Alert was a new boat to come on the river in 1835, as was the Arrow, under Captain James McCord, father of Captain John L. McCord. Other boats that year were the A.S. Bennett, the Pocahontas No. 1, the St. Charles, the Cumberland Valley, the Euphrasie and the Antelope. The Euphrasie was named for the beautiful wife of the wealthy George Collier of St. Charles. The Antelope made the long voyage that year for the Missouri Fur Company.

This company in 1836 sent out the Trapper, and in July of that year the St. Charles burned at Richmond Landing, opposite Lexington. The Oceana, under Captain Miller, the Rhine, under Captain James McCord, the Boonville, the Ione and the Haidee were new on the river that year.

In 1837, the Missouri Fur Company sent out the St. Peters under Captain Chouteau, while the rival American Fur Company sent out the Elk. It was on this trip of the St. Peters that smallpox broke out on the boat, the disease quickly spreading to the Indian tribes of the upper river, causing widespread loss of life among the tribesmen. The Amaranth, under Captain George W. Atchison, the Pirate, under Captain Moore, the Tempest No. 1, the Clarion, and the Washington also made their bow that year, and the Phillos, Kanzas, Howard, Bridgewater and Fayette were reported as having arrived at St. Charles, with the Dart, owned by Captain John Cleveland of Glasgow, being "still above." Also on the river that year was the Chariton, Perkins, master.

During the year 1837, one hundred steamboats landed at Jefferson City, where twelve years before only one had stopped.

Captain Dan Able was on the river in 1838 with the fast J.H. Dickey and in one of the early races of the river, his boat beat the Peerless, causing an admiring editor to remark that "Captain Able is an old river fox and hard to head." Other boats making their initial runs that year were the St. Anthony No.1, the Glaucus, under Captain field, and the Little Red, named for the indomitable but unfortunate Senator David Barton. It was under command of Captain Enoch Price, veteran of the river.

That year, there were two hundred and sixty-four steamboat arrivals at Jefferson City, compared with the one hundred landings made two years before, and the solitary landing of 1826.

In the year 1840, the river came alive with steamboats. The American Fur Company sent out the Emilie No. 1 under Captain J.W. Keiser. Captain James McCord had the ill-fated Edna, which blew up two years later at Green Island at the mouth of the Missouri River, killing fifty-five German immigrants. Captain Martin had bought an interest and was in charge though not responsible when the disaster occurred. Captain McCord had the Naomi on the river that year, too. Another boat to make its appearance was the Big Hatchie. The Bowling Green and the Nodaway were boats belonging to the wealthy Captain John J. Roe of St. Louis. In 1843 the Nodaway brought six hundred and fifty Indians, assisted by the Republic, from Cincinnati to the mouth of the Kaw River. These were the last of the Wyandots to migrate to their new home in Kansas.

The Dakota, under Captain Finch, the Nimrod and the Thames, both under Captain Dennis, the Yucatan under

Captain S. Banks, the Bertrand under Captain James Yore, the Osage Valley under Captain Young, the Carroll No. 1 under Captain Weath, and the Wapello under Captain Nathaniel Jackson Eaton, made their bow that year, as did the Columbian, Corvette, Geneva No.1, John Aull, Lynchburg, St. Croix No. 1, the Warsaw and the Charles H. Green. The Transient and the Huntsville, too, were on the river that year, but the latter, returning to its wonted route between St. Louis and eastern ports, "took a sheer" on its pilot while in the Cumberland River and was lost. That year, too, the Albany, the Jim Brown, the Bedford, the Rhine and the Mail were on the river.

The Nimrod, under Captain Dennis, landed at Bellevue in 1844 with a large quantity of whisky concealed in barrels of flour to evade the inspection of Indian Agent Miller, a former Methodist minister. The agent discovered the deception, but too late to stop the shipment that was intended for upriver Indians. However, his official complaint of the trickery set up reverberations that caused trouble and embarrassment to the American Fur Company, owner of the boat. In 1846 James W. Magoffin and three others were passengers on the Nimrod, Independence to St. Louis, carrying forty thousand dollars in specie. One of his companions was Edward James Glasgow, who with Dr. Henry Connelly had embarked in the Santa Fe trade. He later served as commercial agent for the United States at Chihuahua. Magoffin had just arrived at Independence with a wagon train from Santa Fe and was on his way to Washington for a conference with President Polk. Having a great deal of influence with the Mexicans, he has been credited with smoothing the way for an easy conquest by American troops entering Santa Fe.

Captain Yore's Bertrand is thought to have been named for Joseph Bertrand, Jr., a fur trader. Hiram Bersie was captain of the St. Croix No. 1. The Thames had as a passenger in 1840, Tixier, who had been in Indian country and had come down the Osage, boarding the boat just below the mouth of the Osage. The Warsaw was a small boat, built under the supervision of Captain McCourtney at

Boonville in 1840 and intended for use in the Osage River trade.

"A very agreeable man," according to Alfred S. Waugh, artist, who rode the boat from St. Louis to Jefferson City, captained the Wapello, named for a chief in the Sauk and Fox tribe. In May 1846, it brought Missouri volunteer soldiers upriver to Fort Leavenworth to take part in Doniphan's great march on Mexico. Eaton had entered the national military academy in 1832 as a cadet from Massachusetts, had become a first lieutenant in 1836, and was dropped in 1837. His military service was performed at the Jefferson Barracks, 1827 to 1835, during which time he participated in the Black Hawk War. From 1837 to 1849 he was master of various steamboats on the western rivers. He died in 1883 at St. Louis, where he had been post warden of the harbor.

Sir William Drummond Stewart, a Scotchman, who had come to America to hunt buffalo, organized a party of about eighty men at St. Louis in 1843. The party left St. Louis in April on the John Aull, named for the Lexington merchant, outfitter of mountain men and Santa Fe traders. Father De Smet was to accompany the party as far as Westport. At Glasgow the John Aull was overtaken by the Omega, carrying the celebrated artist and naturalist, John James Audubon. Some of the party went aboard the Omega and talked with Audubon, whose long gray hair gave him a romantic wildness of aspect. The artist was most interested in the missionary and his work among the Indians. The Stewart party left the John Aull at Westport Landing to set out across the plains led by the veteran mountain man, William L. Sublette.

In 1844 Captain Middleton took over the fast Missouri Mail and was reported "up for a pleasure trip to Council Bluffs."

Steamboating on the Missouri River had not been entered upon in 1819 without considerable justifiable trepidation. As such things go, it was but a whisper of time back to the stark experiments of Fitch and Fulton, while Roosevelt's first hazardous adventure with a steamboat on western waterways was but a yesterday away. Undoubtedly, Captain Nelson's Independence was a clumsy, awkward thing, its mechanical driving force an experiment, feeling its way through a channel fraught with unseen and even unknown dangers.

This held true for the boats that were to follow it, though the danger grew less as the operators learned more of the mechanism of their craft and to adopt whatever innovations in machinery as seemed to enhance speed and endurance, or to promote the safety of passengers. There was less danger from the treacherous river itself as pilots came to know and recognize and avoid the danger spots. From the fifty-ton Independence, it was a far cry to the boats several times its size, multiplied in numbers, carrying goods on a river that from the viewpoint of traffic potentials had tripled in length. And a far cry, too, from the time when steamboating was synonymous with suicide to the quarter century later when a veteran riverain could be reported as bringing his steamboat upriver "for a pleasure trip to Council Bluffs."

Chapter Seven

Gem of the River Towns

Hardeman's Gardens, about six miles above Old Franklin, was one of the most interesting places on the whole river, a tract of ten acres laid out by John Hardeman in 1819. With its more than six hundred different plants, mostly European, the plots set off and separated by neat and winding shell walks, it was a show place of the West. A large part of the garden was swept away by floodwaters in 1826. Hardeman died in New Orleans in 1829 and by 1837 only a neglected corner of the garden remained. His antecedents shrouded in mystery, he was one of the best-posted horticulturists of his day and, according to the Glasgow Missourian, author of several books on the subject.

He belonged to a small coterie of intellectuals, who lived in the neighborhood, including Genera Thomas A. Smith, who had left the management of Fort Bellefontaine, going upriver to Old Franklin to become registrar of lands, and had a farm nearby comprising five thousand acres. Also included would have been Beverly Tucker, who had abandoned his hollow-tree law office near Fort Belle-fontaine to cast his lot in the vicinity of Old Franklin. His estate, called "Ardmore," was a magnificent place of many acres, quite in contrast with his former abode.

Dr. John A. Sappington of Arrow Rock made a fourth in the group, and also was the writer of a book, a treatise on the use of quinine, a new drug at the time, from which he derived the foundation of a fortune.

Arrow Rock, just above Hardeman's Gardens, was laid out as a town in 1820, though a settlement had existed for a decade previous. Brackenridge described the scene in 1811; "The hills rise with a most delightful ascent from the water's edge, to the height of forty or fifty feet... The settlement is but one year old, but is already considerable and increasing rapidly; it consists of seventy-five families, the greater part living on the bank of the river."

The town became an important point for Santa Fe traders and was beginning to take note of the increasing river traffic in 1830 when Joseph Huston built his famed Arrow Rock Tavern which was to dispense hospitality to travelers by trail or water – traders, trappers, bullwhackers, pilots, politicians, homeseekers, land sharks, lawyers, soldiers and merchants.

In time Arrow Rock became an important shipping point, gaining from the steamboats what it had lost when the initial point of the Santa Fe Trail moved farther west. Steamboats carrying freight up and down the river would unload it there to be hauled by wagons to the neighboring inland towns. One of these boats, the Ohio, struck a snag and sank near Arrow Rock in 1846. This gave an opposition paper opportunity to take a dig at the administration; "This is the second steamboat that has sunk with government stores in the Missouri River since the veto of the river and harbors bill. So much for the economy of our locofoco president."

With the passing of the river trade, Arrow Rock became a sleepy little town, a sleepy old town, one of the oldest towns on the river.

A few miles above Arrow Rock was the town of Lisbon, and just beyond that, but yet short perhaps two miles of the present Glasgow, was Bluffport, now only a name and even its exact location unknown.

Some fifteen miles or more upriver from Arrow Rock there developed near the mouth of the Chariton River a nest of towns, or a series of towns, beginning with Chariton, which was established in 1816 by Duff Green. He was then about thirty years of age, well educated, both generally and in the law, practicing in Missouri River towns as far west as Bluffton, which he helped establish. He was considered wealthy and took an active part in state and national politics. He went to Washington to establish the United States Telegram, organ of opposition to John Quincy Adams. For thirty years he conducted newspapers in Washington, being credited with immense party power. He became the center of what Senator Benton called "the cabal of intriguers for the annexation of Texas." He died in Dalton, Georgia, in 1875.

By 1822 Chariton had one hundred and seventy-seven inhabitants. Excitement ran high and the town was expected to rival St. Louis. By 1826 the place had attained a population of two thousand. After ten years, in which it was one of the liveliest towns on the river, it was decided the site was unhealthy and most of the town was moved to higher ground a mile inland, the new place being given the name of Monticello. After three years of this, the site was changed again, to a spit of land thrusting into the Missouri River from the mouth of the Chariton, the place being called Thorntonburg after one of its merchants. This place was soon changed to Louisville-on-the-Missouri River.

But Chariton never yielded in prestige to these newer towns; its name still being a household word along the river after their names were forgotten. As late as 1937, Duff Green's pretentious brick home was being used as "an excellent house of entertainment." The home of William Cabanne was destroyed by fire as late as 1916.

It was not until 1837 that there arose what was to become Chartion's real successor – the town of Glasgow, two miles downstream, named for James Glasgow, early settler.

The importance of steamboat navigation to this new town became at once apparent to its citizens, many of them being interested in the ownership or operation of steam-boats. All steamboats, coming and going, landed at this port and all the town's business was transacted at the river's brink. Water Street was a mile long and in the heyday of steamboating all of its seven landings at times were occupied while some boats had to wait their turn to get in. It was called the gem of the river towns.

Captain John Cleveland owned the Dart and ran it between Glasgow and St. Louis. Lewis D. Dameron and John D. Perry, also of Glasgow, were interested in steamboating. Both went to St. Louis and became successful businessmen. While living in Glasgow, Perry maintained a large home overlooking the river and when his boat, the John D. Perry, made her maiden landing in 1857 it was a holiday in Glasgow. It cost fifty thousand dollars, was two hundred and twenty feet long and considered one of the best on the river. It ran for twelve years before it burned at Duvall's Bluff on the White River in Arkansas. Near the Perry residence was the hospitable home of big John (Dutch) Davis, who became a steamboat captain on the Missouri. The young folks of the town especially enjoyed downriver excursions on the moonlit deck of the Kate Howard, where they danced to the music of fiddle and banjo as guests of Captain "Joe" Nanson.

The Martha Jewett, owned principally by Glasgow capital, was named for the sister or Captain "Dandy" Jewett, whose home was said to have been in Glasgow, but being a bachelor, he had not established a residence. Stricken with cholera in 1854 on his boat, he was taken to the home of Captain W.J. Stratton in Glasgow where he died within a few days. Some historians, who have said he died in St. Louis, apparently have overlooked his obituary in the Glasgow Weekly Times of July 13, 1854. Captain Edward T. Herndon was master of the William J. Lewis, built especially for the mountain trade, and it was on this boat that Captain George W. Vaughan learned the river. In his later years he became a lecturer and writer of historical articles pertaining to the old days on the river.

Captain Henry McPherson commanded the C.W. Sombart, named for a wealthy Boonville judge, running it between Glasgow and downriver ports until it was destroyed by fire in 1858 when he bought the Carrier and ran it for three years. The popular Captain Ben Glime was interested with others in having built the St. Nicholas, intending it for the lower Mississippi trade. His wedding to a belle of Glasgow was a gala event, taking place on the new boat tied up at the wharf. The maiden voyage of the St. Nicholas became the honeymoon trip of the newlyweds. But tragedy stalked the honeymoon. Somewhere below St. Louis, the boilers blew up, the boat was lost and nearly all on board were burned to death or drowned, the list including Captain Glime and his bride.

Captain William D. Swinney came from Virginia in 1832 and settled near the site of Glasgow, becoming the town's leading citizen of all time, interested in tobacco and steamboats and piling up a large fortune. It was for his daughter the steamboat Kate Swinney was named in 1849.

The most extensive tobacco-manufacturing firm in Glasgow was B.W. Lewis & Brother and the steamboat Ben W. Lewis was named for and largely owned by the head of this firm. A few miles above Old Chariton the town of Cambridge existed as early as 1833. Its main street, on which were the general stores, ran parallel with the river, the levee being paved with limestone. Long a flourishing river town, it was more than a hundred years old before it joined the lengthening list of ghost towns of the river.

Three miles upriver from this town had been Jefferson, now usually spoken of as Old Jefferson, established in 1820. As early as 1837, it was referred to as "once a deserted village, now improving or taking on a second growth." But two years later a traveler referred to it as "Old Jefferson, the remains of a townsite, six mile above Glasgow." In time it faded and New Frankfort now occupies the site. Just above was Hamilton, which existed only on paper.

The Rev. Thomas Keytes, who named the town for his old home in England, laid out Brunswick, ten miles above Glasgow and one mile below Grand River, in 1836. He also founded Keytesville Landing, noted as the home of General Sterling Price. For ten years or more Brunswick was the nearest steamboat landing for towns almost as far north as the Iowa line. It gave the river at least two steamboat captains. One, Captain DeWitt Clinton Basey, whose father was a hotelkeeper in Brunswick, was born in 1837 and went out on the river when he was fifteen. He became a well-known river man and went on the Yukon River in 1898 during the great gold rush. Captain Jasper Marion Peery went to Brunswick in 1854, being then twenty-two. He became captain of the David Tatum, named for a famous Boonville steamboat pilot, and ran it between Brunswick and St. Louis.

In time, the river changed its course and Brunswick was left far inland. In 1848, a Colonel Whistler of the United States army laid off a town just west of Brunswick, which he called Grand River City, but the place seemed quickly to have joined the list of ghost towns.

DeWitt, a few miles above Brunswick, was laid out also in 1837, but by 1852 was known as Winsor City and reference was made to this "recently laid out town."

Across the river and four miles above DeWitt, the town of Greenville was platted in 1838 by Henry Ferrill, who had been operating a ferry at that point, the name being changed to Miami in 1841. It was here the Burrus family of rivermen lived and operated such boats as the A.C. Bird, the Lucy Lee, the Mattie Lee, the Columbia, the Commodore and the Lloyd. The town quickly superseded Doyleston, a few miles east on the Missouri River near the old Miami Indian fort, which had been chartered by William Doyle, dentist. Somewhere near Miami was the river town of Philadelphia, built a mile or so back from the river. Around 1827 it was a promising village, but now not even a pile of stones remains to mark its location.

Next above Miami was Malta Ben, named for Captain Joseph W. Throckmorton's steamboat Malta, which sank there in 1841. When a town was platted at that point in 1867 it was given the name of Malta Bend.

In 1845, Washington Shroyer platted Middleton, the name being changed three years later to Waverly. Colonel John Dennis Thomas, who had settled there in 1822, founded St. Thomas in 1850, on land adjoining to the east. The towns merged and now are known as Waverly.

This was the home of Jo Shelby, Confederate general, who refused to follow Lee into surrender and who took his brigade into Old Mexico and placed it at the disposal of Emperor Maximilian. When he married his cousin, Miss Elizabeth Shelby, at Waverly, two steamboats were chartered to take the wedding party to St. Louis.

Though several miles back from the river, Carrollton was rated a river town, known in 1839 as "the devil's headquarters." Its contact with the river was made at Caton's Landing and at Hill's Landing, known locally as "Shanghai," home of Captain William Baker. William's home was used as a hotel for steamboat travelers. The home of Captain Woolfolk was nearby and across the river was Wells Landing and Old Buffington Landing. Above the latter was Webb's Landing, in 1833 considered an important shipping point.

Next came Mill's Point, Fine's Landing, the quaint little village of Dover, which had been platted in 1833, Berlin, Mount Vernon, and after that the important river town of Lexington.

Chapter Eight

Tragedy at Dead Man's Bend

The nucleus of Lexington was formed when William Jack and his wife went there from Tennessee in 1820 to establish a ferry on the Missouri River near the mouth of Rupe Creek, though the need for a ferry at that point was not plain. However, more and more settlers, mostly from Kentucky and Tennessee, were beginning to take up claims on both sides of the river in that vicinity. The ambitious Duff Green was offering lots for sale in Bluffton on the north side of the river and only a few miles upstream from the site of the new ferry. His town of Chariton, eighty-five miles downstream, was the first town east of Jack's Ferry, and with the exception of Arrow Rock, the only town between Old Franklin and the site of Lexington. The latter was laid out in 1822 on a high crest overlooking the Missouri River, the first location becoming known as "old town" when "new town" was platted in 1836.

There appeared to be hardly any more excuse for establishing a town at Jack's Ferry than there had been in the first place for the ferry. There was a good natural landing for the keelboats, and far-seeing promoters probably envisaged a western metropolis at that point should there come an expansion of traffic due to the steamboats, just then making their initial appearance on the Missouri. These town-builders did not see their vision of the future wholly realized, but the stature and importance that Lexington finally gained must have been a source of much personal satisfaction as well as an exemplification of the soundness of their theories. In those early days as the population movement proceeded upriver with almost the inevitable tread of destiny, it became the unique position of town after town to serve as the jumping-off place for western-bound immigrants and ox-team freighters and as the terminal point for the steamboats. Each such town hoped some day to develop into the great metropolis of the Missouri River and of the West. Lexington was no exception.

Lexington might have been called the town that hemp built, for this was its most important industry and the cause of the town's steady growth from the time of its founding until emancipation of the Negro slaves rendered hemp production unprofitable. Slave labor was essential to the profitable growing of hemp, hence important to the continued success and prosperity of Lexington.

To take care of the hemp and other trade, warehouses and rope walks soon were established in Lexington, among them being that of Alfred K. Stevens. Stevens was given a permit as early as August 6, 1822, to build a warehouse on the river for the storage and inspection of tobacco. Other warehouses were the large warehouse and rope walk of Oliver Anderson and his sons, where all kinds of produce were accepted for shipment. Another was the establishment of the McGrew brothers at the upper landing where a rope factory was maintained and the proprietors had the reputation of buying "anything from drove of hogs to a wagon load of hoop poles."

John Aull, who had a store in Chariton, was the pioneer in the commission and trading business of Lexington, having in 1822 built a store and warehouse on the river bank. In 1825, his brothers James and Robert joined him, the concern branching out to nearby towns and becoming the leading supply firm of the frontier. They sent "sand and hammered" dollars to their agents in St. Louis, the coins concealed in the heads of barrels of freight and the barrels marked. These probably were the Mexican silver dollars in use in western Missouri around 1830.

Nearly all the town's business was done down by the river, in that part of Lexington referred to as "under the hill." This was particularly true from the late 1830's on, when the volume of steamboat traffic was on the increase. The levee was two hundred feet wide and four hundred feet long and as many as thirty steamboats stopped at Lexington in a single day. Merchants from nearby towns and from southwest Missouri came or sent their big Santa Fe wagons, drawn by four or five yoke of oxen. These wagons were loaded with hemp and other products, often forming long lines to move down Broadway to the warehouses where the product was sold and stored. For the return trip these wagons would be loaded with groceries, salt, flour, whisky, rope, plows, stoves and other items. Conditions were so crowded "under the hill" that there was hardly room for these long wagon trains to turn, so that they usually proceeded down to the river via Broadway, but returned over the road through "Irishtown."

While Lexington "under the hill" was booming with its warehouses, rope factories, flour mill, sawmill, coal mines, and foundry, that part of the town on the bluff also was making progress. The tavern of Elisha Green in "old town" had given way to Poole's Tavern in "new town." Green's tavern had once been where the judges of the county court had held their sessions when Lexington first took the county seat away from Mount Vernon, six miles downriver. After Poole's burned down, it was succeeded by Burtis Hotel, named for its builder, but sometimes called the Grand Central. Burtis was a big man, a courageous Whig who owned slaves but opposed slavery. Town rounders were refused the rum which he kept on sale to better trade. His one weakness, apparently, was staying up all night to gamble on one of the steamboats usually to be found lying over at Lexington for the night. This hostelry later called the City Hotel and run by William F. Walton, was a popular resort during the old steamboat days. It was torn down in 1905.

A year after "new town" was platted; Lexington was described as "One of the towns from which outfits are made in merchandise, mules, oxen and wagons for the Santa Fe or Mexican trade. The fur traders who pass to the mountains by land make this town a rendezvous, and frequently are going out and coming in with their wagons and pack mules, at the same period of coming and going that is chosen by the Mexican traders. Lexington is, therefore, occasionally a thoroughfare of traders of great enterprise and caravans of infinite value."

The town of Lexington had a dual personality – one, having its exegis on the hill, where the colleges and seminaries and churches with graceful spires and the ornate brick residences supplied all that was needful for a background of culture and gracious living. Here was the private school, now the public library, kept by young James Lane Allen, who later was to become famous for such books as A Kentucky Cardinal and Choir Invisible. Here were the homes of the merchant princes, situated to afford a view of the river, up and down, for many miles, where they could see and hear the steamboats. Here were the homes of the educators, the lawyers, the ministers, the bankers, the editors – in short, this was the abode of the gentry, citizens of a staid, contented attitude.

This was the polite side of Lexington, for which A.B. Jackson gave a series of lessons in the polite accomplishment of dancing, at the Mansion House, teaching quadrilles, waltzes, mescolanzes, and Spanish dances, "the ladies' class to meet in the afternoon and the gentlemen's class at early candlelight." It was the social crowd that gave the elaborate balls on the second floor of the Arcanum Hall, gliding to the strains of Henry Switzer's orchestra; sometimes listening to the Lafayette Silver Cornet band, or later, to the Zeiler brothers.

The other side of the picture was presented by "under the hill." Here were the saloons and dives catering to those Lexingtonians who lived by the sweat of their brows and the exercise of their brawny arms – coal miners, railroaders and riverains. On frequent occasions they spilled over their natural confines and went roistering up Broadway or along the "Irishtown" road, arriving uptown in such a hilarious state as to completely upset the aplomb of the better citizens. This caused the Lexington Express to note that "marauding night brawlers continue their depredations unwhipped of justice, and we hear of no provisions making to better the present state of things."

However much they might have resented the incursions of hoi polloi from below, gentlemen from on the hill on occasion sought recreation "under the hill." When Lewis W. Stofer, editor of the Expositor, engaged in a little game on the steamboat A.B. Chambers, a difficulty arose and he was shot in the head by a gambler named Clark. There was a great excitement and the levee was crowded with men bent on a lynching, but authorities succeeded in landing Clark in the county jail. The jail was a miserable wooden structure on the outskirts of town, whose chief claim to fame was that it once held Murrell, the South's most noted outlaw. It had been described as "a goods-box jail."

Lexington in time became one of the most important steamboat towns on the river. When a steamboat approached the landing there would be a scene of activity in the livery barns. This was where two or four horses would be hitched to big red coaches which dashed about town to collect passengers who might have been booked for several days, remaining in a state of expectancy and unrest, waiting for the whistle of their boat. Such delay in the arrival of the steamboats was not unusual nor was it unexpected. The boats frequently were several days late, having been caught on a sand bar or held up for other reasons. One such delay at Lexington's Dead Man's Bend, plus the impatience of a steamboat captain, resulted in the greatest tragedy in the history of the Missouri River, the sinking of the steamboat Saluda on April 9, 1852.

This has become a legend of the river. Much has been written about it and much romancing has been done. The boat, under Captain F.T. Belt, arrived at Dead Man's Bend on April 6, but the spring thaw was on and the river, full of ice, was racing around the curve. Pilot Charles La Barge vainly tried for three days to negotiate the bend. After each trial, he was forced back to the levee. On the morning of the third day, the boat had gone but a little distance from shore when there was a loud explosion, the Saluda shivered and then seemed to fall apart. Wreckage and bodies flew through the air. Peter Conrad was blown to shore. Captain Belt and La Barge lost their lives. It has been said that Captain Belt ordered the engineer to make all steam possible, saying he "would either round the point or blow the boat to hell." His family in St. Louis immediately took steps to disprove this assertion, but the picturesque legend lingers on. The forward deck was crowded with passengers, most of them emigrants for Utah, when all the boilers exploded, causing a complete wreck of that part of the boat above the lower deck and extending back to the wheelhouse. The current threw the wrecked boat back against the shore, where it was partly submerged. Captain Belt, a large man, was found on shore, his body denuded, where he had "sailed through the air like a blue rock." Every physician in town and most of the male population went to the levee to help in the rescue work. A large brick house at the upper end of the levee served as a temporary hospital. Taking care of the wounded, dying and dead was like working on a battlefield. Sixteen babies under one year old were laid out side by side. One baby was picked up a mile downstream, still sleeping in its crib.

Despite all the articles that have been written about the sinking of the Saluda, the current account, given by the Express of April 10, probably kept closest to the facts;

"At half-past seven the Saluda blew up as she was leaving the wharf on her upward trip to the Council Bluffs. The first clerk informs us there were one hundred seventy-five persons on board, only fifty of whom survived. Captain Belt and Pilots La Barge and Lewis Tepo were killed. Captain Miller of the Isabel refused to land alongside the Saluda, saying he believed the boat, with its old boilers, to be a menace."

Upbound steamboats were crowding the river, carrying passengers to the frontier. In 1845, the John Golong with William W. Baker as master had been the first boat up the river. It had been fitted up expressly to run as a regular packet between Weston and St. Louis. During its October trip, Father Bernard Donnelly, to become a celebrated Catholic leader in Kansas City, was one of its passengers. The river was at its lowest stage and he wrote; "After a toilsome journey of eleven days over sand bars, often close to snags and always against the current, Mr. Golong reached Owens or Blue Mills Landing in safety." This was the steamboat landing for Independence, the intervening distance of seven miles being covered in a hack.

In April 1846, young Francis Parkman went up the river on the Radnor, of which J.R. Douglas was captain, his destination being Westport Landing. This was where he would set out on that "tour of curiosity and amusement to the Rocky Mountains" which was to furnish material for his western classic, The Oregon Trail. The boat was crammed with wagons and goods for the Santa Fe trade and provisions for Oregon immigrants. In the cabin he noted Santa Fe traders, gamblers, speculators and adventurers. In steerage were the mountain men, Negroes, and a party of Kansas Indians returning from a visit to St. Louis. These were signs of a new life on the river. The mid-century was to see the packet trade flourish as never before in the brief history of steamboating on the Missouri, to usher in the era of the palatial packets.

The spectacular explosion of the Missouri River steamboat
SALUDA at Lexington, Mo. in 1852. Over 100 lives were lost.

Chapter Nine

Palatial Packets on Parade

Romance rode the river in the days of the packet, with its gingerbread superstructure of scrollwork and bright paint, its blazing furnaces and belching smokestacks, its gilded ballroom, and its staterooms done in blue and pink and yellow. Every boat was a "floating palace," cabins and saloons finished in the finest mahogany and furnished with silken draperies and rich carpets. Table china was imported, decorated with a picture of the boat, and monogrammed linen was on the tables. The cabin was a marvel of beauty in its snow-white splendor, with generally a landscape scene painted on the panel of each stateroom door and a beautiful oil painting hung in the after part of the ladies' cabin. There were porcelain knobs on the doors, filigree work overhead in the cabins, touched with gilding, big chandeliers with dazzling glass prisms that glistened and reflected every color of the rainbow as rays of sunlight penetrated through the colored-glass skylights. Staterooms opened on the deck and awning-covered promenades stretched from stem to stern. Argand lamps were used, named for their inventor, Aime Argand of Geneva. This was the lamp with a tubular wick that admitted a current of air inside as well as outside the flame. Elaborate glass chandeliers multiplied the brilliance of the many lights. That was the packet in her days of white paint and gold, when the sound of her whistle blowing for a landing, low, melodious and leisurely, would have caused the levee to be lined with beautiful women in hoopskirts and beaux in stocks and tight trousers.

Originally, packets were vessels employed by the government to convey dispatches of mail, but by the mid-forties the term was applied also to boats carrying passengers and goods and operating on fixed schedules.

The Amazon in 1846 took three hundred and twenty-three Indians from St. Louis to the Kansas River from where they went overland to the Osage River agency on Little Sugar Creek. In 1856, under Captain H. Hazlett, it was the first boat on the river to have a calliope, that instrument having been invented the year before by J.C. Stoddard of Worcester, Massachusetts.

The Annawan in 1843 had brought John James Audubon down from Alton, Illinois, to St. Louis where he boarded the Omega for a trip to the upper Missouri River. In his party were John G. Bell, Isaac Sprague, Lewis Squires, and Edward Harris. The latter has given a complete description of that trip in his Up the River with Audubon. Captain Joseph A. Sire of the Omega was born in LaRochelle, France, in 1799, and came to St. Louis from Philadelphia in 1821 and died there in 1854. He married Victoire Labadie and was therefore a cousin by marriage of Pierre Chouteau, junior, and Peter B. Sarpy.

The General Brooke was named for General George M. Brooke, doughty Virginian, and then division commander in the West. A Chouteau boat, it was sent to the Yellowstone in 1845 with Captain Throckmorton in command. Shown on its paddle boxes were the face and bust of the general in full regimentals.

The Henry Bry was at the Westport Landing that year with John Charles Fremont and a company of sixty men heading for the West.

The Lewis F. Linn was named for the United States senator from Missouri who because of his interest in promoting the northwest country became known as the father of Oregon. The Mendota had been named for one of the posts of the American Fur Company. The Martha, Captain Joseph La Barge, brought John Charles Fremont and a party of thirty-five to the Westport Landing for another of his journeys through the West, this time through Cimarron country, led by the scout and guide Kit Carson, who met him at Westport. This time, the Pathfinder was accompanied as far as Westport by the "immortal wife," Jessie, daughter of Senator Thomas Hart Benton.

It was a custom of the packets to give free excursions, sometimes up the river, sometimes down. These excursions were usually at night. The boat kept slowly on the move, returning to its home port just before daylight. There was a fascination in the picture to be seen from the deck of a river packet at night, the lights shining across the water in rippling ribbons, the moon and the stars visible over the smooth surface of the river, stabbing and accentuating the darkness.

The social life on the packets was lively, each boat having a piano and a string band, a dance being always in order at night. This might have been the Sir Roger de Coverly, a stately form of the Virginia reel, or a polka, or the varsuvienne. At all towns along the river it was the custom for young people to go aboard for an excursion. The steamboat business was romantic in the days of the packets, and is one of the most picturesque and delightful memories of the American frontier.

The popularity of a packet depended not alone on its speed or its magnificent furnishings. Cuisine was an important factor and the best chefs and the best waiters were obtained. It was a matter of pride with hotel dining rooms along the river to advertise the services of a former steamboat chef.

Trouble with Mexico developed into a shooting war in 1846 and Missouri River steamboats were useful in helping our soldiers over the first leg of their journey to the scene of conflict. Fort Leavenworth was the receiving center for volunteers preparatory to their overland march to Santa Fe. Volunteers from Howard County, Missouri, embarked at Glasgow May 23, 1846, on the Wapello. The

Galena was reported on the river with soldiers in September, and the following spring Governor William Walker of Nebraska, which then included Kansas, noted in his diary: "Today our Wyandott volunteers set out on board the Amelia for the seat of war." Ben Holladay, who had come up to Weston on a steamboat a decade before, began hauling war material and laying the foundation for the fortune which would enable him to build up his empire on wheels.

The river was becoming more and more the highway of settlers heading for the Southwest or for the Northwest. In 1847-48 it was crowded with boats and the boats were crowded with emigrants, for the packets afforded the only water route westward.

Mark Twain had been a sub-pilot on the Paul Jones, and according to his Life on the Mississippi, a snag knocked her bottom out and she sank like a pot because there was a gray mare and a preacher aboard.

The steamboat pilots, in their fine ruffled shirts, tight fitting boots, long black coats and plug hats, were the ✴ dandies of the river towns, matrimonial catches for whom the belles eagerly set their caps. The pilot might have been a Jim Gunsollis with a weakness for wearing diamonds, who received and spent a salary of eight hundred dollars a month and died in poverty. Or he might have been a Joe Oldham, who wore the largest, heaviest and most expensive gold watch on the river. The watch was ornamented with a five-hundred-dollar diamond and hung from Oldham's neck by a large gold chain. He, too, died in poverty.

Discovery of gold in California placed a new burden on Missouri River transportation. The rush of gold seekers was in the early stages in the years 1849-50, the crowds being carried by such boats as the Duroc, under Captain William H. Parkinson; the Sacramento, under Captain John Rogers; the El Paso, under Captain T. H. Brierly; the Pocahontas, under Captain Henry J. Moore; the St. Paul, Monroe, L.L. McLean, General Lane, Tuscumbia, Mary Blane, James Mulligan, Hungarian, St. Ange, Princeton,

Cambria, Robert Campbell, and the Ne Plus Ultra.

Captain James A. Pritchard boarded the Cambria at Petersburg, Kentucky, April 10, 1849, at which time there already were aboard several other companies of gold seekers from different states. According to a passenger on the boat when it landed at St. Louis, there was a large company on board, most for California, among them about thirty "real live Yankees from Maine – some of them always shooting guns and pistols." The Cambria unloaded its cargo of Argonauts at Wayne City. Among the passengers on the Embassy was Alonzo Delano from Indiana, who claimed in California to be a businessman first and a writer second, and actually was in charge of the Wells-Fargo Banking and exchange office in Grass Valley. Writing as "Old Block," his Tales of California Life became a classic of the gold rush. The Bay State was reported as crowded with Forty-niners. From Glasgow to Fort Leavenworth, the Algoma carried in May the party of General John Wilson, lawyer, newly appointed Indian agent for Salt Lake and naval agent for San Francisco. His adventures in reaching the gold fields could have filled a book.

As one method of whiling away the time on long and tedious river voyages, gambling was commonly indulged in, faro being the rule. Play frequently ran high and sometimes a gambler held the "dead man's hand," two black jacks, two red sevens, and any fifth card. Rough voyageurs, back from the mountains and the gold fields, enlivened proceedings as they tried to drink all the liquor on board and played cards all the way to St. Louis, their gambling aboard the packets rendering pale the feats of Monte Carlo. Many of the boats were infested with professional gamblers, often in league with and giving commissions to the dignified bartender, who did not himself descend to the vulgarity of mixing drinks, but employed help for that purpose. These gamblers fleeced the frenzied gold seekers and more particularly the successful ones returning downriver. The gamblers never took long trips, but after making a killing on one boat would disembark and board another. They generally operated in small groups, were quiet, well dressed, courteous and soft-spoken. Their favorite game was poker, yet any game of chance would find them participating. There was little or no restriction on gambling, games being started in the cabin every evening, frequently continuing all night, with the ladies often playing, and for high stakes. Joseph Latrobe, in The Rambler in North America, referred to the small apartment found on some steamboats, called "social hall," as "a den of sharpers and blacklegs, where from morning till night the dirty packs of cards passed from hand to hand."

Joseph Latrobe, with Washington Irving, had been bound for Independence, which, with Westport, was a base for the wagon trains heading for the West.

To keep the packets going when the West depended on river traffic, Snagboats cleared trees and roots out of the channels.

Chapter Ten

When Long
Caravans Rolled

Independence became the successor of Fort Osage as rendezvous and jumping-off place for those adventurers who paused there to make sure that all was in readiness before plunging into that vast grassy ocean lying to the west. In setting out over the long rails that led from Independence, some sought romance, some sought adventure, but most sought wealth. These were the impelling forces that sent men out on far journeys to build strong forts, erect proud states, and found glittering cities. For many, the desert plunge spelled oblivion from whence they never returned, while others went on to attain high and exalted places in the worlds of politics, of education, and of finance, or to become otherwise noted. Independence was the successor of Fort Osage because of an important difference. Where a mere trickle of travel had passed in the heyday of Fort Osage, the volume of travel through Independence grew and grew with every passing year, reaching its apogee in a frenzied outpouring of men, women, children, vehicles and beasts of burden of every description. The little frontier city became the fountainhead from which the streams of immigration flowed over three nationally important trails: one leading west to Bent's Fort in Colorado, then north to Salt Lake, thence to California; one leading northwest to Fort Laramie, the South Pass and the

Oregon country. The third was the Santa Fe Trail, running as the traders said, "from civilization to sundown." The Santa Fe Trail was the making of Independence.

After the steamboats became practical factors in moving goods upriver, that is, the late thirties, the goods for the Santa Fe trade were discharged at Blue Mills Landing, as Prine's Ferry had come to be known. For a time Blue Mills was called Livingstone in honor of Edward Livingstone, secretary of state in President Jackson's cabinet.

As a port for Independence, this place was superseded by Wayne City, which formerly had been known as Ducker's Ferry. One traveler, getting off a steamboat there in 1850, described it as "the most miserable of all wretched collections of log huts that were ever inhabited by pickpockets, grog vendors and vagabonds of every shade, name and nature." There was a railroad running the three or four miles to Independence, which, with possibly one exception, was the first railroad to the West.

Independence, by virtue of its advantageous location near the big bend of the Missouri, immediately became the point of articulation of river traffic with both the Santa Fe and the mountain trade.

When Lilburn W. Boggs, assistant factor at Fort Osage, laid out the town of Independence in 1827 he "anchored" business to the town square, around which the storehouses became clustered. About the square, or in the vicinity, were numerous "groceries" as the grog shops were called. Each of these places was equipped with its gambling tables and otherwise prepared to furnish whatever vice was necessary for a prolonged spree when the greasy, dirty mountain men with their long hair and buckskin suits brought in their peltries or the traders returned from Santa Fe. Then were times of high carnival in the frontier town of Independence.

In the early thirties, young Washington Irving came with his friend, Joseph Latrobe, and others, looking at the country, a survey that Irving recorded in his Tour of the Prairies. He visited his sister, who was married and living in Independence at the time.

Soon after the town of Independence was laid out, there came from Ohio one Joseph Smith, preaching a gospel both strange and new to the Missourians, a gospel from the Book of Mormon. The natives looked with high disfavor upon any religion other than the Protestant type they had brought from Tennessee and Kentucky. Feelings became ever more bitter between the Mormons and the Missourians, until there came a clash of armed men. The equipment of the Mormon newspaper, the Evening Star, was dumped into the Missouri River and the Mormons driven to the north of the river and eventually to Nauvoo in Illinois.

Independence was born just in time to reap full benefit from the westward thrust of immigration that was being heightened by the growing practicality of the steamboat as a means of navigation on the Missouri River. This river traffic had its serious beginning in the early 1830s and reached its apogee about 1870. The town expanded to take care of the traffic over the Santa Fe Trail, growing in volume and importance. If the town were crowded to take care of the traffic of the Santa Fe Trail, it must have stretched almost to the bursting point when it became the eastern terminus of the Oregon Trail. This trail was a highway that followed the Santa Fe Trail a few miles into Kansas, then branched northwestwardly across the prairies where a crude sign pointed, "Road to Oregon."

Independence knew, too, the Argonauts, those gold-hungry men who crowded its streets in the days of forty-nine, when word went out that gold had been found in Sutter's millrace in California. John A. Sutter, a young Swiss emigrant, had quit his job in a St. Charles store, going to Independence for the purpose of engaging in the Santa Fe trade. He had little dreaming that the trade eventually would carry him to California and that his name would forever be linked with the discovery of gold in California. Independence was excited over the news of the gold discoveries and instantly was seething with new movements toward the West. Gold seekers came from all over the country, joining those desert-faring leaders already in Independence. They left for the gold fields in wagons and on horseback, some even using pushcarts.

About mid-century, or shortly thereafter, Independence began to slow up. The termini of its three important trails had moved farther upriver. But the most important factor was that the steamboats had been developed to the point where they were carrying freight and passengers in ever-greater numbers far beyond the landings that had represented Independence on the Missouri River. First of these rival towns was Westport, approximately fifteen miles away, with its landing on the river.

Westport was founded in 1833 by John Calvin McCoy at a point where he had set up a general store in a two-story log building where the only public road running west from Independence intersected a road running south from Chouteau's trading post on the Kaw River. In this wilderness he dared to believe, a town would grow. He later wrote; "I reasoned it out that eventually steamboats would be coming up to the mouth of the Kaw, and the intersection where my store stood would be an outfitting place for people crossing the plains." He reasoned well.

He told also of persuading the captain of the steamboat John Hancock to unload a bill of goods at what later became Westport Landing, four miles from Westport. There was no landing there then, and the goods were tumbled out among the fallen timbers and brush. McCoy says he cut a road through the dense brush and with three ox-teams hauled the goods to Westport, although Pierre Roi, who ran a ferry at Westport Landing, is also credited with having built the first road between that point and Westport.

As the Westport Landing came more and more into use as a receiving point for Santa Fe goods shipped upriver by steamboat, the traders found it less advantageous to use Independence as the eastern terminal point of their journey. It was in 1845 that Bent & St. Vrain, the famous traders of the Santa Fe Trail, received the first consignment of goods from the East at the Westport Landing. Each day, almost, the stagecoach brought passengers from the steamboat landing, while the outfitters, the traders and the travelers gathered at the Harris House.

As it proselyted the trail, mountain, and river trade from its older rival, Independence, the new town of Wesport became a great outfitting station, going in for the manufacture of everything relating to transportation. It was the gathering place for hunters, trappers, traders, and Indians—every type of man of the West being represented on its streets. Long caravans of covered wagons, drawn by oxen, rolled down Main Street from morning till night. These caravans were piloted by trainmen, bronzed from the glare of the trail, in leather leggings and deerskin shirts. Gold and silver bullion worth hundreds of thousands of dollars baled in bullhides was stacked on the sidewalks.

The colorful John A. Sutter, one of early Westport's most picturesque settlers, who had taken a wagon train out of Independence, returned over the trail from New Mexico. He arrived at Christmas time in 1836, bringing with him a retinue of Mexican servants and herdsmen, a few wagons, and two-score or more of mules. He was a large, soldierly-looking man with a great deal of dash and restless energy, wearing high-topped boots and a splendid blue-green cloth cloak, its capes reaching nearly to the ground. He bought out the trading firm of Lucas & Kavanaugh, but set out again in 1839, headed for the West with a friend named Welter. He had been grubstaked by McCoy and left as security "some remnants of very fine cloth, a few pictures, and a gold watch chain."

Due perhaps to the example set by Sutter, perhaps because of the Oregon fever which was beginning to stir men, a number of Westporters under the leadership of Colonel John Bartleson set out for the West in 1842. In the party were Robert Rickman, Charles Hopper, Joseph McDowell, Aaron Overton, Grove Cook and William Baldridge. The latter, arriving in California, constructed the mill for Sutter which soon became famous with the discovery of gold.

The business community of the growing town was being constantly augmented. Colonel Albert G. Boone and Van Boone, merchants, traders, and freighters, located in

Westport and established a large outfitting and supply business with many trains on the plains. Alexander Majors opened a packinghouse, or slaughterhouse as it was called.

John C. Fremont appeared in Westport in 1842 heading a party composed largely of Frenchmen and Canadian Frenchmen gathered up around St. Louis. The expedition, the first of this celebrated pathfinder to the Far West, had been organized at the trading house of Cyprian Chouteau on the Kaw River about seven miles from Westport.

Fremont's principal guide was Kit Carson, while the hunter for the party was Lucien Maxwell, also noted on the frontier. His second expedition was organized at Westport the following year, Maxwell again being the hunter, but Carson's place as guide was taken by Thomas Fitzpatrick, known throughout the West as "Broken Hand."

It was in 1843 that the immense tide of the "great migration" broke over the prairies of the West. In 1845 nearly three thousand migrants left Westport and other Missouri River towns, and in 1847, the number was between four thousand and five thousand. Long lines of prairie schooners passed through Westport with their sleek teams and shining harness, marshaled for the start of the long journey to the Far West. They formed a stream of human life surging along the highway like the rising of the tide, one train scarcely having passed out of sight before another followed in its wake and "camp fires gleamed along its border like diamonds in a necklace."

The Oregon migration was still in progress in 1849, when the gold rush struck the country and forty thousand immigrants were outfitted in Westport. The tents of the immigrants and the tepees of the Indians made a vast transient city south and west of Westport. There was shooting and cutting, and the clatter of spurs on the streets, the whir of roulette wheels, the clink of glasses, the drone of the dance halls, the rattle of money in the gambling halls. Despite all this, Westport never acquired a reputation as one of the "wild and woolly" towns of the frontier.

By 1855, the border war was on and Westport became a headquarters for pro-slavery men who crowded into the town, described then as "a thriving, bustling, muddy little city of eight hundred with two churches, two large hotels, several bar-rooms, and a weekly newspaper."

This newspaper, the Border Star, edited by young Joseph Hodgson, reported in 1858 that, "Mexican trains and traders are arriving daily with gold, silver, furs, pelts, and wool. At Bernard & Company's we see a pile of silver rocks. At the same place a piece of pure gold as large as an apple dumpling. The streets are crowded with wagon trains, it sometimes being difficult to tread one's way across the streets on account of the blockade of wagons, mules, cattle, bales and boxes."

The following year it was reported that nearly eight hundred wagons were sold in Westport, as indicative of the extent of the trail trade. However, when the Civil War began, the great western trade moved upriver to safer towns such as Fort Leavenworth, Atchison and Nebraska City. It was never resumed to a great extent at Westport.

But after the war it was picked up by its neighbor on the river, the erstwhile landing for the Westport trade. Destined to engulf Westport, Independence, Parkville and Liberty, to become a city of first magnitude with magnificent buildings to pierce the sky, it already was a full-fledged rival of those towns and sporting the new name, the Town of Kansas.

Chapter Eleven

Fort Osage, Frontier Gibraltar

Standing on a bold headland overlooking the Missouri, Fort Osage, near Sibley, Missouri, gave a view of the river for many miles, both up and down the stream. This dramatic view greeted the eye of explorers, hunters and trappers in the early days, and was beheld later by rivermen, soldiers, and pioneer settlers. On the summit of the high river bluff, the river's contour has yielded in no essential to the mutations of a century and a half since the fort was in its heyday. Yet, until only a comparatively recent date, it would have been necessary to search through a tangle of wild vines, shrubs and trees to come upon the site, where no vestige of the fort remained; but searching further, one would have found the old graveyard. The graveyard, with its "gaunt, wind-torn cedar," a few weather-beaten headstones (but none for Zenas Leonard, mountain man and author of Narrative of the Adventures of Zenas Leonard), and a cairn marking the communal burial place of a number of dragoons who had died of the "black tongue." The Native Sons of Kansas City restored the old fort in 1940.

The river was narrow at this point, its current running swiftly along the north bank, compelling all manners of river craft to seek the easier water of the south bank. Following the path of the current was a necessity that would have brought every boat passing that way within easy range of the guns of a fort situated on the bluff. The strategic value of the situation was at once apparent to Lewis and Clark as they moved upstream in the summer of 1804. It was characteristic of Clark's forthrightness of perception that he was able, even then, to visualize a citadel on that promontory, having a command of the river which would make of it a veritable Gibraltar of the frontier. Within four years he was to support his judgment by overruling another location and supervising the building of a fort at this point, know in its earlier days as Fort Clark.

Government officials had been quick to see that Fort Bellefontaine had been outmoded as a protector of the frontier almost before it had been finished. It was felt a more appropriate location would be where the Missouri met the Osage, near Cote sans Dessein. But Clark, who had been allowed considerable discretion in selection of the site, boldly jumped the frontier westward by a hundred and fifty miles when he built Fort Osage near the western boundary of Missouri.

As a preliminary move, the government in 1808 bought six square miles of ground from the Osage Indians, purposing that the area should serve as the demesne of the proposed fort and trading post. This purchase became known as the Six Mile District.

The fort was meant to encourage and assist those in the fur business of the Northwest or those who soon would engage in the trade with Santa Fe. Trade with the Indians was important, too, being drawn from the tribes along the Missouri and Kansas (or Kaw) rivers and from the Osage tribes to the south and southwest.

In August, 1808, the personnel of the various forces whose task it would be to build, protect and serve the new fort, moved out from Fort Bellefontaine, eighty-one by boat, under the leadership of Captain Eli Clemson; perhaps as many by land, under General Clark as their leader. George C. Sibley, who had been assistant factor at Fort Bellefontaine, was to serve as factor in the new Fort Osage. A Mr. Prince was to be sutler to the garrison, one of the boats carrying his goods; another, owned by the Morrison brothers, carried goods for the commissary. Sibley had twenty thousand dollars worth of goods on four other boats, intended for the Indian trade.

The method of getting those keelboats upstream was by a cordelle or warp. The men would take a rope in a skiff and row up the river as far as they thought the rope would reach, then let the rope play out in the river till it reached the boat. The men on board then secured the line and pulled the boat up to the skiff. Sometimes they had to lay three or four warps in going around a bluff.

Clark lay out and built the fort in the form of a square with an outwork. This was to be defended with four block-houses in the main works and a single blockhouse at the point. The walls of the fort were logs set upright, or poteau style. The principal buildings were the barracks and the factor's house.

Among the personnel at the fort in its earlier days were Reuben Lewis, Dr. John H. Robinson, Isaac Rawlings, and Jim Bridger. Lewis was the younger brother of Meriwether Lewis, appointed to serve as sub-agent of Indian affairs at Fort Osage. In the following year he became a member of the Missouri Fur Company and yield-ed his post to Dr. Robinson. Dr. Robinson came in the spring, after the completion of the fort. He had been with the expedition of Zebulon M. Pike in 1806, had visited Santa Fe and had been thrown in a Chihuahua jail. His wife and children joined him at the fort and young Sibley became one of their boarders. In the fall of 1810, young Isaac Rawlings of Maryland came to be Sibley's assistant. Afterwards he was in charge of the trading post at Chickasaw Bluffs on the Mississippi, and a number of years later was one of the founders of Memphis. Jim Bridger was a stripling lad from St. Louis, working peltries, doing anything about the fort that Sibley wanted him to do, serving his apprenticeship as a frontiersman, a career that some day would cause his name to be written in tall letters on the scroll of western history.

In November, 1810, Wilson Price Hunt came to Fort

Osage, having withdrawn from his large merchandising store in St. Louis to throw in his fortunes with the John Jacob Astor fur interests. He was leading the vanguard of the Astorians, some forty or fifty men. Hunt was accompanied by Ramsey C. Crooks, Joseph Miller, and Donald McKenzie; the party sojourning several days. The next spring the main body of the Astorians tied up at the landing.

A year after this, another expedition arrived, that of the Missouri Fur Company, outgrowth of the St. Louis Fur Company, its president being General Clark, builder of Fort Osage, and its operating head "Uncle Manuel" Lisa. The concern's roster included such leaders of St. Louis as Sylvestre Labadie, Charles Gratiot, Pierre Menard, Pierre Chouteau, Auguste P. Chouteau, Andrew Henry and the Reuben Lewis who had been located earlier at Fort Osage.

By the summer of 1813, the war with Britain had taken such a turn that the advisability of trying to retain Fort Osage was in doubt. Together with the nature of the terrain between the fort and the vicinity of the Boone's Lick where the nearest white settlers already were "forting up" to protect themselves, and in view of the type of warfare that would be waged by the Indian allies of the British, it was deemed expedient to move the personnel of the fort downriver a considerable distance. Officers of the fort wrote to the secretary of war that, under the existing circumstances, Fort Osage constituted "a moth in the public purse." Permission was granted, and the equipment of the fort was moved down to Arrow Rock, approximately across the river from the Boone salt works, being returned to its original site in 1816.

In the meantime romance had come into Sibley's life, and the second period of his residence at Fort Osage as factor was to be a halcyon one as the husband of Mary Easton, daughter of Rufus Easton, one of the wealthiest and most influential men in St. Louis. Born in Baltimore, educated in Lexington, Kentucky, she was a remarkably talented young woman, skilled musician, ardent horsewoman, and an accomplished linguist. Sibley wrote of her: "Mary is a splendid woman, fifteen years of age, in splendid health and full of courage and determination." Their honeymoon, one of the earliest romances on the river, was spent on the keelboat that brought them from St. Louis to the fort.

Every living thing in and about the fort responded to and was caught up by the contagious elan of this slender, vital girl bride. It seemed that there was added sheen and lustre to the bright red and green plumage of the myriad paroquets, or love birds, that inhabited the wooded area; even the wild flowers vied in their efforts to match her "bright-colored cashmere and merino dresses." Active, mentally and physically, she doubtless took a supervisory interest in the "fine garden, well stocked poultry yard, and ice house" of which Sibley wrote, and sometimes she was on the river. In the small boat she had named Six Mile. Again she was riding Old Trudge, the faithful tall roan that rounded out its twenty-eighth year of life after the Sibleys had moved to St. Charles. She entranced the Indians and attaches of the fort when she played her piano with drum and fife attachment, the first instrument of its kind west of St. Louis. Sometimes she taught the little girls of the frontier outpost, giving a foreglimpse of Lindenwood College, the splendid school for young women she and her husband were able to establish in later life at St. Charles.

One of the frontier children to receive tutelage at the hands of Mrs. Sibley doubtless had been Susie, the little daughter of William S. Williams, employed by Sibley as interpreter. He had grown up on a farm near the site of Fort Bellefontaine with Osage Indian boys as playmates. At seventeen, he had gone up the valley to preach the gospel as best he could without having been trained for the work. He preached "hell-fire and brimstone," but gradually lost the spark, becoming more and more as one of the Indians with whom he consorted. He was an expert shot with a rifle, and was described by Pike as "a man about six feet one in height, gaunt, red-headed, with a weather-beaten face, marked deeply with the smallpox, all muscle and sinew, and the most indefatigable hunter and trapper in the world." He accompanied Sibley to Taos, and in time, as

"Old Bill" Williams, he became one of the most famous of all the mountain men.

Sibley built Fountain Cottage for his bride, a home she made noted for its charm and hospitality, becoming hostess to all travelers of repute up and down the river. Alfonso Wetmore, an early traveler and writer, wrote that Sibley's "hospitable mansion and amiable family at an early period robbed the wilderness of its terrors and crude aspect and imposed an agreeable surprise on the weary and necessitous traveler." Chester Harding, famous painter and author of My Egoistography, painted Mrs. Sibley's portrait. He came west to serve the elite of St.Louis, went to the Bonne Femme to paint his celebrated portrait of Daniel Boone, and later was the most sought-after portraitist in London. In his book, he does not mention visiting Fort Osage.

Fort Osage, which had served as a springboard for fur seekers going upriver, was to prove a jumping-off place of an entirely different sort. When William S. Becknell's wagon train came moiling up the narrow river road from Franklin, it paused a while before pushing out into the desert wilderness to establish trade with Santa Fe. He was followed by more and ever more similar trains and in 1825 Sibley with two others were commissioned by the federal government to survey the Santa Fe Trail. The fort remained an important station on that trail until superseded by the new town of Independence, a few miles to the southwest, which had been laid out by Lilburn W. Boggs, assistant factor at Fort Osage.

But the frontier was becoming restless, and ready to move on to the West. Word came that Fort Osage was to be abandoned in favor of another government post to be built approximately fifty miles farther up the Missouri River. One day a tiny steamboat chugged and wheezed its way past the fort, carrying as passenger Colonel Henry W. Leavenworth, to be commandant of the new outpost that was to bear his name — and old Fort Osage became a memory.

Dr. Kate L. Gregg, in the peroration of her scholarly

monograph on Fort Osage, Westward With Dragoons, said, "The soldiers were gone; the settlers had come in their place. There is a certain symbolism in the fact that before long the very logs and beams of the frontier post were incorporated in the dwellings of the newcomers and on the site where it once had stood, not a vestige remained. The frontier had passed westward."

In nearly two decades it stood as the government's far outpost (1808-1822) on the western frontier. Fort Osage, through the feeling of security it gave to all Americans whose interests lay in the west, encouraged further expansion toward the setting sun. This was true, because of the important part it had played in the development of trade over the Santa Fe Trail, opening up broad vistas of commercial intercourse with a foreign nation. It was true too, because of that fuller development of trade in the valley itself that had resulted from the great influx of home-seekers which its propinquity had fostered. The life of the fort, brief though it had been, had constituted an essential link in the history of the river. The day of Fort Osage was done, but a new and greater life was coming to the Missouri and the river was about to live as never before.

Being the highway over which the bulk of traffic must travel, the tempo of the traffic necessarily was keyed to the pace set by the cumbersome keelboat. But now, entering the twilight of obsolescence, the keelboat was about to be superseded by the steamboat, which was to become the most important factor by far in the long life of the river.

Fort Osage overlooking the Missouri River near Sibley, Missouri.

Chapter Twelve

Rocky Bluffs and the River Meet

Gabriel Prudhomme, paddling up the Missouri River with a band of Canadian Voyageurs around the year 1820, was impressed by the rugged beauty of the terrain on the south bank of the river shortly before he came to the mouth of its tributary, the Kaw (Kansas). The voyageurs originally from Trois Rivieres in Canada, claiming Canada as their homes but being, actually, river wanderers, soon effected a fur-trading post at the mouth of the Kaw. A decade passed, however, before Gabriel, remembering his early impressions, homesteaded the farm that was to form the nucleus of Kansas City. Despite the rough, wooded hills and ravines and the wild, forbidding aspect of the land near the Prudhomme farm, it gradually became a rendezvous of the French-Canadian trappers, hunters and traders. Many of who squatted upon the land along the riverfront in defiance of the treaty that would have reserved that part of western Missouri for Osage Indians.

Perhaps at two-miles east of the Prudhomme farm, Francois Gesseau Chouteau and his brother Cyprian had in 1821 built a warehouse nearly opposite the Randolph Bluffs, probably being the site of "Old Calisse" Montardeau's ferry, reported to have been slightly to the west of Randolph. Before the town of Kanzas was thought of, Chouteau's warehouse had been a rendezvous of boatmen and mountain men. In charge had been Grandlouis Bartholet, so-called to distinguish him from his son, Petitlouis Bartholet. Grandlouis and his wife are reported to have gone up river as early as 1800, probably to Randolph Bluffs, returning to St. Charles for a few years, then back to the site of Kansas City.

Just to the west of Chouteau's warehouse, from 1825 to 1827 was the Kaw Indian agency, with Antoine Francois (sometimes called Baronet or Barnett) Vasquez acting as sub-agent. He was a Spaniard from St. Louis who, in 1806, acted as an interpreter for Zebulon M. Pike on the latter's expedition to the Rocky Mountains. He died of cholera in 1827.

West of Prudhomme's farm and very near the mouth of the Kaw River, the French had a settlement of a dozen cabins sometimes called Kawsmouth. So it appeared the little cabins of the Frenchmen were strung along the south bank of the river from a point nearly opposite Randolph Bluffs to the very mouth of the Kaw, a distance of four miles. Included would have been the cabins of Grandlouis Bartholet, Gabriel and Louis Phillibert, Louis Uneau, Louis Tremble (Tromley), Louis Tourjon, M. Vertefeuylle, Louis Ferrier, M. Cabori, and John La Sarge. Other cabins included those of Calisse Montardeau, the ferryman, and his good wife Helois, of Pierre La Liberte, sometimes called Joe Barter, who deserted the Lewis and Clark expedition, of Benjamin Laugatherie, who in 1836 married Charlotte, the daughter of John and Marianne (Naketihou) Gray, both Iroquois; of James Fornais, who became known as "Old Pino" and died in Kansas City in 1871 at the age of one hundred and twenty-four. One cabin, that of Clement Lessert, Father Charles La Croix, the missionary, held mass in 1822 before any church had been built and sometimes gave sanction to marriages that had already been consummated by the Frenchmen and their Indian brides "in the absence of a priest." There also was the cabin of Major Andrew Drips. Major Drips was a noted figure on the Missouri frontier in the pioneer period, and was for many years in the employ of the American Fur Company. He was associated with Lucian Fontenelle in the operation of a trading post in the vicinity of Laramie. He became United States agent for the Indian tribes of the upper Missouri. In 1840 he was commander of the caravan when Father De Smet made an expedition to the Rocky Mountains. His first wife, Mary (Ottonata), was buried (before 1846) at the early burying-ground, "at the summit of the angle of the bluff" just east of the foot of Grand Avenue. His second wife, Louise Geroux, was a Yankton Sioux. Born in Pennsylvania in 1789 of Dutch parentage, he died in Kansas City in 1860.

These French enjoyed simple pastimes, particularly dancing, with the brothers Joseph and Peter Revard, parish fiddlers, furnishing the music. When a dance was held in one of the cabins, the host was expected to furnish the pot de bouillon, a rich, palatable soup, containing chicken, wild fowl, venison and seasoning.

On an early day visit to Randolph, Thomas Hart Benton is reputed to have pointed toward the site of Kansas City, across the river and three miles upstream, and said, "Where yonder rocky bluffs meet the river, a great city will arise."

Indian title was extinguished in 1825 and in 1828 the white men opened the land to settlement, the first patent being obtained by James H. McGee on land south of the Prudhomme farm. In that year, too, Louis Roi settled on the riverfront and his son Pierre began the operation of a crude ferry at that point.

In November 1838, Gabriel Prudhomme having died, his farm was acquired by a townsite company, the fourteen members of which were William L. Sublette, Fry P. McGee, William M. Chick, William Gillis, James Smart, Moses C. Wilson, Abraham Fonda, Oliver Caldwell, George W. Tate, Jacob Ragan, William Collins, Samuel G. Owen, Russell Hicks and John C. McCoy.

Sublette was an Indian trader and fur trapper of the Rocky Mountains, who each year had made the trip back and forth from St. Louis to the mountains. He and his brother Milton, and Robert Campbell, had become heads of the Rocky Mountain Fur Company as early as 1830, succeeding its founder, General Ashley. Colonel William Miles Chick, who had won his title in the War of 1812, had come up the river from Chariton in 1836 and bought McCoy's store in Westport. William Gillis had been a personal friend of William Henry Harrison at Cincinnati, and had fought under him through the Tippecanoe campaign. He helped in the removal of Indians from Ohio to the West, becoming an Indian trader. Abraham Fonda, from Holland, a newcomer in the West, was a gentleman of means living off the income from his investments. Samuel Combs Owen was a storekeeper in Independence. Hicks of Independence was a leading attorney of western Missouri. McCoy was the founder of Westport.

Sublette, on behalf of the company, bid on the Prudhomme farm for a little over four thousand dollars and the fourteen founders retired to the log tavern of "One-Eyed" Ellis on the river bank to work out the details. This tavern, which had been the cabin of Louis Uneau, became the germinal dot of Kansas City.

As early as 1838, there was a store on the riverfront, owned by a Frenchman, and Isaac Richards's saloon, where the Indians and trappers resorted. The first trade of the town came from contacts with fur traders, boatmen and nearby Indians. The latter would bring in their annuity moneys and their ponies; the trappers and boatmen their peltries and trinkets. Soon there were a dozen stores including that of William P. Jarboe and some of the steamboat men called the place Jarboe's Landing. Then it was not uncommon, when the Mackinaw boats swept downstream with the mountain men from a winter of trapping, to see three or four hundred men on the levee of the little town, all of them eager to purchase the wares of the traders.

After the John Hancock in 1834 had landed a shipment of goods at the point for John C. McCoy's Westport store, other captains and shippers, learning of the excellent rock landing, so much better than the shallow, muddy landing at Wayne City, brought their cargoes to the Westport Landing. In a few years it became the chief steamboat landing and outfitting point for the commerce of the prairies.

The Town of Kanzas, located mainly on the levee, for a few years grew slowly if at all. But it was a busy place, with its Santa Fe and other trade, even as Independence and Westport were, but was not seriously considered as a rival for either of the latter towns, being jocularly and all too truly referred to as "the Westport landing."

The town hardly had time to settle down after the Mexican War before word came of the gold strikes in California and the Town of Kanzas became host to hordes of gold seekers en route to California and its precious metal.

It probably was in response to the demand created by these Argonauts that Dr. Benoist Troost erected the Gillis House on the riverfront between Wyandotte and Delaware streets, the finest hostelry of its time, which in two years took care of twenty-seven thousand persons.

In 1853 the town was chartered as the City of Kansas, being then a string of houses, a mile in length, stretching along the levee, a place where Doubting Thomases stopped until they decided to stay where they were, go on over into Kansas, or follow the Santa Fe Trail. The stretch was crowded with covered wagons, mules, Mexican teamsters and emigrants. The town was described as " a miserable dirty little town, stuck among hills and hollows," and in truth the new city with its population of three hundred was, aside from the houses along the levee, little more than a few rough warehouses. A place with a small number of cabins hanging perilously to the hills that walled in the levee where the citizens went daily to see the churning steamboats unloaded.

The steamboat traffic daily became of greater importance to the town, a number of Kansas Citians becoming interested in the trade, such as Captain Pierre M. Chouteau, owner of the Amazon; his brother-in-law, Captain Ashley Hopkins, owner of the Asa Wilgus; and Captain Alexander Gillham, owner of the A.B. Chambers. The latter was one of the favorite boats of the younger set for moonlight excursions, and for dances when it was tied up for the winter.

The levee was piled high with stacks of smoked bacon, plows, cases of silk dress goods, new wagons, kegs of nails, barrels of whisky, kegs of powder, barrels of molasses, guns, groceries, and sometimes a piano. Indians were on the streets, begging and trading. Backwoodsmen, greasers, traders of the trail, and riverains crowded the saloons where business was active day and night and on Sundays as well.

In 1851, a Mr. Kennedy had established the town's first newspaper, the Kansas Ledger, which he published for about fifteen months and then sold to a Mr. Eperson, who continued its publication for another fifteen months.

Despite the fact the paper was "ably and satisfactori-ly conducted by both editors, Mr. Eperson found it neces-sary to sell the equipment to a group of men who used it in Independence in getting out the Western Reporter. After some eighteen months without a newspaper, several of the leading citizens met at the Gillis House to underwrite the establishment of another paper. Mayor M.J. Payne was sent to St. Louis where he purchased the necessary equipment for the Kansas City Enterprise, which made its bow September 23, 1854, under the editorship of W.A. Strong, a lawyer, the mechanical department being in charge of D.K. Abeel, a practical printer. They rented the second floor of the brick building at the southeast corner of Main Street and the levee, the first floor of which was occupied by "Kit" Cole's saloon. In August of the following year the paper was purchased by R.T. Van Horn, a Kansas City leader of first importance.

Kansas City by 1857 had become a very important point, engaged in a neck-and-neck race with Leavenworth and St. Joseph for the rich prize of the great commercial metropolis of the Far West. The city perched on a high bluff commanding a fine view of the river for miles below, its broad bouldered landing sloping down to the water's edge. There, one was presented with a confused picture of immense piles of freight, horse, ox, and mule teams receiv-ing merchandise from steamboats, scores of immigrant wagons, and a busy crowd of whites, Indians, half-breeds,

Negroes and Mexicans. There were solid brick houses and low frame shanties along the levee and scattered unfinished buildings on the hill above, where the grade was being cut fifteen or twenty feet deep, through abrupt bluffs. The town had approximately five thousand persons and was growing rapidly.

Kansas City, and indeed the whole area up and down the river, was seething with feelings engendered by the struggle then in progress over the slavery question. Its population was about evenly divided on the issue of whether Kansas should be slave or free. At all the river towns there appeared to be active preparation for war, armed mobs frequently assembling at the levees to turn back steamboats carrying passengers destined for the scene of impending conflict. The friction was greater in Kansas City for the simple reason that neither side had been dominant. The friction resulted in a tendency to lawlessness and the town became embroiled in the border war.

One hot August day in 1858 M. Bordeaux brought to town the news that gold had been discovered along Cherry Creek in the Rocky Mountains, some six hundred miles to the west. This brought a rush of unattached men, most of them coming upriver by steamboat on their way to the gold fields.

Kansas City's first growth had stemmed from the Santa Fe trade and the steamboat traffic on the Missouri River. The troublous times of the Civil War were the lines of demarcation between the frontier village and the young metropolis. But in the 1850s there had been tremendous growth by both the city and the steamboat traffic.

Steamboat YELLOWSTONE near Fort Osage in 1833. (from a painting by Carl Bodmer). —*Native Sons Collection, Western Historical Manuscripts UMKC.*

Chapter Thirteen

Paradise of Western Towns

The gradual and continuous progress of the European race toward the Rocky Mountains had the solemnity of a proverbial event, according to De Toqueville in Democracy in America, who likened it to "a deluge of men, rising unabatedly, and driven daily onward by the hand of God." By the middle 1830s, hamlets were strung along the Missouri River from St. Charles to the western limits of Missouri, represented at that time by the frontier village of Barry, about ten miles north of the present site of Kansas City. Between Lexington and Barry, there were a dozen river towns, some of which soon sank out of sight. None brought to fruition the splendid dreams of the men who founded them.

On the south bank of the river and above Lexington were the towns of Wellington, Napoleon and Sibley, all of which are still on the map. The first named town was platted in 1837, following by a year the establishment of Poston's Landing, which later became Lisbon, honoring the founder's wife, and finally was given the name of Napoleon. Above Napoleon, adjacent to the site of old Fort Osage, the town of Sibley was platted in 1836. It was founded by Archibald Gamble of St. Louis and named in honor of George C. Sibley, who had been the factor at Fort Osage.

On the north bank of the river at Lexington, there was a landing known variously as North Lexington, Richmond Landing, Farmville and Moore's Landing. The latter was for Colonel William Moore, who went to Missouri from Tennessee or Virginia in 1830 and bought a large acreage north of Lexington. He died in 1854 and the town fell into the river.

Next above North Lexington had been Bluffton, an important town that became a ghost town even in the early days. It had been laid out in 1819 by Duff Green and Dr. B.F. Edwards, the latter acting as local agent. Local historians believe there had been a settlement of some sort there as early as 1816.

The town was on the first pioneer trail along the Missouri River. This old trail crossed the river at Jack's Ferry and ran west through the bottoms to the bluff on which Bluffton was situated; thence on the point where Liberty afterwards was located. When malarial fever struck, due to the miasmatic conditions in the river bottoms, the inland town of Richmond was established to become the seat of justice and Bluffton dwindled away and disappeared.

At the foot of the bluffs, two miles east of old Bluffton, there arose the important river town of Camden, described in 1837 as "a new town, a little below Bluffton, with several stores." In time it became the biggest shipping point between St. Louis and Omaha, the steamboats bringing goods to the local merchants and taking away tobacco, hemp, cattle and horses. In 1843 a six-story brick building was erected and used for years as a hotel during the steamboat era. When the channel of the river changed, the importance of the town was gone.

A few miles to the west of Camden, north of the present village of Orrick, the town of Albany was laid out in 1856. Famous as a gambling resort, it is remembered chiefly as the place where Bill Anderson, noted guerilla of the Civil War, was shot to death by a detachment of Union soldiers.

In 1822, the new frontier town of Liberty had a dozen

houses and two stores around its public square. It soon became the trade center and social mecca of the area. John Baxter was proprietor of a harness and saddle shop in Liberty and was the ferryman at Liberty Landing on the river.

By 1829, Liberty was regarded as "the paradise of western towns – a thriving town, Richmond and Lexington and Independence scarcely deserving the names of towns in comparison." In the late 1830s, a newspaper called the Far West was published at Liberty, being, with the exception of the short-lived Mormon paper at Independence, the first newspaper west of Old Franklin. Its editor was Peter H. Burnett, young lawyer, destined to become supreme justice in Oregon and first governor of California. He was among the first to catch the Oregon fever, leading a group in 1843.

In 1838 the first of the Oregon-bound settlers went out under the leadership of T.J. Farnham. Four years later a larger group set out, piloted by Elijah White. Another year and Whitman led a thousand settlers toward the Oregon country.

Then the war with Mexico broke out and Colonel Doniphan marched his regiment of Missourians out of Liberty for the long trek to Mexico, first holding silent worship in Liberty's Christian church.

In 1855 a band of Liberty pro-slavery men seized the arsenal three miles south of Liberty, taking guns and ammunition to be used in the border war then beginning to flare on both sides of the Missouri River. Six years later the place again was raided, and it was the first act of aggression against the government of the United States after Fort Sumter.

A few miles east of Liberty Landing, Missouri City had its beginning in 1834 when Shrewsbury Williams established a ferry. By 1846 the place was called Richfield. Nearby came the towns of St. Bernard and Atchison. The three were consolidated in1859 as Missouri City. A few miles to the west was Randolph Bluffs, established in 1800 as a trading post.

The little inland hamlet of Barry was situated on the line of the western border of Missouri and represented "thus far and no farther" for the homeseekers, speculators and adventurers. They had for fifteen years had been eyeing hungrily that area of land, now comprising the six northwestern counties of Missouri. It was Indian land, belonging to the Sac and Fox and Iowa tribes.

When the Platte Purchase was opened in 1837, young Burnett, who galloped into town from Liberty yelling and swinging his hat, brought the news to Barry. The purchase price given the Indians for the six counties was said to have been seven thousand five hundred dollars in cash, an interpreter, a blacksmith and a grindstone. While not strictly accurate, this succinctly conveys the spirit of the transaction, known as the treaty of Prairie du Chien.

Settlers choked the roads into the purchase in the years 1837, 1838 and 1839. Leaving their homes in the East, they followed the call of adventure and romance typified by the West, and sought their fortunes on the far side of the new state of Missouri. Then it was still the beginning of the great unknown, the opening of the treacherous gateway to the prairies and the mountains, the last post of organized government. There, in the rude western hamlets and the towns along the riverfront, teemed the life of a new country.

One of the first fruits of the opening was the town of Parkville, on the north bank of the Missouri just a few miles inside the line of the purchase. White Aloe, a French trapper, had "caved up" near there as early as 1823, his name being still retained in the creek that meanders by Parkville. Early steamboat men knew the place as English Landing, for Steve English, who first homesteaded the land and erected on the riverbank, at what became the foot of Main Street in Parkville, a log warehouse as a steamboat landing. Colonel George S. Park, a Vermonter, having returned from the Texas war in 1838, bought the English interests and built a home below the White Aloe branch. In 1844 he laid off Parkville, sold out lots, and built the stone warehouse at the foot of Main Street and erected the stone hotel that later became the nucleus of Park College. It immediately became one of the most important towns on the Missouri River. Joseph Winston laid Winston out just a few hundred feet to the west of Parkville in 1839 or 1840, but the town never acquired a foothold.

Parkville probably reached its highest level around 1853, a booming little town of three hundred, all hurry and bustle, what with settlers hurrying to Kansas, and all western Missouri in a prosperous condition. As many as nine steamboats could be seen at the landing loading and unloading at one time.

It was inevitable that Park, a courageous and outspoken man, would be drawn into the vortex of the border troubles. They had been precipitated by passage of the Kansas-Nebraska Act in 1854, a momentous piece of legislation which repealed the Missouri compromise, reopened the slavery question, made of the soil of Kansas a battle ground, and assured the coming of the Civil War.

Park had founded a newspaper at Parkville, the Industrial Luminary, which, following the Kansas election of March 30, 1855, printed a very sharp editorial of "squatter sovereignty." The repercussion was immediate and sufficient.

Within a few days a dozen men rode in from the country, went to the printing office and put the editor, Patterson, under guard. Park happened to be out of town. By noon, two hundred men had arrived. The press was taken down and a speaker said they had come with the determination "to black tar and feather and ride on a rail, G.S. Park and W. J. Patterson." The latter's wife clung to him and the crowd abandoned its idea of tar and feathers. However, it adopted a resolution to the effect that the Luminary was a nuisance, that the editors were traitors, that if they remained in town at a subsequent date they should be thrown into the Missouri River, that if they fled to Kansas they should be followed and hanged.

The press was then shouldered with a white cap drawn over its head and labeled "Boston Aid," marched up through town to the upper landing, and with three hearty cheers was thrown into the river.

Horace Greeley in his New York Tribune printed thunderous editorials denouncing the outrage, and Park printed glorious editorials defending his position, but left Parkville nevertheless, never to return, except in death. But he never lost interest in the town that bore his name, and much of the fortune he made in Illinois was lavished on the town he had founded and the college that honored his name. He is buried at Parkville under a twenty-two-ton column of granite.

An interesting river town with a history antedating the opening of the purchase, was Rialto. It since has joined the long list of ghost towns of the river. Valentine Bernard is credited with having pushed through the wilderness to establish a trading post at Rialto, a mile below the present Weston. Some people were said to have located at the site around 1819 – squatters who sold liquor to the soldiers from Leavenworth when that cantonment was established in 1827 – and were ousted by the government. The place was first known as Pensineau's Landing, being immediately across the river from the trading house kept by a Frenchman of that name. Another threat to Weston that faded was the laying out in 1857 of St. Mary at the mouth of Bee Creek.

Iatan, a few miles beyond Weston, was founded in 1837 by John Dougherty and first was known as Dougherty's Landing. It was farthest west of the river towns. John Dougherty ran a way from home at the age of fifteen and made his way among the Indians, and later as Indian agent for the tribes along the Missouri River was a man of great influence, loved and respected by his wards. His honeymoon trip in 1824 was a steamboat ride to Fort Atkinson. As much as possible of the town's outgoing freight was saved for the new steamboat Iatan, named for a chief of the Otoes, a visitor to Major Long in 1819.

Weston was laid out in 1837 in the elbow of the bend of the river, on the north bank, its founder having been Joseph Moore, a former soldier from Fort Leavenworth across the river.

Two years after the town's founding, John Bidwell came walking from Ohio, a youth of twenty. He took up a claim, but yielded to a claim jumper. Hearing one of the Robidoux family telling of the merits of California, he organized the Western Emigration Society and on May 12, 1841, set out with sixty-nine persons in a caravan guided by Thomas Fitzpatrick.

Another to try his fortune in Weston was Ben Holladay, who came from Kentucky in 1838 and set up a dramshop. The Mexican War opened a door of opportunity and the Civil War afforded further opportunity. He became the Salt Lake trader, the railroad constructor, the stage coach king, the New York millionaire and the owner of Ophir Farm.

In February of 1849 word was brought to Weston of the discovery of gold in California. When spring came, Weston was a heaving metropolis of gold seekers who took anything in the shape of vehicles and animals and started for the West. Men were coming by steamboat from all quarters of the country and every steamboat on the river was jammed with gold seekers.

Weston was ten and for the next few years at the height of its glory. This was when the city of Leavenworth had not been thought of; neither Omaha nor Denver had been laid out; there was no Atchison, Kansas City was a mere steamboat landing and St. Joseph only a trading post. Weston was the big steamboat headquarters of the West and the biggest town in the United States west of St. Louis.

The prosperity of Weston suffered its first blow in June, 1858, when the river left its traditional course and moved a mile away, destroying the usefulness of the port.

Today, the little town, finding new pride in being the tobacco capital of the West, nestles among the high bluffs where spreading trees shelter lingering old houses, and where the old cathedral on the hill stands as a sentinel of passing time and quiet peace.

Chapter Fourteen

Joe Town, Cock of the West

Joseph Robidoux first appeared at the Blacksnake Hills in 1803. In connection with this trading post, which eventually grew into the city of St. Joseph, he was made, in 1809, Indian agent at the Council Bluffs, above the present Omaha. In 1819, with Chouteau, Berthold and Papin, he had a trading post at the mouth of the Nishnabotna River, a few miles above the Blacksnake Hills. The place became known as Robidoux's Landing. There on the red, crumbling earth of a hillside, he built his home of logs with a stone basement and above the mouth of the creek he built his store.

When the Platte Purchase was opened in 1837, the Blacksnake Hills became the object of an immigration rush, the announcement being the signal for general movement into the new country, settlers arriving by steamboat, by ox wagon and on foot. People poured in through the woods, over the prairies and up the river.

In 1843, Robidoux laid out the town of St. Joseph, and Audubon called it "a delightful site for a populous city." Within two years the town had six hundred and eighty-two inhabitants, three hotels, a newspaper and twelve mercantile establishments.

With the inrush of new settlers, it was inevitable that Robidoux's little French fur-trading village would become subject to lively competition, most of it from newly established upriver trading posts. In 1842 Nodaway was laid out and then Owen's Landing. In 1846 came Sonora and Linden. All have disappeared.

In November 1848, a small party arrived in St. Joseph bringing gold dust from the Feather River in California. It was pronounced pure gold by a local chemist.

By the following spring the rush for the gold fields of California was on, St. Joseph's star was in the ascendancy and the little village of wooden stores began to take on the airs of a city. It was more convenient than Independence as a point of departure for the gold fields, being a full two-day journey by steamboat up the river from Independence and considered seventy miles farther west than its older rival, the equal of four days of steady travel by ox team. A continuous line of wagons, extending east as far as the eye could see, fed the two ferryboats a prospering stream. Oxen drew some of the wagons. Many of the gold seekers pushed their worldly belongings before them in handcarts.

From April1 to June 1, that year, fifteen hundred wagons, averaging four men to the wagon, crossed the "Big Muddy" at St. Joseph. Many, waiting for the ferry, were camped upon the plain below the town, the tents of the emigrants and the white covers of their wagons being visible for miles around. All day long, day after day, prairie schooners drawn by oxen came into St. Joseph, and the steamboats came, five or ten a day, loaded to the guards with travelers, provisions and ammunition. There were college graduates from the East mingling with unwashed Indians from Nebraska; there were farmers, clerks, shopkeepers, levee roustabouts, lawyers, editors, preachers – all yielding to the seductive dream of easily acquired wealth. To those hopeful travelers no story of the vast gold deposits was too wild to be believed, no story of dangers so vivid as to deter them.

An incident of the gold rush occurred on the steamboat Tuscumbia about two miles above St. Joseph which involved Charles Crocker, a young man on the way to California where he became one of the big four that dominated almost every phase of activity on the Pacific slope. Early in 1850 he organized a small group of gold seekers which included two of his four brothers and set out from Marshall County, Indiana, where he had been interested in an iron works. Reaching Quincy, Illinois, he instructed his party to proceed with the wagons across muddy Iowa while he went by boat to St. Louis to purchase provisions that would be essential in crossing the plains.

Having bought his provisions, he arranged for their shipment up the Missouri on the Tuscumbia and took passage on the same boat. About May 1 the boat arrived at Sandusky, called "Jimtown" by the forty-niners for whom it was an important river crossing. There the captain declared his intention of unloading the boat, giving as his excuse that it was dangerous to operate a steamboat through the shoal waters that would be encountered farther upstream.

"Big Charlie" Crocker, believing he was being duped, had no intention of playing the role. The twenty-eight-year old giant, weighing two hundred and fifty pounds, was wrathful. With that same driving force he later employed in building railroads and financial empires, he let it be known his goods were going through as contracted. It was one of the few instances, perhaps the only one, in which a hardboiled Missouri River steamboat captain bowed to a landlubber. The goods went through.

For two years the gold rush continued, in which time thousands of emigrants had swarmed through St. Joseph, but by 1851 steamboat competition had cut in, taking freight and gold seekers to Florence and Council Bluffs. But even as late as May 1853, the steamer Alton was employed three days ferrying emigrants over the river at St. Joseph, taking two hundred and twelve wagons and nearly eight thousand head of cattle.

St Joseph had become so firmly established by the trade with the Argonauts that it had little to fear from its self-declared rivals, the upriver hamlets in the immediate vicinity. These would have included Forest City and Nodaway. In 1851 the name of the latter town was changed to Boston. Nodaway City had a rival in Elizabethtown. In 1857 Amazonia was started nearby and the four names were used rather indiscriminately for what virtually was one town, best remembered as Amazonia, a town which ceased to exist when a shift of the river's course left it over a mile inland.

Forest City, also an 1857 product, became a noted shipping point and was the scene of bustle and animation and thronging steamboats. One day in June 1868, the Katy P. Kountz tied up at Forest City, took on freight and departed. Next day the river was more than two miles from the town. Other river towns in the vicinity, now only names, were Scott City, Kalamazoo, El Paso and Sacramento City. All were washed away by the shifting Missouri River.

The first gold rush, to California, had put St. Joseph on a solid commercial basis and assured its continuing growth. When the word began to drift back to the Missouri River towns in the fall of 1858 that gold had been discovered in the Pike's Peak area, a new contest was opened. This time, however, St. Joseph had heavier competition, with the new towns of Leavenworth, Atchison, Nebraska City and Omaha seeking to obtain a share of the traffic. Although it failed to obtain a lion's share of the traffic, St. Joseph emerged as the leading city on the Missouri River, the 1860 census showing : St. Joseph, 8.932; Independence, 3,164; Kansas City, 4,418; Leavenworth, 7,379; Weston, 2,921; Atchison, 2,611; Council Bluffs, 2,011; Omaha, 1,881. St. Joseph was the largest and busiest town on the river.

The steamboat had been an important factor in the development of the Northwest and the traffic had reached its height about the time of the Pike's Peak gold rush in 1858, many gold seekers following the river route as far as possible.

It was at the time of that gold rush, according to Billy Alford, an old-time riverman of St. Joseph, that a gambler was hanged on Cat Island, a well-known landmark just above St. Joseph. He had tried to fleece a youth on board the steamer Henrietta, but something had gone wrong with his deal. His opponent was about to rake in nine thousand dollars when the gambler seized a handful of money and ran, stuffed the money in his pocket, jumped overboard and made for the shore. A boatload of armed men overtook him while the Henrietta headed for Cat Island where the mate and a dozen men swung the gambler to the breeze under a big tree then prominent on the island.

In 1858 sixty regular packets were engaged in the trade, probably the most profitable year in the history of Missouri River navigation. Much of the popularity of St. Joseph as disembarkation and outfitting point was due to its ferry facilities. It had two steamboats going from shore to shore, one to Elwood, directly across the river, the other to Bellemont, a few miles upstream.

After the Hannibal & St. Joseph railroad was completed in 1859, the St. Joseph & Omaha Packet Company was organized to make connections between those two points. This venture, under Captain Rufus Ford, met a ready demand. Whether the steamboat men realized it or not, and they probably did not, the steamboat was on the way out when the locomotive came in. Ironically enough, a steamboat brought the first locomotives upriver from St. Louis to operate on the western end of the St. Joseph & Hannibal railroad. As the boat came in sight of St. Joseph, its whistle sounded continuously, setting off a concatenation of church bells in the city so that sleepy citizens rubbed their eyes and then headed for the levee to see the iron horse sitting serenely in the bow of the boat.

From nearby river towns the citizens came by every available vehicle to augment the crowd and to participate in a daylong celebration that included the continuous firing of anvils. The strains of "Wait for the Wagon" and "Pop Goes the Weasel" arose from the several brass bands that had been hastily assembled for the occasion. A pier was thrust into the river from which the crowd was sprayed with oratory, a place of honor being given "Old Joe" Robidoux, founder of the city, who smiled benignly. A changeful constituency was saying, though unawares, "the steamboat is dead; long live the locomotive!" But before the railroad was to be crowned the king of speed, it was to be challenged once more by a primitive type of locomotion, the pony, bodied forth and glorified in the Pony Express.

That colossal enterprise, called by some a magnificent failure, is said to have had its inception in the brain of Senator William F. Glynn of California, who had traveled across the West on his way to Washington. He, in turn, might have received inspiration for the thought from the rides of F.X. Aubrey, ending at Independence. As a matter of fact, many men might have, and probably did have, the same thought. But Glynn did something about it. He spoke to his friend William Russell of Russell, Majors & Waddell. This was probably the only firm in existence capable of making the dream become a living reality. It was the only firm or combination of men with a sufficiently comprehensive background of meeting and overcoming transportation difficulties over the vast expanses of the West. It was the only firm with the requisite experience and organization; and it was the only firm with the essential credit and material resources to send the horses of the Pony Express flashing across the plains.

William H. Russell went to Lexington, Missouri, in the early 1830s and was employed by James and Robert Aull in 1833. William Waddell also went to the vicinity of Lexington in the early 1830s. In 1855, Alexander Majors, who had been freighting out of Independence over the Santa Fe Trail, went to Lexington where the three men became partners in transporting commodities to the West. Russell and Waddell are buried in Machpelah Cemetery, Lexington; Majors in Union Cemetery, Kansas City.

The St. Joseph Weekly West of April 7, 1860, said that late in the afternoon of April 3, William Richardson, former sailor, sprang into the saddle in front of the express offices of Russell, Majors & Waddell and the Wells-Fargo companies on Third Street, just south of Felix, and headed his horse down Jule Street to the ferry that was waiting to take him over to Elwood. He carried a revolver, a bowie knife and a Bible.

There has been controversy as to the place of departure of the first rider and as to his identity. Local historians for years mistakenly assumed the ride was begun from the Pike's Peak stables in Pattee Park, but research has developed that those stables were not established until several weeks after April 3. Likewise there was error for years in honoring Johnny Frey as the first rider of the Pony Express. Claims have been made for Henry Wallace and Alex Carlyle.

When expected government assistance was not forthcoming, the financial weight of the Pony Express proved too great even for the gigantic structure of Russell, Majors & Waddell. The firm crashed and the partners were reduced to the status of poverty stricken litigants. But though the venture spelled death for the great transportation firm, it had been good advertising for St. Joseph. The town was revered as the largest, most widely advertised town in the West – a man's town, for the eyes of men were alight at the mention of Joe Town, or St. Joe, as it was affectionately called.

In time it outgrew the appellation and as befitted the name St. Joseph, it became a larger town, a richer town, with more of dignity and more of culture. But there are those who will argue that in many respects the city reached its pinnacle I that year of 1860 when it was the mecca of railroaders, riverains and riders of the Pony Express – when it was Joe Town, cock of the West.

Chapter Fifteen

The Call of California Gold

Towns along the Missouri River were the first to feel the great awakening caused by the news that gold had been found in California. There had at first been only a slow reaction to the impact of the word and then when realization came of what it could mean to the individual economy of tens of thousands, the response was little short of mass hysteria. Because the vast majority of gold seekers favored the overland route, believing it to be the poor man's road to the gold fields, a throng of adventurers moved up the Missouri River by steamboat, thus shortening the overland trek by two or three hundred miles. Others, driving their ox or mule teams, followed the course of the river because it would bring them to one of the jumping-off places on the river which were vying for the trade of the Argonauts.

A favorite route of gold seekers from the East was by way of Pittsburgh where a steamboat could be boarded to take them down the Ohio and up the Mississippi to St. Louis at which place they would take steamboats up the Missouri.

In St. Louis the rush was tremendous with hundreds of gold adventurers arriving every day, filling the hotels, boarding houses, and even finding accommodations in some of the steamboats. Camps were formed in the neighborhood to accommodate some of the companies of gold seekers that were operating in a semi-military manner. It was said that if fairly set upon the route, the cavalcade might be made to extend the whole distance from western Missouri to the gold region.

One small group leaving St. Louis consisted of George Mifflin Harker, a newspaper reporter, and two companions, Milton Rains Elstner and Theodore R. Keyes of Crittenden, Kentucky. They started out from Morgan Street, heading for the gold fields. Harker wrote:

"We must have made a grotesque appearance. We created a sensation. Two of us were leading mules upon the backs of which were fastened real old-fashioned American packsaddles. One of us was perched upon a spring seat in front of a large, dashing red wagon, covered with India rubber cloth, holding in one hand the lines, in the other a long whip, and driving four fiery little mules with the dexterity and pride of a Yankee stage driver. Old women, fair damsels, and little children along the route all were anxious to catch a glimpse of the strange procession. Some little boys were singing 'I'm bound for California with my washboard on my knee.' Saucier lads parodied an old Negro song, "A jackass before and behind, Old Joe." The second day out we overtook a young couple bound for California in a wagon drawn by two yoke of oxen. They were connected with no company. The female was a buxom lass of some twenty-five summers, quite good looking and apparently able to endure the privations and hardships of the tedious journey across the plains."

Because Harker was one of the most articulate of the Argonauts, we may pursue his journey further, as reported in Glimpses of the Past, a publication of the Missouri Historical Society, St. Louis;

"We are taking it rough and tumble, sleeping in the open air, driving stupid, contrary donkeys, shooting prairie fowls and squirrels. This is kind of initiatory lesson that we are conning preparatory to crossing the plains. The number of persons going from this state to California is almost incredible. I am informed that almost a hundred wagons left Calloway County alone. A company of about a hundred young men left Columbia last week and a large company left Rocheport a day or two since; and companies are still being raised in this and adjoining counties. We crossed the river at Rocheport in a miserable horse ferryboat. That night we camped a mile this side of Boonville on a high bluff of the river—a lovely spot. In the edge of the grove a party of fifty Bostonians was camped. There was one woman in the group, a Mrs. Hutchins of St. Louis, who was accompanying her husband." Arriving at Independence, Harker reported:

"We passed some fifty California teams between Rocheport and this place, and heard of several companies that were about starting from the counties through which we passed, perhaps two hundred in all, mostly driving ox teams. Everything here is in confusion, with cholera prevailing. Many already have become dissatisfied and are returning home. Many have gambled away their money and are obliged to take the back track. The almighty dollar seems to have engrossed the whole attention of this place and they think of nothing else. Turner and Allen's company, the Pioneer Line, has been encamped for a few days nine miles out from this place on the Santa Fe Road and was to have left yesterday. As near as I can learn, some nine or ten thousand persons have reached points on the Missouri River above St. Louis this spring on the way to California. Of these, two-thirds are poorly equipped and some have not teams of sufficient force to move them from one extremity of Illinois to the other, let alone a trip of upwards of two thousand miles.

We will start early tomorrow morning and overtake some forty or fifty Kentuckians, all supplied with first rate mule teams and good outfits. We will travel with them."

In St. Louis the gold seekers were clambering aboard the up bound steamboats, their usual destination being Independence, Weston, or St. Joseph, paying the moderate fare to save the time and trouble entailed in crossing the state by wagon. From any of these points to the south fork of the Platte River, a distance of more than four hundred miles, they would encounter fine rolling prairie, abundant-ly supplied with water and covered with rich grass.

All the steamers leaving St. Louis were crowded so that when J. Goldsborough Bruff arrived, heading a company of more than sixty young Argonauts from the city of Washington, he found it necessary to divide his party and make the upriver leg of the journey on three separate steamboats. The names and ages of members of his party were printed in the local newspaper, showing a remarkable preponderance in the age group around twenty to twenty-two years. This would have held good for most other groups of Argonauts. It was a young man's hegira.

Bruff's company held to the militaristic formula, as did many other groups bound for the gold regions. Their uniform consisted of a short gray frock coat, single-breasted, with gilt eagle buttons; cassimere pantaloons of the same color, with black stripe; glazed forage cap with the initials of the company in front, and white shoulder straps.

Some of Bruff's party left for St. Joseph on the steamer Alice, "already pretty full of California emigrants." St. Louis was thronged with them. Steamers arrived and departed almost every hour with additional thousands to swell the grand overland concourse. Others of his party left on the Cambria, which, "like all the other steamers 'bound up' was crowded to excess."

Bruff and the balance of his party boarded the Belle Creole with emigrants from all parts of the country, though principally Illinoisans and New Englanders. Bruff noted; "We were on board amid such a dense medley of Hoosiers, Wolverines, Yankees, Buckeyes, and Yorkers, including blacklegs and swindlers of every grade of proficiency and celebrity, as is seldom to be found together, even on our western rivers." The Daily Republican reported; "The fast running Belle Creole left this city last evening for the Missouri River, with between three and four hundred passengers, nearly all California bound with the gold fever."

The Belle Creole was larger than most steamboats essaying the upriver trip and what with the water being at low stage had to proceed cautiously. It lay alongside the bank at night, as snags rendered night navigation very hazardous. Arriving at Camden, it was unable to go farther, unloading many of the gold seekers and their equipment to finish the journey by land. Others were taken to Lexington, a few miles downstream, and the Belle Creole returned to St. Louis. Those who had been set down at Lexington boarded the Meteor and reached St. Joseph without further incident.

"Gold! Gold! Gold!" exclaimed the Glasgow Weekly Times. "The country seems to be in a complete ferment about the gold of California. It is established beyond doubt that gold exists there, in great abundance, and that those on the ground are lining their pockets at the rate of from ten to fifty dollars per day. This news has caused no little fluttering and anxiety on the part of many, who are talking about going to California." Six weeks later, it said; "Many of our young men, captivated with these accounts and stimulated with the desire of amassing a great fortune, in a short time, are preparing to risk their all in the venture, without counting the cost." When the weather had become clement, the Times reported; "The flood of emigration is still rolling to our frontier, in order to be ready to make an early start for the Eldorado of the world. Almost every boat that passes up is crowded, while the roads are crowded with wagons. A man from Hannibal said he was never out of sight of a California wagon and that the ferry at Hannibal could not cross them fast enough."

A portion of the Howard County emigrants left Glasgow on April 12. Others left on April 22 to rendezvous at Weston and perfect their organization. The Weekly Democrat at Boonville carried an advertisement February 23, saying: "All persons in Cooper County, who design going to California in the spring with mule teams are requested to meet in the upper room of the courthouse in the City of Boonville."

And so it went. As every state in the Union was said to have been represented by a party of gold seekers, so every county in Missouri had a contingent heading for "the most interesting part of the earth, the richest gold mines ever known." Missouri was both native state and point of departure for many of the Forty-niners in the most colorful and dramatic phase in the saga of the western movement.

The People's Organ, St. Louis, in its issue of April 16, 1849, estimated that twenty thousand persons, four thousand wagons and thirty thousand mules would be crossing the plains by June of that year. Most of these would have followed or crossed the Missouri in the earlier stages of their trek.

The Frontier Guardian at Council Bluffs believed between six hundred and a thousand wagons were heading for that place from Iowa, Wisconsin, and Michigan, all on their way to the gold regions.

The St. Joseph Adventure reported not less than fifty or sixty thousand oxen, mules, and horses, with several teams abreast in some instances, crossing the plains of Nebraska and Wyoming. The St. Joseph Gazette figured that in that stretch of the river between St. Joseph and Council Bluffs seventeen thousand persons and thirty-four thousand animals had crossed the river.

One man, who issued a map of the emigrant road from Independence to San Francisco, noted that taking packsaddles instead of wagons would be the safest and most expeditious way of travel, "even for women and children.' He warned that sidesaddles should be discarded and that women should wear hunting frocks, loose pantaloons, men's hats and shoes, "and ride the same as men." There is no indication, however, that the ladies heeded his advice.

One of the most imposing and best known gold seekers from Missouri was William Muldrow of Marion County, in which Hannibal is located, on the Mississippi River. This Kentuckian who had come to Missouri in 1821 was more than six feet tall, was a big man. In the 1830s he had launched plans to build a metropolis, Marion City, on the banks of the Mississippi; to erect a college; and to construct a railroad to the Pacific Ocean. Eastern capitalists furnished the initial funds. But the river soon took the dream city, which Charles Dickens satirized as "Eden" in Martin Chuzzlewit, having Mark Tapley and Martin pay a visit to their forty-acre lot in the God-forsaken place. Grading was commenced on the railroad, but the road remained an unfulfilled dream. Muldrow was a big man with big ideas and his favorite expression was "there's millions in it" an expression caught up by Mark Twain, who knew him personally, when he immortalized him as "Colonel Mulberry Sellers" in The American Claimant.

With a party of gold seekers Muldrow left Marion County, April 17, 1849, and arrived at Weaversville, California, October 13. The records do not show whether he succeeded in finding gold, but in 1859 he was speculating again, being the owner of John Sutter's Fort Ross and the Bodega tract. He returned to Missouri in 1869 and died in 1872.

Like the myriad other youths that had been part of that great complex, the gold rush, he had returned from that trail of the long chance to a more serene life. And like them, when life ebbed away with the coming of age, his obituary could proudly point to the highlight of his life; "He crossed the plains in '49."

Chapter Sixteen

Steamboats
in Their Glory

Freight traffic was slack in the season of 1851-52, but the packets were able to make a profit off the emigrant trade, all upriver boats being crowded to capacity. The California and Oregon migration was in full swing, and it was reported that in May 1852, four hundred immigrants left St. Louis by steamer bound for the Pacific Coast. There were many other passengers bound for Missouri and Iowa points, besides the Mormons taking the river route, as many as two hundred and forty of them being loaded onto Captain Gormley's steamboat, the Banner State, bound for Council Bluffs in May, 1851. The next year the Robert Campbell took a similar load. A passenger that year on the Clipper No.2 wrote, " We are upbound on an old worn-out boat, the officers caring for nothing but the gold they are making. This is the largest crowd that ever traveled up this river on one boat."

The Delaware, according to Frank A. Root, historian, took the first two steam engines up the Missouri, destined for use on the Hannibal & St. Joseph Railroad. They were named the Buchanan and the St. Joseph. Root was in Quindaro at the time, June 9, 1857, and from the upper story of the Chindowan newspaper, located on the levee a few rods from the river, saw the boat and the engines. There is other authority for saying it was the Saranac No. 3

that carried the engines. The latter, under Captain Saltmarsh, went up to Council Bluffs in May, 1850, to get a cargo, some forty-five thousand buffalo robes and thirty mountain men, employees of the Union Fur Company, owner of the furs and the Saranac No. 3. Officers of the boat reported eight or ten thousand emigrants with three thousand wagons encamped around Kanesville (the early name for Council Bluffs).

The El Paso, under Captain John Durack, went to the mountains in 1850 and reached a point three hundred and fifty miles above the Yellowstone, a record for that time. In April, 1855, it was one of the numerous boats bringing New England emigrants to Kansas City, from where they went into Kansas for the purpose of influencing the future of that territory.

The Allegheny Mail, Captain Preston Brown, carried the minstrel show of Dan Rice in the middle of the century when he was making a tour of the rivers. It is believed, in some quarters that the Isabel was named for the wife of Zenas Leonard, who had a store at Sibley and owned one or more steamboats. It first was advertised in the Kansas Public Ledger for July 4, 1851, about the time of Leonard's death.

The Sam Cloon brought parties of New England emigrants bound for Kansas to the Kansas City landing in October 1854, and again in April 1855. It was described then by one of its passengers as "a miserable old boat." The Elvira in May 1851 took a boatload of Mormons to Council Bluffs. In May 1852, Governor Walker noted in his diary; "Yesterday the Wyandot delegation for Washington set out, on board the Elvira." So limited were hotel accommodations in the early 1850s that a Colonel S.H. Hunt converted the new St. Paul into a hotel at the mouth of the Kaw River in the town of Wyandotte.

Before the middle 1850s, when the railroad competition began to be felt, the river traffic made wonderful strides. The freight rates varied from season to season and from year to year, performing an arc between 1850 and 1855, going up, then down. In 1859, the captains, clerks, and mates of the packets were fighting the freight away, all the packets going out of St. Louis being jammed with passengers, the first effort being to accommodate the unprecedented rush of passengers bound for the Pike's Peak country. Frequently, however, western-bound persons took the train from St. Louis, changing at Hermann to the packets bound upriver and later at Jefferson City when the railroad was extended that far west.

As a rule there was keen competition for the river trade, although the captains had in 1845 agreed upon a uniform rate. In 1855, a still tighter combination was formed, to the indignation of many shippers and some newspapers. When the Missouri River Packet Lines engaged all the pilots licensed to run boats on the Missouri, it was pointed out that the number of pilots was none too great for the demands of the trade. Even when working, it was much less when being paid to walk leisurely about the streets of St. Louis. The consequence of this being that "a very few boats, comparatively, have monopolized all the carrying trade of one of the most important rivers in the West, and at a time, too, when the development of the country, the improvements in western Missouri and the settlement of Kansas and Nebraska have greatly increased the demand for boats on that river," a quote from the St. Louis Intelligencer, April 13, 1855.

The Liberty Tribune of the same date said the steamboat monopoly was literally crushing the lifeblood out of the people. They pointed out that the boat owners had combined, bought off all the Missouri River pilots in order to keep out boats from the Ohio and the Mississippi, the result being to keep up freight rates. The paper mentioned further that "Ninety percent of the boats are owned by St. Louis men and of course they are parties to the thieving monopoly now existing. If the monopoly continues what are we to do for salt, sugar, coffee, iron, nails, etc., and what are we to do with our hemp, tobacco, corn and wheat? Will not our merchants, rather than suffer this monopoly to continue, go to work and build packet boats for next year's trade?"

But in the years 1853-55, the proud packets were doing an enormous business, and it seemed no time to worry about indignant shippers or travelers or newspapers, nor yet the incipient threat of railroad competition. (chart here)

Captain La Barge's St. Mary was named for a town just below Council Bluffs. The Sam Getty was named for a wealthy foundry owner in St. Louis, who had been a bound boy in Pennsylvania, of the Getty family for which Gettysburg was named. He became a foundry worker before going to St. Louis where he established his own foundry, became rich and took an active interest in politics.

William H. Parkinson, captain of the Star of the West, was born in Pennsylvania in 1814 and was in command of a steamboat on the Ohio when he was eighteen. He came on the Missouri in 1842 where he continued until 1858. Retiring to Colorado in 1858 he helped lay out Denver and lived there several years. He died at Boulder, Montana, August 12, 1892. The Star of the West landed at Kansas City in April 1856, with a hundred emigrants from Georgia, Alabama, South Carolina and Kentucky. On her next trip upriver, in June, she had abolitionists as passengers and ran into difficulties at Weston where the inhabitants of the town and surrounding country refused to let the passengers come ashore. The party was part of the Army of the North, organized by James H. Lane. The boat earlier had been detained at Lexington, where a mob of Missourians, headed by Colonel Jo Shelby, relieved the Northerners of their firearms.

Another boat was the "new and splendid packet," the F.X. Aubrey, under command of Captain Ambrose Reeder. Between the smokestacks of this boat was the figure of a man riding at full speed on horseback, honoring the famous ride from Santa Fe to Independence, made by F.X. Aubrey. Then there was Captain Andrew Wineland's new boat; her construction superintended in Louisville by the captain himself. This was the James H. Lucas, named for a rich man in St. Louis. A Glasgow paper, the Weekly Times of April 6, 1854, said, "Captain Wineland has spared no pains or expense to make her what she is – one of the best boats ever built for the Missouri River trade...speed, convenience and beauty." Still other boats were the Bluff City, under Captain John McCloy, the Fanny Sparhawk, the Reindeer, the "elegant steamer," the Cataract, under Captain Lou A. Welton, the E.A. Ogden, with Captain Baldwin, and the Emma Harmon.

Traffic on the Missouri River had made immense strides, physically and financially, as well a in the nature, value and volume of goods transported, since Captain Nelson and his little steamboat, the Independence, had braved the snag infested river for the first time in 1819. His boat would have looked puny and crude indeed by the side of the floating palaces of the mid-fifties.

Then the river boasted of such steamboats as the Duncan S. Carter, the Fannie Barker, and the John Warner, said to have had the largest and sweetest toned bell on the river. The William S. Campbell traveled then, which had both Tom Scott and William Edds for captains that year of 1856; and Captain Alex Gillham's A.B. Chambers, frequently carrying a string band and being a favorite with the youth and beauty of Independence and Kansas City. (chart here)

It was in the summer of that year that Captain Barton, Captain Able and Captain Louis A. Shelton contracted with the Missouri Pacific Railway, which had progressed as far west as Jefferson City, to pick up passengers there for upriver points. In this service were used the Cataract, the F.X. Aubrey and the Australia. The tie-up was advertised as "By railroad to Jefferson City, thence by a daily line of elegant mail steamers to all points on the river, as high as St. Joseph, connecting there with the various packet and stage lines for Kansas, Nebraska, and Iowa. Fare as low as any other route. Time saved over the river route full thirty hours."

Thus in the heyday of their prosperity the steamboats themselves were sowing the seeds of a competition which soon would rise and destroy them. For by this pact, through passenger traffic from below Jefferson City was forever lost to the steamboats – the beginning of an end not discernible then when every steamboat on the river was jammed "to the gunnels" with passengers and freight. Each year then saw additional boats being added in answer to the transportation demands of emigrants pouring into the West despite the slavery dispute.

All the growth had not been confined to the steamboats or to those towns between Lexington and Kansas City on the south side of the river. There had been an equally exciting expansion going on along the north banks of the stream from Lexington to St. Joseph.

—Native Sons Collection, Western Historical Manuscripts UMKC.

Chapter Seventeen

When Kansas Was a 'Bleeding

Kansas still was Indian Territory in 1842 when the Wyandottes of Ohio sent trusted men there to spy out the land preparatory to removal of the tribe from its traditional hunting grounds. The aging John Hicks, last of the hereditary chiefs, led his tribesmen to their new home in the West, the site of the town of Wyandotte, located at the point of land formed by the junction of the Kaw and Missouri rivers.

Governor Robert J. Walker was a scholarly man who spoke a dozen Indian dialects as well as being versed in Greek and Latin. He spoke albeit with a peppery tongue. Once in his diary he exclaimed; "My execrations upon the captain of the steamboat Manona for landing my lumber on a point opposite Wyandotte City instead of our usual landing place." Like many another of the early settlers, he had arrived at Wyandotte by steamboat, making his first speech in the new territory form the deck of the New Lucy. Other territorial governors arrived by the river. Governor Charles Robinson landed at Kansas City in 1849 from the Ne Plus Ultra. Governor Wilson Shannon arrived in 1855 on the Martha Jewett; Governor Reeder returned in May 1856, on the David Tatum, and in the same year Governor Glick arrived on the Alonzo Child.

By the mid-fifties Wyandotte was the leading town of

the territory, its population represented by nearly every state in the Union and almost every nationality. The lax morals of the town were accepted as the usual concomitants of a frontier town and its heterogeneous population. By that time, too, the race was on between free staters and pro-slavery men, bringing and influx of unusually rugged men.

From 1857, there sprang up a great rivalry between Wyandotte and Quindaro, a new town, some three miles upstream, each town claiming that it was destined to become the future great metropolis of the West.

Quindaro was established January 1, 1857, promoted principally by Abelard Guthrie, and named for his Indian wife, Seh Quindaro Brown, a member of the Big Turtle clan of the Wyandottes. Guthrie was a well-informed man who had been a delegate to the congress from the Nebraska Territory in 1852. He was well liked by the Wyandottes, which helped the growth of his town, located on land that had belonged to his wife. The most important factor in the rapid growth of the new town, however, was that it was favored by the New England Immigrant Aid Society, which was seeking a port of entry for free staters free of the restraint which pro-slavery men exercised at other towns on the Missouri River. The society offered transportation to free state advocates who would go to Kansas to settle. The new town became their mecca; a town remarkably free of the usual frontier lawlessness.

Boatloads of homeseekers, fortune hunters and tradesmen landed at Quindaro, coming from the North and the East. Gold circulated freely, town lots were snapped up at exorbitant prices, and the town grew amazingly. Horace Greeley visited the place and predicted it would become the great city of the West. Water Street and Kansas Avenue bustled with activity. Stages and hacks left every morning for interior towns. The place had a newspaper, the Chindowan. But after only four years, with the coming of the Civil War, Quindaro was snuffed out like a candle.

During the 1850s a number of little villages sprang up

along the Missouri River frontier on the eastern edge of Kansas. These were where free state men were flocking in anticipation of and in preparation for the struggle between free state and pro-slavery men, the turbulent times of border warfare when men whipped and murdered each other and the term "Bleeding Kansas" was coined. Of such towns were Leavenworth, Fort Williams and Delaware. It was a period of intense land speculation with fortune seekers crowding the steamboats that touched Kansas ports and with new towns springing up over night.

Delaware, sometimes called Delaware Crossing or Delaware Point, was founded in August, 1855. Halfway between Wyandotte and Leavenworth, its lots immediately sold at fabulous prices and it outdistanced both the new town of Leavenworth and the older town of Kickapoo. In 1858 Leavenworth forged to the front and all Delaware's business houses were moved there. Then a contemporary historian noted: "The town of Delaware has come to nothing – people are leaving for the Colorado mines."

The new town of Leavenworth, established in 1854, had the benefit of the nearby fort as a sustaining influence to help it survive the high mortality among towns of the Kansas border. The fort had been established in 1827 by Colonel Henry Leavenworth to succeed Fort Osage as the government's farthest outpost. It was the supply depot for the Army of the West during the Mexican War, being the only government fort on the Missouri River.

As Leavenworth grew up near the fort and as other towns were laid out along the river in the 1850s, the competition became keen for the honor and the profits that went with being the point of supply. As government transportation across the plains grew in volume, Leavenworth grew in importance as a shipping point for government stores to the Indians and military forces of the West and Southwest. The town was able to hold a virtual monopoly except for the period between 1858 and 1861 when it was lost to Kansas City, the opening of the Civil War forcing the traffic back to Leavenworth where it remained until the twilight of overland freighting.

The town's first hotel was the Leavenworth House, catering to free state men. The H.P. "Hog" Johnson started the Planters, a block from the levee, where no free staters were admitted until 1857 when new owners took over. Stephen A. Douglass spoke from the ornate balcony of this hostelry and his great rival, Lincoln, was a guest, but spoke at Sedgewick Hall. The Planters for two decades was the scene of Leavenworth's most interesting life, popular and prosperous until the disappearance of the steamboat from the Missouri.

The founding of Leavenworth in 1854 by pro-slavery men from Weston was a significant corollary of the passage of the Kansas-Nebraska Act of the same year. It was an Act that made Kansas the central figure in a vast drama, a tremendous conflict that was to be a prelude to the civil war. There along the shores of the Missouri, the Civil War was fought in miniature, but no whit less bloody or violent. Then, as one orator put it, "the prairies were aflame and the hearts of men were hot with controversy." There ensued a wild scramble by partisans of both sides to secure Kansas, the steamboats of the Missouri River being, at first, the principal means of conveying men to the scene of strife. But a majority of the masters of those steamboats was favorable to the pro-slavery elements and it became increasingly difficult for free state men to reach Kansas. They were subjected to offensive and insulting remarks of bystanders at nearly all river towns in Missouri; were, in some cases, relieved of their arms; and finally their boats were ordered to turn about and head downstream without unloading the passengers. This happened to the Star of the West with a hundred and twenty-five free staters aboard it, it being turned back at Leavenworth. Then passengers aboard the Sultana were similarly treated.

So effective had the steamboat blockade become that by May of 1856, the free state men saw their leaders in prison, their newspapers thrown into the river, and blood running down the streets of Leavenworth.

Almost from the day of its founding to the opening of the Civil War, Leavenworth experienced a half-dozen years filled with violence and lawlessness. In April of 1855, Malcolm Clark, a leading pro-slavery man, was killed in a row with Cole McCrea. The latter was arrested and indicted for murder, but escaped. The next month, William Phillips, free stater, was tarred and feathered, then taken to Weston, tarred and feathered again, ridden on a rail, sold on the block by a Negro. In January of 1856, Captain R.P. Brown, a free stater, was murdered by a mob, the killing being condoned by the pro-slavery Herald. Brown's slayers spat tobacco juice into his wounds, saying, "anything would make a damned abolitionist feel better."

Marking the arrival of the gala girls on the frontier, "Curly Jack" ran a house of ill fame in connection with his saloon and gambling den. Addison Rogers kept a dramshop and gambling place on the levee and was shot by a gambler named Brush. In August of 1856 one Fuget killed and scalped a man named Hoppe, but was acquitted at his trial. The following month, ruffians killed the William Phillips who had so been mistreated the year before. One Harrison, who had been a gambler in New York and had been run out of San Francisco in 1856, had acquired an unsavory reputation in Leavenworth. Counting up eleven men he had killed, he declared he would have a jury of his own try him in hell and fired a bullet into an inoffensive old shoemaker at work across the street. Harrison succeeded in evading a mob that formed to lynch him. In July 1857, James Stephens was murdered and robbed. His murderers, John C. Quarles and W.M. Bayes, were taken from the jail and lynched "near the sawmill." By the fall of 1858, the Leavenworth Journal was crying: "Run them out! Our city at the present time is completely filled with gamblers, thieves and pickpockets... Why should we have a horde of robbers and murderers quartered upon us this winter? We are decidedly opposed to mob law, but think such an example as set them two years ago, would have a beneficial effect." Despite this plea, John J. Ingalls noted on January 2: "Since Christmas there have been five murders in the city limits, all of the worst description, in the worst places."

While the turbulence due to the border troubles was

at its height, in September, 1858, E.V. King walked into a Leavenworth bank with a quill of gold dust from Pike's Peak. William H. Larimer quickly organized a party of gold seekers. By the following April the town was in the midst of a rush of Pike's Peakers. Two or three steamboats arrived each day loaded with people bound for the new gold region. The levee swarmed with people who sat on piles of dry goods boxes, stood in knots at the street corners or clustered about the Planters or the Leavenworth House or the Leavenworth & Pike's Peak express office.

William H. Russell and John S. Jones had organized this transportation company. The eastern terminus later was moved from Leavenworth to Atchison. The Lexington triumvirate of transportation, Russell, Majors & Waddell, in 1855 had obtained a contract to carry all government material from Leavenworth to the plains and mountain posts. By the opening of the Colorado gold rush, their fleet had increased to thirty-five wagons and forty thousand oxen, and they were employing four thousand men. A local newspaper called this huge firm, "the mariners of the plains."

Besides the countless varied types of newcomers arriving from the eastern states, the streets were full of soldiers from the nearby fort, Indians of many tribes in their picturesque costumes, Mexicans in gay dress, cowboys form the cattle trails and bullwhackers from the long wagon trains that constantly were going to and coming from the great West. Wagons all but obstructed the levee and the vicinity of the large outfitting houses near by. The men were buying outfits and selecting from the wagons and cattle that were for sale on virtually every vacant lot in the town. The wagons were being stocked with flour, bacon and groceries preparatory for the final start. The horizon on every side was lighted by the campfires of the companies already in camp along Three-Mile and Salt creeks.

Profiting from the demand for housing facilities, a Cincinnati firm had shipped by steamboat large quantities of what probably were the first prefabricated houses, the Hinkle cottages, more popularly "Cincinnati houses." So many were put up the western part of the town was called "Cincinnati."

In the next two yeas, as the excitement of the gold rush died down, there came a lull also in the fighting between the free staters and the pro-slavery men – perhaps it was the lull before the storm. For, in the spring of 1861, the Civil War burst in all its fury and the free state of Kansas was born amid high drama. In far-away Washington, distinguished sons of the South were arising to announce their resignation from the senate of the United States an their adherence to the Confederate States of America. As one after another the walked out of the senate chamber, an observant senator noted that the southern majority had vanished, and he quietly rose to move that Kansas be admitted as a free state into the Union. The territorial delegate, believing the news would interest his friend, the editor, sent a telegram to D.R. Anthony of Leavenworth.

That fiery and fighting editor had just printed the regular edition of the Leavenworth Conservative, but quickly printed an extra edition, blazing the news that Kansas had become a free state. He walked the streets, spread the news and gave away his extras. He carried a copy of the Kansas statutes, which were the Missouri statutes forced upon Kansas. When the extras were gone, in a characteristic gesture, he crammed the hated statutes into the maw of Old Kickapoo; a squat cannon captured in the Mexican War, and fired them back across the Missouri River, whence they came.

Chapter Eighteen

To the Stars – the Hard Way

In the days when the territory of Kansas was striving mightily toward its destiny, there arose a string of towns along the river which formed its eastern border – there being perhaps a dozen between Fort Leavenworth and the Nebraska line. Though Atchison eventually emerged as the important city along that stretch of the river, there were others, considered in their heyday quite important towns – such as White Cloud, Iowa Point, Palermo, Doniphan, Geary City, Elwood, Sumner, Fort Williams, and Kickapoo. The latter, six miles above Leavenworth dated back to the time of the Kickapoo Indian occupancy in 1832, when its diminutive chieftain, Wathena, led the tribe there. In the early 1840s it was a principal steamboat landing, reaching its apogee around 1854-56, when it was considered the superior of the upstart towns of Leavenworth and Atchison. In its earlier days, mail had been brought across from Weston, making Kickapoo an important distribution point for the postal service. But the town was unfortunately located on a rough and broken site, almost inaccessible from the backcountry. In the late 1850s, beset by rivalry of Leavenworth and Atchison, the town began to decline, and its dreams of greatness vanished when the capricious Big Muddy changed its channel. This succeeded in wiping out part of the townsite, then swinging back to the Missouri bluffs, leaving a huge sand bar at the front door of Kickapoo.

Beyond Kickapoo was Port Williams, a small place that had its beginning in 1855. The town never attained any size, but was well known.

Sumner, five miles above Port Williams, was a free state town, founded by John P. Wheeler, twenty-one-year-old surveyor from Massachusetts – red-headed, blue-eyed, slim, freckled, and enthusiastic enough to interest George Sumner, brother of the famous statesman, Charles Sumner, in buying lots in the new town. And it was George, not Charles, whose name was honored. The rugged, picturesque and well-nigh inaccessible site was located in what the early French voyageurs had called the Grand Detour of the Missouri River. From its founding in1856, it had a rapid growth, reflecting the determined spirit of the men from Massachusetts who pre-dominated among its earliest settlers. The flood time of the town's prosperity was 1856-1859, when it acquired a newspaper and several commodious buildings. It was at this time that its streets were filled with the clamor of busy traffic as thousands of oxen and mules labored to transport the products of the East across the great American desert to the Rocky Mountains. For a short while the city was said to have a population of twenty-five hundred.

A washerwoman in Sumner kept boarders while her husband worked at his trade in nearby Leavenworth. A nine-year-old daughter helped serve the boarders. Years later, the little girl became the renowned prima donna, Minnie Hauk, whose voice charmed two continents and who married Count Wartegg. Sumner for a while was also the home of Albert Deane Richardson, correspondent for the Boston Journal until 1859, when he went to Pike's Peak with Villard and Greeley. After that he went with the New York Tribune until he was shot and killed at his desk in the Tribune office in 1869.

Most important of Sumner's alumnus was John J. Ingalls, who as a young college graduate went to Sumner after having been attracted by handsome lithographs which made the new town present an imposing aspect in no wise a true representation of its actual state. Nevertheless, the young Ingalls stood on the hurricane deck of the Duncan S. Carter and prophesied that one day he would become the United States senator from Kansas – a prophecy that was fulfilled. And Ingalls was loyal to Sumner until its star had set and Atchison's sun had risen. This was when the railroad had come to Atchison, its smoke drifting down over Sumner like a pall. Then began an exodus of citizens; houses were torn down and the timbers hauled away. Today, beneath the shadow cast by mighty oaks and sighing cottonwoods, Sumner lies forgotten.

The town of Atchison was organized in 1854 by a group of prominent Missourians meeting at Weston. It was named for Senator David R. Atchison. It was his idea, and that of his associates, that by organizing the town and populating it with citizens who favored the extension of slavery into Kansas that it would serve as an outpost for his followers and also serve to impede the flow of abolitionists into the territory. And there was no flaw discernible in his ratiocination until James H. Lane made his appearance on the scene. Then the whole border struggle shaped up as a trial of strength between these two master strategists – with Lane, the free soiler, victorious in the end.

Atchison was strongly, not to say violently, pro-slavery. Dr. John T. Stringfellow, right-hand man of Senator Atchison, and the fiery Robert S. Kelley edited its first newspaper, the Squatter Sovereign, official organ of the pro-slavery element. Free soilers who inadvertently got into Atchison and forgot to be discreet in their utterances were warned to leave town. "Else," a publicly adopted resolution stated, "they will meet the reward which their nefarious designs so justly merit – hemp."

This failed to squelch one Pardee Butler, a preacher who lived near Atchison. He spoke his conviction as a free soiler once too often in Atchison and was given a coat of tar and cotton. He then was placed upon a small and hastily-built raft adorned with several placards bearing jeering comments, and turned loose upon the bosom of the Missouri, his departure being under the auspices of a regatta of small craft manned by pro-slavery men. A few miles downstream, Butler was rescued by friendly persons and set free.

Atchison grew great on the freighting trade, and within two years of its founding, several freighters, important in the Utah trade, had used it as a shipping point. They helped with their freight to crowd the levee where immense quantities of freight were stacked up for several blocks and warehouses were packed with groceries, provisions, clothing, boots and shoes. The Mormon trade then was regarded as the greatest of all western markets and Atchison apparently had a monopoly on it. It was a big day of big business along the levee, where the steamboats disgorged their burden of freight to have it picked up by the freighters to be hauled into the hinterland.

Atchison, being on the great western bend of the Missouri River, was advertised as the best crossing and the nearest and most convenient point to all the territory north of the Kansas River and as a starting point for all emigrants, to California, Oregon and Salt Lake. It was a natural trade terminal, with roads radiating to the north, south and west, and an immense freighting business was carried on. In 1859 D.W. Adams & Company had seven hundred wagons, nine hundred men and hauled more than three million pounds of merchandise. A.S. Parker & Company had two hundred forty-five wagons, two hundred sixty-eight men and hauled more than a million pounds of merchandise, according to the Atchison Union of July 23.

When the gold fever struck Atchison in the fall of 1858, the loyal editors were sure there was but one desirable route the pilgrims might take to the Cherry Creek mines and that was the "First Standard Parallel Route" west from Atchison. If, in their loyalty and enthusiasm, the editors mentioned bridges, ferries and good roads "along level divides," which as a matter of fact did not exist, it was but in the spirit of the times. Many went out in the spring and summer of 1859 and when some of the pilgrims came back from the diggings to report that from eight dollars to thirty dollars a day could be made by hand washing, with no machinery, the gold fever mounted and raged and gold digging was all the talk in Atchison. Every steamboat that nosed in at the landing was crowded with men bound for the mines. Some were so naïve as to believe Pike's Peak might be reached in an afternoon's walk from Atchison. More Peakers outfitted in Atchison in 1860 than in the previous year, covered wagons were everywhere and stores were crowded with outfitters, while the roads leading west were thronged with vehicles of every type, western-bound pilgrims passing successful gold seekers returning, anxious to dispose of their gold and get home.

Atchison was booming, becoming famous as a depot and notorious as a town of grog shops and bawdy houses. The shops and stores were open on Sundays and the saloons, billiard halls and ten-pin alleys did a thriving business. Its rise as a river town and as an important city of the West was rapid and dramatic, the several contributing factors being the steamboat traffic, the opening of the West to settlers, the discovery of gold, and the huge freighting business. Its veriest beginning was due to the opening of the territory; the river trade contributed much to its growth; the outfitting trade was a significant part of its economic history; but its dominance as a trade center was owed most of all to the freighting business.

It was an important station on the Pony Express route. Many freighters made their headquarters there, including eventually the gigantic outfit of those mariners of the plains, Russell Majors & Waddell.

As early as the spring of 1861, though its streets still teemed with emigrants and freighters, there was a slight diminution in the traffic; emigration was not as heavy as it had been in the preceding year. After the middle 1860s the town declined as a factor in the westward movement. In 1866, with railroad competition established across Kansas and across Nebraska, the overland stage ceased operation, and long trains of Concord stages, express coaches, hacks and other rolling stock went out of the stables and yards on

Second Street, leaving Atchison forever. Young men tramped in the streets, idle, hungry, and shelterless. Even some of the prostitutes had to leave town. Atchison's hope of becoming the hub of the universe had faded. Its colorful days were over.

But its leaders turned to more prosaic and perhaps more basically sound methods of building a city so that its position as the dominant city between Leavenworth and Nebraska was never endangered. Other river towns, which had given bright promise in the early territorial days, fell by the wayside. Doniphan, three miles above Atchison, had been organized in 1854, on the site of an ancient Indian village said to be the headquarters of Bourgmont, the French explorer, when he ascended the river in 1724. The town attained a population of a thousand, had a newspaper, became important politically and to some extent head of navigation of the Missouri River because of Smith Bar, a mile above town, extending across the river and rendering passage difficult for the deep draught steamboats. The Indian channel, above Doniphan, was a dangerous passage and between 1852 and 1871 saw the destruction of the Pontiac, the Delaware, the Sully and the Viola Belle. Doniphan no longer is a river town, there being several miles of land between it and the river.

In 1856 the town of Roseport was laid out across the river from St. Joseph, the name being changed to Elwood the next year. It was a good outfitting point for traders and trappers and profited from the Pike's Peak trade around 1858. Its population increased to two thousand and it had a newspaper, the Weekly Advertiser, and was mentioned in eastern newspapers as a likely rival of St. Joseph. It was host overnight to Abraham Lincoln, who came over from St. Joseph where he "sat in the dirt waiting for the ferry-boat." To make a speech that essentially was the same he delivered later at Cooper Institute in New York.

Wathena Landing was three miles above Elwood, and two miles above that was Whitehead, which later became Bellemont. In 1841, William Banks, who had been a deck hand on the Yellowstone in 1832 and was well known as a river man, chartered the Thames and landed on the Missouri side near Forest City. He started a store and also became a woodhawk. He called his place Iowa Point. Later he established a ferry and another Iowa Point grew up on the Kansas side. This was for many years a noted crossing on the Missouri River. In 1858 the town was claiming to be a rival of Leavenworth. It had several wholesale houses and was built up rapidly with brick buildings. In 1862 it experienced a devastating fire, from which it never recovered.

White Cloud, last river town in Kansas before the Nebraska line was reached, was named for an Indian chief, the son-in-law of Joseph Robidoux, founder of St. Joseph. Its birth had been a gala Fourth of July event in 1857, the town company chartered the Watosa, the Emma and the Morning Star to bring prospective buyers from far up and down the river and a grand ball was held that night on the Morning Star. The town had one of the best natural landings and back of it an opening in the bluffs.

Someone of a classic, not to say prophetic, turn, gave Kansas the motto, "Ad astra per aspera," interpreted as, "to the stars through difficulties." It had its difficulties, all right, through the territorial days when it was called bleeding Kansas, through the war-torn years and after, when it was advised to "raise less corn and more hell!" Eventually Kansas did reach the stars, but none will deny it was done the hard way.

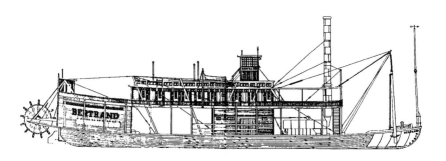

The Boats that Wore the Horns

The Missouri River's tortuous course was not adapted to steamboat racing of the neck-and-neck variety that became famous on the lower Mississippi River. Its history cannot produce any such contest as that between the Natchez and Robert E. Lee. Nevertheless, there were fast boats on the Missouri and the crew of any steamer, from captain to cabin boy, exulted in being identified with the boat that wore the horns and knowing that every other boat on the river had to "take her wash." To make the quickest trip became a matter of pride with all steamboatmen. The boat making the fastest time would "carry the horns" – usually a pair of elk's antlers, highly polished and gold or silver mounted – upon her pilothouse or at the guard rail under her bow. It was the sporting thing, when one's record had been lowered, to hand over the cherished trophies to the captain of the speedier boat.

Thus when the Polar Star left St. Louis, made all landings for freight and passengers and arrived at Liberty Landing in fifty-two hours and forty-seven minutes – beating the Martha Jewett to Lexington by ten hours, the editor of the Liberty Tribune, noting that it was the fastest time ever made up the Missouri River, said, "the Jewett should immediately hand over the horns."

This speed record set by the Polar Star seems to have

137

specially notable, judging from the comment made
[i]e press and in other quarters. In that same race against
[o]ne and a gallant rival, the Polar Star went from St. Louis
to Jefferson City in twenty hours and forty minutes, beating the Martha Jewett's time more than five hours. When
Captain Thomas H. Brierly, wealthy owner of the Polar
Star, arrived at his home port of St. Joseph in sixty-four
hours from St. Louis, the prominent citizens of the town
presented him with a fine pair of elk horns, mounted with
silver, with an appropriate inscription. That evening the
Polar Star, advertised as "an entirely new and elegant
steamer, unsurpassed for speed, passenger accommodations and all the requisites of the Missouri River, " was the
scene of a gala ball in which the elite of St. Joseph participated, dancing until dawn. The Polar Star became the flagship of General Grant's fleet at Vicksburg in the historic
battle there. Its splendid speed record was allowed to stand
only three years.

In July, 1856, the James H. Lucas, with Captain
Andrew Wineland, "the old river fox,' in command, covered the same route in sixty hours and fifty-seven minutes.
The boat was then two years old, having been built in the
spring of 1854, at which time one river town newspaper
said "Captain A. Wineland's new boat, the James H. Lucas,
passed up the other evening and attracted no little attention. She is of Louisville build, and Capt. W. himself superintended her construction. The accounts that preceded her,
thought by many to be exaggerated scarcely came up to the
mark. Capt. W. has spared no pains or expense to make her
what she is – one of the best boats ever built for the
Missouri River trade. The object has been to combine
speed, convenience and beauty, and there is no part of this
handsome structure which does not bear evidence that
these requisites of a first class boat have been attained."
The boat was named for a St. Louis millionaire. Its record
probably never was exceeded, although the New Lucy, the
Polar Star, the Luke Sharp, the Silver Heels and the
Morning Star made unsuccessful attempts to lower it. The
Post Boy was described as wearing the horns in 1868. The

New Lucy burned November 25,1857, opposite DeWitt, trying to beat "the record of the Polar Star" to St. Joseph, though that record had already been lowered by the James H. Lucas.

One of the fastest boats on the river was the Minnehaha. She took the horns for the fastest rip between St. Louis and St. Joseph, only to have her record lowered by the Peerless; a St. Joseph owned boat.

The matter of racing against the record of another boat goes back to 1824, when Mandan, under Captain William Linn, and the General Neville left the Council Bluffs at the same time and the Mandan reached St. Louis first. The Missouri Republican in its August 9 issue declared the round trip of the Mandan, St. Louis to the Council Bluffs that was made in forty-six days, the shortest trip on record at that time.

In 1840, the steamer Mail, which after beating all her contemporaries on the Ohio, played the same pranks on the Missouri, according to the Missouri Argus of May 21, 1840, which said: "She has just returned from Lexington, having been absent only five days, ten hours. Time from St. Louis to Jefferson City, twenty-four hours, twenty minutes; and to Boonville, thirty-six hours. This is the best speed yet made upon the waters above St. Louis."

There seem to be discrepancies in the editorial viewpoint as to the spread of the boats, for when one newspaper is reporting a speed of twenty-four hours and twenty minutes between St. Louis and Jefferson City, another is saying that the requisite time was forty-eight hours. One year ago, thirty-six hours was considered a speedy trip. This year, it is traversed in twenty-four hours by several boats, and the Empire made her trip last week in twenty-two hours and fifteen minutes, which we believe, is the shortest time on record for the one hundred and fifty miles." In 1843, the Eden broke a record when it arrived at Lexington in two days, fifteen hours, and thirty minutes, including all stoppages for wood, and to discharge freight. The Lexington Express of August 13, said: "This is the quickest trip ever made by a steamboat from St. Louis to Lexington."

Pride of the river in 1845 was the Lewis F. Linn, bearing the name of the popular junior United States senator from Missouri. She was a long, slim boat with the appearance of a greyhound, built for speed and for two years had been showing her heels to everything on the Missouri River. While her record for speed justified the efforts of her builders, it was inevitable that she would have to meet stern competition. This appeared in the form of the Algoma, "graceful as a beautiful woman," brought out for the express purpose of wresting the Glasgow trade from the proud and haughty Lewis F. Linn.

From the owners of the new boat came a challenge that was promptly accepted by the owners of the Linn. The match was arranged for a certain day, the course to be St. Louis to Glasgow. The boats were advertised to leave St. Louis at a given hour on a certain day. Residents along the river thus could figure pretty close to the exact hour the boats would pass any given point. Crowds lined the riverbanks, particularly at Boonville where residents had sought vantage points on both sides of the river from which to view the race. An old newspaper account takes up the race at that point:

"The boats rounded the bluffs below Boonville about twelve o'clock at night. Heavy clouds obscured the moon and almost pitchy darkness covered the turbulent stream, lighted only by the fitful flashes from their furnaces and the lamps of their cabins and lanterns hung upon their decks. The smokestacks appeared to be a dull red, from the hurricane decks to their very topmost tips, and the steam came from their escape valves with a hissing that indicated that every drop of water in their boilers had been reduced to the highest pressure of steam. The figure of the Negro firemen, as they danced around the furnace doors, piling cottonwood, pine knots, lard, bacon-sides and almost every other kind of combustible into the hollow depths of the flames, presented a picture that might have been, without any stretch of the imagination, taken for a true presentation of the devil and his imps stoking the fires of the infernal regions…"

"They passed the center of the town running nose and nose – apparently not an inch of difference between them... Possibly it required ten minutes of time to pass the town, and during that time not a sound came from the crowd on shore, not a word from the boats, not a whistle sounded. It was as if two slender steeds with ears laid back, eyes bulging and nostrils extended, were straining every nerve under the lash and spur to reach the goal first or die in the attempt."

"The crowds at Boonville remained on the banks until the steamers could only be distinguished by their red-hot chimneys in passing the opening between the island just above Arrow Rock and the main shore, twelve miles away. The boats reached Glasgow early the next day, as they had passed Boonville, running nose and nose, and although much money had been wagered on the result, none was lost, for the race was declared a tie."

The foregoing graphic description of the race between the Linn and the Algoma, written, or at least printed, fifty-eight years after the event actually transpired, was published in the Boonville Advance for December 31, 1903. It may have been a rewrite from some obscure or forgotten diary kept by an actual eyewitness of the titanic struggle between the town boats; or it may have been a writer's skillful expansion of a relation by some elderly person who had witnessed the race.

It would seem that the mania for speed had reached its height on the Missouri River in the 1850s. More expensive boats might have been built in the years that followed, but that was the daring decade.

The Silver Heels was one of the darlings of the river then and to be considered in all speed contests. Of one of its trips, the Lexington Expositor, June 5, 1857 said:

"We learn from the second clerk of the steamer Silver Heels, Mr. G.T. Tillery, that this excellent boat left St. Joseph on Monday the 18th inst., at three in the evening, discharging fifty tons of way freight, landing passengers at various points on the river, losing three hours on Sonora Bar, and arriving at Council Bluffs on Tuesday, the 19th, at four o'clock. This is the quickest time ever made. Time out from St. Joseph to Council Bluffs thirty-seven hours." In that same year the Silver Heels made the record time from St. Louis to Omaha in five days and fifteen hours.

The Memphis Commercial in the steamboat days devoted considerable space to the activities of the riverains. In an undated article quoted in the Jefferson City Tribune of September 3, 1893, it describes a noted race between the Martha Aull, carrying the proud name of one of Lexington's first families, and the steamboat Johnstone:

"One of the greatest races ever seen on the Missouri River was that between the Martha Aull and the Henry K. Johnstone, which took place in the early fifties. The boats left the St. Louis wharf within a half-hour of each other. Each was loaded with merchandise, most of the passengers being men in search of a fortune in the boundless West."

"In the light of early morning, both had turned into the Missouri and were so close that a taunt from Captain Bristow's Johnstone caused Captain Jorgenson of the Martha Aull to say; "I didn't come here to race, but if they want to know what kind of boat this is, I'll show 'em."

"The boats began to tear through the water and the race was on. All day the boats sped along, and each hour the Aull gained a trifle. Another evening found the sky again clear – a perfect night for racing on the river. Not a breath of air stirred. The stillness was broken only by the regular deep-toned throb of the engines as the boats cut through the water. Washington, Portland, Jefferson City – the little state capital high on the bluff – all had been passed in the afternoon with a whistle that had brought the inhabitants out to see the speeding boats."

"Sides of bacon were used and the Johnstone spurted, in increased speed being noted at once. So close together did the throbs of the engines come that they appeared like a steady vibration. The Johnstone gained steadily. Soon the Aull was so close that her outlines were plainly visible in the brilliant moonlight. As they came abreast, the order was given to pile on the bacon. Inch by inch the Johnstone moved ahead."

"A lady passenger on the Aull offered to pay for butter as fuel. So butter in cakes and baskets was smeared over sticks of wood and fed to the greedy flames in the boat's furnace. There was a bend ahead where the bluff broke for a few feet, only to rise higher than ever a few yards beyond. This was the goal. A mighty shout went up from the deck of the Johnstone as it rounded the bend and the Aull could not be seen. The Johnstone had won."

There was a very real and tangible affinity between these greyhounds of the river and the young city of St. Joseph, where some of their chief owners lived. It was the home of Captain Thomas H. Brierly and his less famous brother, Captain Thomas Brierly; Captain Pat Yore and his brother, Captain Jim Yore; and Captains John E. Barrow, Frank B. Kercheval, Dan Silvers and William Bell. The boats and their captains seemed to personify that eager competitive spirit that characterized the new town that was striving mightily to become the great metropolis of the river. There was an elan that was shared by the boats, their owners, and the city.

Chapter Twenty

When They Sang Along the River

Singing along the Missouri had its beginning in the rondeaux of the French voyageurs as they sped their light craft over the turbid waters. Their little songs usually pointed out that the singer was a man of unusual prowess, excelling as a hunter, oarsman, and lover – these three subjects constituting, in the main, his repertoire. The chansons of these Frenchmen awakened the echoes of the river bluffs, the voyageurs singing lustily as they strove with oar, pole and cordelle.

Manuel Lisa, father of the navigation on the Missouri, used to steer with the long oar and hearten his crew with a nonsensical thing about a prince, some ducks, and a shepherdess. He sang the verses and his men sang the refrain. No matter how weary, the men were always animated to new vigor by Lisa's little song.

Those brought to the western waters by keelboatmen who came down the Ohio from Pittsburgh succeeded the songs of the voyageurs. Typical of these might have been the one sang by Mike Fink, king of the keelboatmen, his young friend Carpenter, and "Pittsburgh Blue," and "All the way from Shawneetown, long time ago." This might have been the ancestor, or merely a variant of the cabin and nursery song, presumed to be of Negro origin, heard later in Missouri, "The little black bull came over the mountain, long time ago."

Introduction of "The Arkansaw Traveler" into the West by the same river route from Pittsburgh, brought an adaptation of an air from the folksong of Italy, set to words in the East, and popular with the drivers of the huge Conestoga wagons who patronized the taverns and cabarets in the first half of the century.

Of a little later vintage were "The Maid from Prairie du Chien" and the spirited "Buffalo Gals." The latter, particularly adapted to the violin, was a favorite with many of the boatmen who whiled away the hours by playing their fiddles. "Natchez Under the Hill" was a lively air that might have celebrated the utter wickedness and abandon of the town on the lower Mississippi where the boatmen so often fought and frolicked.

Up past the Mamelles and over the Boone's Lick Trail settlers from Kentucky, Tennessee, Georgia and Virginia, poured into the valley of the Missouri, bringing with them the songs they had learned from their foreparents as far back as the time when they had lived in the Carolinas. These old ballads, with their plaintive, keening airs, had been brought over the ocean from old England.

One of these songs, "Two Babes in the Woods," was said to have been based upon an incident of history several hundred years before and is mentioned by Bishop Percy in his Reliques. Probably most frequently heard was "Barbara Allen, " a song with almost countless variations, mentioned by Pepys in his diary.

Other songs brought in by the settlers would have been "The Cambric Shirt," "Willia Came Over the Ocean," "The Pretty Golden Queen," "Polly and William," "The King's Seven Daughters," and "Pretty Polly," all having their origins or being variants of "The Elfin Knight." This particular ballad is one of the most persistent and widespread of ballads, known throughout Europe, although Professor Francis J. Childs gives its provenance as Ireland.

Another popular ballad was "The Two Sisters," appearing also as "The Old Man in the North Countree," "My Sister Kate" and "The West Countree," going back hundreds of years to Lancashire and Kent. "Lord Randal" was widely known and sung by these descendants of the English, Scotch, and Irish, and generally is accredited as "an old English ballad," though as a matter of fact it seems to have had its origin in Italy in the sixteenth century.

The Scottish ballad of "Lord Thomas and Fair Annet" had a wide vogue; the title encountered being more frequently "Lord Thomas," "The Brown Girl," or "Fair Eleanor." Another of the old ballads having many variations was "Little Musgrave and Lady Barnard," the title being corrupted at times to "Little Mathy Groves."

Still others were "The House Carpenter," derived from "James Harris"; the robust and ribald "Our Goodman"; "The Little Mohee," puzzling as to provenance; and the story of a rejected lover as related in "The Lonesome Scenes of Winter." The story of a lover not rejected, or at least that is the implication, ran through "The Nightingale," the theme being as old as the twenty-seventh idyll of Theocritus, appearing again in one of the stories of Bocaccio's Decameron and having its ballad beginning in the nineteenth-century "The Nightingale's Song, or the "Soldier's Rare Musick", and "Maid's Recreation."

The story of a cabin boy who single-handedly scuttled an enemy ship, as told in the "Golden Vanity," also was known in Missouri, but not by that name. By some strange mutation, through which the old ballads frequently went, it became "The Turkey Revelee."

Following these old songs that came with the first settlers was "Old Rosin, the Beau," an old song in its own right, which is mentioned as having furnished the air for improvised songs written to cheer Santa Fe traders and Oregon settlers on their way at Independence. This song had been popular in the South, sung in New York in the 1830s, but as a matter of fact its origin is "lost in antiquity."

Others of the time were "Old Grimes is Dead," "Little Brown Jug," "The Jolly Miller," and "Shule Aroon," a popular Irish song.

"The Hunters of Kentucky," celebrating Andrew Jackson's great victory at New Orleans was especially popular with the settlers crowding into the valley of the

Missouri. They were the very "half-horse, half-alligators" who had made up Jackson's army when he had dealt the final blow to Pakenham, British commander at the Battle of New Orleans. Sometimes the song was sung as "Packing Ham," and again as "Old Pakenham." It was sung to the tune of "Miss Bailey's Ghost," according to one authority, but would seem to fit better the still earlier "The Unfortunate Miss Bailey," who had an affair in Montreal and was "hanged by her garters."

"The Waggoner" was popular as a fiddle tune, the song telling of adventures of another and earlier generation of settlers, in the vicinity of the Yadkin River. "Fuller and Warren" and "McAfee's Confession," topical songs of murder in the frontier states of Indiana and Ohio, respectively, were sung and the cases discussed around all the campfires of the West.

The "log cabin and hard cider" campaign of 1840 produced, among other campaign songs, "When This Old Hat Was New," which is reported to have been sung as far west as Liberty and Westport, the excited interest in that political battle extending all the way up the Missouri to those frontier towns.

Within a few years the war with Mexico brought out such songs as "Pretty Little Pink," "Plains of Mexico," and "Buena Vista." Steamboats were loaded with soldiers bound upstream for Fort Leavenworth, thence to the scene of conflict. The most popular song of that particular war was furnished by no less distinguished a poet than Robert Burns, with every soldier singing "Green Grow the Rashes O!" So universal was this song on the border that the Mexicans called the American soldiers "Green Grows" or "Gringos."

Play-party games, so-called because some of the older generation frowned upon the word "dancing," were: "Under the Juniper Tree," "Weevily Wheat," "We've Round the Levy," "Little Brown Jug," "Skip to My Lou," "Make a Cake for Charley," "We'll All Go Up to Rowser's" and "Old Brass Wagon." Closely allied to these were "Old Dan Tucker," "Rye Whisky," "Plant Your 'Taters in the

Sandy Land," and the immensely popular "Wait for the Wagon."

In the late 1840s the varsuvienne came in, a dance lively enough, not so stately as the Virginia reel, but more dignified than the waltz, a new dance which was considered by the more conservative to be vulgar. A haunting fragment of the varsuvienne still may be heard occasionally along the Missouri in a little air with the words:

Put your foot down, put your foot down,
Put your foot down right there;
Don't you see my, don't you see my
Don't you see my new shoes?

When in 1849 a horde of men along the Missouri River by steamboat, bound for golgonda represented by the name California, their spirits were kept up, if such needed to be, by a song composed by the young bookkeeper of a Cincinnati steamboat concern, still unknown to name. Stephen Foster's "O! Susanna" was carried all the way to California and back again. This song was adopted by the Argonauts, but one written especially for them was "Joe Bowers," the ballad of a lovesick gold seeker from Missouri. There had been considerable controversy as to whether the ballad was written by one of a party of Missourians on the way to California or by an actor "writing on a rum-soaked bar" in San Francisco.

The flatboatmen, with little to do except avoid snags, sawyers and sand bars, led a happy carefree life, floating down stream, fishing, shooting at marks along the shore, playing old sledge or joining in one of the boat songs that came over the water with a melody peculiarly their own. These choruses consisted of frequently recurring refrains, sung in concert, separated by verses improvised by a leader. One of these, "De Boatman's Dance" frequently was heard on the Missouri River.

Pleasing, sometimes touching, was the singing of the Negro deckhands as they arrived or departed from the port. After a hard time loading or unloading the boats, the crew often, as the boat got under way sang those tuneful and touching melodies peculiar to the African throat. Sometimes a sound of hilarious joy, a stirring, trumpet-like shout; more often, perhaps, a tender, melancholy cadence that touched the heart of the hearer – some such song, perhaps, as "Kitty Wells." Then the pendulum might swing back to a mood of jollity while they sang "Old Virginny Never Tire."

When a London street song came out with the ever-recurring refrain, "Pop! Goes the Weasel," it had such a catchy tune that it soon crossed the waters and became popular in the rural sections of this country. Incidentally, a weasel is a tool used by London hatmakers; a pop was a slang word meaning to pawn. Thus, the hatmakers carousing "Up and down the City Road, in and out the Eagle" (a well-known tavern), saw their money vanish and found it necessary to "pop the weasel." First heard in 1852, the song has shown such vitality that some authorities even now mistakenly class it as of American origin.

When John Charles Fremont, "the Pathfinder," became the first Republican candidate for president of the United States, the adherents of "Ten-Cent Jimmy" Buchanan, his opponent, as passengers on the Missouri River steamers would chant;

> *Fremont rides the woolly horse,*
> *Buchanan rides the eagle;*
> *That's the way the money goes,*
> *Pop! Goes the Weasel.*

"Jim Along Josey" and "Old Zip Coon" were popular among the so-called comics. Of another and later type were the universally love "Lorena," and "Sweet Evalina, " while "Darling Sweet Nora O'Neal," "Sweet Belle Mahone," and "The Rock Beside the Sea" were favorites. The waltz was gaining in favor and brought out, among others, the tender and dreamy "Sweet Kitty Maguire, Come Home," "The Steamboat Waltz" and at least one dedicated to a steamboat, the "Kate Kearny Waltz." None of these, however, was so popular as the "Rose Waltz." These were approximately of the Civil War period, as were "Bonnie Eloise (the Belle of Mohawk Vale)," "Listen to the Mockingbird,"

"Little Brown Church in the Vale," "Big Sunflower," "O Dem Golden Slippers," "Little Old Log Cabin in the Lane" and "Old Shady."

A favorite of the Civil War, but of ancient lineage, "The Girl I Left Behind Me" was a lively song that went through many transformations. "Root, Hog, or Die" was popular during the war and a parody with endless verses was sung by the bullwhackers on the plains.

When the railroads began reaching toward the West, they were met at their outposts by cowboys driving herds and having a repertoire of songs peculiarly their own. For a few decades some of the river towns became cow towns as well – such places as Kansas City, St. Joseph, Omaha, and Sioux City. The songs of the cowboys became popular with the people of the Missouri River valley and in the towns along the river one could hear; "The Yellow Rose of Texas," "The Fort Smith Jail," "Bury Me Not on the Lone Prairie," "The Chisholm Trail," and the ever-tender "Red River Valley."

These were their folk songs, as Carl Sandburg beautifully puts it; "Living things of the heart and mind, out of love, fun, grief – a panorama of events and people."

Chapter Twenty-One

The Golden Age of Steamboating

The season of 1857 saw on the river the Spread Eagle, which had the words, "E Pluribus Unum," painted on each side of the wheelhouse, together with a large eagle. Her captain, Ben Johnson, told the yahoos along the river that the words meant, "Every tub stands on her own bottom." Other boats were the Washington City, Captain John Fisher; the Asa Wilgus, the Consignee, the Violet, the Council Bluffs, Captain Sam Lewis; the D.A. January, Captain M. Oldham; the Equinox, Captain Sam Boyce; the Kate Howard, Captain Joseph S. Nanson; the Low Water and the Meteor, under Captain Draffen. In that year, Captain James Gormley was master of the A.B. Chambers, and the splendid new Silver Heels made its bow under Captain D. H. Silvers. "Dave" Silvers boasted that he had twenty-five "likely boys in pure linen jackets" to wait on his tables, and that his passengers preferred an extra meal on his boat to an early arrival.

The Violet was destroyed during the Civil War at Van Buren on the western edge of Arkansas.

Other boats noted were the Adalia, Abeonia, William Baird, Ben Bolt, Cataract, Australia, Champion, Gladiator, Hesperian, Mansfield, Michigan, E.A. Ogden, J.H. Oglesby, Prairie Rose, Progress, and Saracen. Mrs. Miriam B. Colt, author of Went to Kansas, made the journey from St. Louis to Kansas City on the Cataract in April 1856.

Steamboating on the Missouri River reached its all-time peak in the year 1858, when the emigration pouring into the West by way of the river was given the powerful stimulus of the discovery of gold in the Cherry Creek area of what now is Colorado. Then there were sixty regular packets on the river, augmented by thirty or forty tramp steamers. Some of those boats were the John D. Perry, the David Tatum, the Kate Swinney, Alonzo Child, D.S. Carter, Eclipse, Empire State, Jenny Lewis, Minnehaha, War Eagle, Southwestern, C.W. Sombart, Tropic and Twilight.

Others would have been the Emma, under Captain Cheeves; the E.M. Ryland, Captain Blount; the Iatan, Captain Eaton; the Isabella, Captain John W. Keiser; the Peerless, Captain Bissell; the Platte Valley, Captain William C. Postal; the Sioux City, Captain C.K. Baker; the White Cloud, Captain William Conley, and the W.H. Russell, Captain Kinney. The White Cloud, built in 1858, conveyed Governor Claiborne F. Jackson and other state officers of Missouri from Jefferson City to Boonville on June 19, 1861, on their way to Neosho to establish a new (Confederate) state capital of Missouri. This capital later was removed to Marshall, Texas.

At a time when men with a stake were heading for the West and successful gold seekers were crowding the downstream boats, it was certain that the professional gamblers would seek out such a fertile field. The unwary were plucked in various manners, not always by the professional card sharp playing for high stakes. One traveler mentioned "One of those lottery jewelers on board picking up stray dimes. He had his prizes arranged on numbers on the table and by throwing dice the number that turned up took the prize answering to the number. He had the valuable prizes arranged on high and low numbers or all threes or all sixes. The numbers that turned up most frequently carried small prizes. One man won a gold watch; all others appeared to lose ten, fifteen, or twenty dollars; many from two to five dollars. I invested fifty cents and drew a comb and brush worth about that amount."

With regard to gambling on the steamboats, one editor waxed so wroth as almost to lead to the belief that he himself had been a victim of the gamblers. His editorial in the Kansas City Journal, August 6, 1858, does not say as much: "It is time that people who travel on steamboats should set their faces against gamblers being allowed to prey upon the public on our Missouri River steamers. On our trip on the W.H. Russell, the present week, a party of three or four got aboard at Hermann, and left before the boat got to Jefferson City, having victimized a gentleman out of one hundred dollars at the game of Mexican Monte. The mode adopted was one to deal his cards, and the others to make false bets, and to induce bystanders to engage in the game. Now, there is not a steamboat officer on the river who does not know that this is a game at which the bettor never wins – of a kin to pigeon-dropping, watch stuffing, and pocket-picking. None but a thief will practice it. Knowing this, it is the duty of the officers to prevent them from engaging in it. It is a duty they owe the public, who believe them gentlemen, sufficient to trust their lives and safety with, as passengers on their boats...Boats that will allow gamblers, thieves and their adjuncts to prey on their passengers cannot much longer expect the patronage of Missouri River people."

By 1859 still greater efficiency was necessary to enable the steamboats to serve the vast numbers of passengers thronging the water route to Pike's Peak – that is to whatever point on the river might have been considered best for starting the long overland trek. In those years just preceding and during the early part of the Civil War, the Skylark was carrying passengers from Jefferson City to upriver points. Other boats on the river in that period included the Chippewa, Captain Crabtree; the Geneva No.2, Captain Throckmorton; the Alice No. 2, Captain Joseph Kinney; the Calypso, Captain A.S. Bryan; the Ed F. Dix; Evening Star, Victoria, St. John, Laconia, Octavia, Stephen A. Bell, Peter Balen, Key West, and the Emilia, named for the wife of its owner, Captain Charles P. Chouteau. The Glasgow, under Captain La Moth, became the subject of song and story when it burned at Bayou Sara on the Mississippi River.

Star of the West, built for the Wisconsin River, came on the Missouri River in 1859 bound for Denver in the Rocky Mountains. Her owner believed his boat, which had only a twenty-six-inch draft, could navigate the Platte to the mountains. When he reached the Kaw River, experienced steamboat men convinced him it couldn't be done. He sold the boat to Captain G.P. Nelson of Wyandotte who ran it on the Kaw where it grounded near Lecompton that fall. The next year the Kansas Valley was built from its salvaged material.

The American Fur Company owned the Spread Eagle in 1859. In that year it went eight hundred and fifty miles above the mouth of the Yellowstone, five hundred and fifty miles higher than any boat had been before. The Western Journal of Commerce at Kansas City in its August 18 issue declared this to be "a most remarkable fact, unparalleled in the world."

The Peter Balen was described as an old tub that had come into the Missouri River from the Ohio during the flush times on the upper river. In the Fort Benton trade she paid for herself several times over, being worth fifteen thousand dollars and earning between sixty and eighty thousand dollars in one trip. She ascended the river to a point higher than any other boat had gone, having on June 16, 1866, gone to the mouth of Belt River, six miles below Great Falls and thirty miles above Fort Benton. This was three thousand eight hundred and fifteen miles from the sea; a point farther than any steamboat in the world had ever reached.

During the war, steamboats were having difficulty traversing the Missouri River, due to the ease with which soldiers or bushwhackers could swoop down upon and capture a boat, or hide along the shore and riddle it with bullets. There were several instances of both having been done, notably the capture of the Sam Gaty by bushwhackers at Sibley when two or three persons were killed, though the records do not bear out the legends of massacre. The bushwhackers were led by a Colonel Hicks, said to have been a member of Todd's guerrillas. Soldiers from Kansas quickly broke up his camp in Jackson County and hanged seventeen of his followers, but the records do not indicate he was hanged with them.

Another incident, in the same vicinity, about the same time, concerned the Marcella. The Lexington Union, September 19, 1863, said; "As the steamer Marcella, on her upward trip, yesterday, approached Berlin Landing, she was ordered to land by about sixty bushwhackers. There being no protection to the pilothouse, there was nothing the pilot could do but obey. As soon as the boat landed she was boarded by the bushwhackers, who robbed the boat and passengers of nine hundred dollars and several cases of boots and shoes and clothing. They then discovered four Union soldiers, took them into the woods a ways and shot them, one of them, however, escaping."

Though some boats had left the Missouri River to ply the upper Mississippi as a safer field during the war, and a number had been pressed into service as gunboats on the lower Mississippi. The Missouri still was being served in the closing years of the war by such steamboats as the Fannie Ogden, Captain Joseph Kinney; the Colorado and the Julian No. 2, Captain John McCloy.
(chart here)

A romantic episode of the period was related by Captain William R. Massie, skipper of the Twilight in 1865, a boat owned by Captains Joseph Kinney, John Keiser, and Henry McPherson. He had on board sixteen young women on their way to Montana to meet their lovers, some of whom for several years been engaged in business at trading posts along the upper Missouri. When the boat got above the mouth of the Yellowstone, the men, bringing their own minister met it. He performed sixteen weddings aboard the Twilight that night. Captain Massie, incidentally, was seated opposite "Wild Bill" Hickok, when that pistoleer was shot and killed in Deadwood. For years, Massie carried the bullet, which had gone through Hickok and into Massie's wrist.

Boats on the river during the balance of the Civil War decade would have included the St. Luke, known to the roustabouts along the river as "the old gray ghost," Captain Joseph Kinney; the Waverly, Captain John P. Keiser; the W.J. Lewis, Captain E.T. Herndon and the Ameranth No. 2.

(chart here)

After the Civil War, the splendor of the steamboats was on the wane as the expanding railroads claimed an ever-greater portion of the east-west traffic. The sands of time were running against the steamboats and the inroads of the railroads constantly forced the boats to seek traffic upstream. Navigation on the Missouri River was hazardous as compared to the railroad, uncertain and limited to short seasons. It was inevitable that they would be unable to compete with the railroads and that their numbers would decrease in the face of competition from the rails. This, along with increasing population in the upper territory accounted for a comparative intensification of steamboat traffic on the river above St. Joseph in the 1870s. This happened when boats as the Emilie La Barge, Captain George Keith, known as "the Little Giant"; Gerard B. Allen, Captain D.L. Keiser; the Stonewall, Captain J.P. McKinney; the Yellowstone, Captain J. McDonald; the Paragon, Captain John McCloy; the W.B. Dance, Captain George W. Boyd; the J. Donald Cameron; the Kate Kinney, Captain J. Kinney; the Octavia, Captain Joseph La Barge; the W.J. Lewis, Captain E.T. Herndon; and the Waverly, Captain Thomas W. Rea were running to Omaha. This, then, was the golden age of the river itself.

The sister ships, the Wyoming and the Dakota wrote the last chapter in the golden age of steamboating on the Missouri River. The Wyoming was built by Captain Coulson at Pittsburg in1877 at a cost of seventy-five thousand dollars. Later its name was changed and it was converted into a dredge – a far cry from the glory of its days of white paint and gold. Sometimes in the dusk of the evening when the mist was rising from the river, she would appear to riverains as a phantom of the old steamboat days. When night covered her with a kindly mantle of dusk, perhaps the river – the ever capricious but ever faithful river – whispered to her of the old friends and of the old days when she was a proud and gleaming beauty.

The steamboat had served its purpose and served it well, and in doing so had rendered a great and valuable service in the development of the West. But the West itself had grown beyond the transportation methods that had made it great and was demanding something more rapid, something more efficient. The day of the railroad was at hand and the day of the steamboat on the lower Missouri was nearing its end. Many of the packets were granted an extension of life on the river or on the lower Mississippi, the Red River, the Atchafalaya, the Bayou Lafourche, the Bayou Terrabonne, the Warrior, or the Tombigbee – wherever there was water enough to drive them ahead.

Chapter Twenty-Two

The West Began at Council Bluffs

The first permanent building on the site of present-day Council Bluffs is said to have been that of a French trader named Hart. His trading post and cabin were on the bluff above the large spring that was well known a half-century later as Mynster Spring. However, in 1824 when the trading post is believed to have been established, the Missouri River ran near the post and the vicinity was known as Lacote de Hart, or Hart's Bluff, to such traders, trappers, and steamboatmen as happened to go there. The river moved away in 1832, leaving Heart's Cutoff, which became a lake above the site of the future city of Council Bluffs. Father Jean De Smet referred to "the old trading post of Mr. Heart" and there are those who believe the original owner of the post was not a Frenchman, but Hard Heart, an Iowa Indian chief, sometimes called Grand Batture or Sand Bar, but whose Indian name was Wang-e-Waha. Members of the Long expedition in 1819 made his acquaintance and described him as "a very intelligent Indian, with solemn dignity of deportment." The weight of authority would seem to favor the Frenchman as owner of the trading post.

In that year of 1824, Francis Guittar, fifteen-year-old steamboat cook from St. Louis, came with other men of the American Fur Company and encamped at the foot of "the handsome, pale-colored bluffs." Becoming a trader for the company, he was frequently in that vicinity in later years, though living a nomadic life, and finally rounded out his career as a storekeeper in Council Bluffs. Guittar furnished the tenuous thread of continuity for the history of the city from its earliest beginnings until he saw it and was a part of it when it had become a modern, thriving city.

For a dozen years after his arrival, all the land on which Council Bluffs now stands was virgin soil and covered by virgin forest. Then it was planned to remove the Pottawatomie Indians to a reservation along the east bank of the Missouri River in Iowa and to establish an Indian agency there along with a model farm where the Indians could receive instructions in practical farming. It also was planned to erect a blockhouse or fort, which could furnish protection from the fierce warriors of the Sioux tribe. The blockhouse was built on a high bluff in 1837 by dragoons from Fort Leavenworth. Colonel Kearny the following year turned it over for use as a school and church for Father De Smet, who arrived on the steamboat Wilmington on May 31, 1838.

The boat landing then was in a part of the river that later became Lake Manawa. A crowd of Pottawatomies greeted the good father whose chief had established a village at the foot of the blockhouse. He was the noted Billy Caldwell (Socanois), a man of fine physique, six feet three, about sixty-one years old at that time. Son of a British officer, he also had been in the British army and was present at the battle of the Thames.

In 1842, according to Pelzer in "Marches of the Dragoons," Lieutenant Burgwin with sixty men from Fort Leavenworth established Fort Fenwick above Council Bluffs, a little below the mouth of the Boyer River. Later, it was called Fort Croghan, but was abandoned in September 1843.

Council Bluffs was an unorganized settlement, with its Indian village, Catholic mission and a few stragglers, hardy men connected with the trading post or doing business with the Indians. The latter removed to Kansas in 1846.

Then the Mormons came.

They had crossed Iowa, moving from river to river, "weeping, smiling, dancing, dying, exhibiting rare fortitude, practicing economy and polygamy." The vanguard, with Brigham Young at its head, on June 14, 1846, first saw the Missouri River "sprawled like a serpent in the sun."

Prominent among the Mormons was Henry William Miller, in whose honor the straggling village was called Miller's Hollow and sometimes Miller's Hill. Then Thomas Leiper Kane came up the river on a steamboat piloted by the famous Captain Joseph La Barge. Kane had been commissioned by the federal government to make an investigation of the Saints. He became so sympathetic that he was looked upon by them as a champion of their cause, and out of gratitude the town for a few years was known as Kanesville and the post office was officially designated Kane.

The Mormons built a log tabernacle, where, on December 29, 1847, Brigham Young was declared president of the church. He went on to Salt Lake with one contingent of Saints and then a second. In 1848 Orson Hyde became the principal leader of the Saints that were left in the city and its vicinity. He was a preacher who had just returned from a mission to England. With a genius for organizing, better educated than Young, and far more brilliant, his became the job of solidifying the Mormons in Missouri. He first built for himself a commodious home in what now is the heart of Council Bluffs and the next year he established a newspaper, the Frontier Guardian. The paper invited Saints to settle there and urged Gentiles to take advantage of its facilities and superior location when equipping themselves to set out for the gold mines of the West. The response was overwhelming.

Within three years of the Mormons' arrival, Kanesville was a pioneer city with several thousand inhabitants, probably the largest and most important town on the Missouri River, with a rough, uncouth population scattered over a considerable territory in groups of log cabins, tents and camps. It was a exceedingly busy place and immigration was pouring in, occasioned by the discoveries of gold in the West. A swelling tide of goldseekers augmented the Mormon emigration. Kanesville became the outfitting place for the vast caravans that were to move out across the Nebraska prairies. Tradesmen in large numbers were operating stores to take advantage of the moneymaking opportunities. By May of 1850, it was said that fourteen thousand people, "mostly Gentiles seeking gold," were milling around the town.

The Guardian, in its issue of June 12, 1850, said the number of teams crossing the Missouri River during the season up to that date was estimated at four thousand five hundred, with probably thirteen thousand five hundred men and about twenty-two thousand horses, mules, oxen and cows. Two or three steamboats were employed all summer in ferrying emigrants across the river, often charging as much as ten dollars ferriage for a single team and wagon.

In that year the tide was running high. With saloons and gambling house opening, the place became a Wild West town. Many who had started to California, sold their teams and remained to make their fortunes. One such was Samuel S. Bayliss, who had started to California by way of St. Louis, becoming a passenger there on the Saluda. At Lexington he quit the boat, believing it unsafe, just before it blew up. At Council Bluffs, he became a leading businessman, interested in a brick kiln, operation of a ferryboat and the building of the Pacific House. Bayliss Park is named for him.

The valley along the Missouri River became a vast field of canvas-covered wagons, and oxen, mules and horses. The streets of the town were thronged by a hardy lot of men – traders, gamblers, horse thieves, murderers and desperadoes, and every conceivable crime was practiced. The gambler applied himself to his occupation at every corner and drinking was common at every shop.

Almon Whiting Babbitt, a Mormon elder who did not like the way in which Hyde was conducting the Guardian, started the Weekly Western Bugle in 1850. Babbitt had been to Salt Lake, probably more than once, as he was credited with altogether having crossed the plains twenty-nine times. In 1849 he had been elected delegate to congress from the proposed state of Deseret, but congress had refused to seat him. When Orson Hyde finally followed Brigham Young to Salt Lake, in 1852, the Bugle, the paper becoming the Weekly Western Bugle and Frontier Guardian, absorbed the Guardian. Later the name was changed to the Weekly Council Bluffs Bugle, having been acquired by Joseph E. Johnson, brother-in-law of Babbitt.

In December of 1854 W.W. Maynard and Jeremiah Folsom, two printers who had made their debut in Council Bluffs by driving a flock of sheep there from Michigan, began publication of the Chronotype. The paper failed to prosper. In 1857, under the urging of General G.M. Dodge, John t. Baldwin and others, Maynard returned from Des Moines, where he had been working as a typesetter, and established the Nonpareil. This paper still is in existence, a strong, virile journal. In 1857, Lysander W. Babbitt became owner of the Bugle, which then was the leading Democratic paper of the state, notorious for its stand in opposing President Lincoln's efforts to preserve the Union by waging war. Babbitt became mayor of Council Bluffs and later was elected to the state legislature, where he introduced a resolution that the capital of the United States be removed from Washington and re-established at Council Bluffs.

On December 10, 1852, the post office name was changed from Kane to Council Bluffs. The sub-agency opposite Bellevue had had a post office designated as Council Bluffs. After that date, the sub-agency was designated as the Traders' Point post office.

On Christmas Day of 1853, the Pacific House was opened with a grand ball. This hotel, famous in its day, was built to meet the demand of goldseekers and Mormons and the rush of emigrants following the opening up of the Oregon country and California. It was for several years the social center of Council Bluffs and the little village of Omaha, which had been started across the river.

The town continued to be full of life, crowded with

emigrants purchasing their equipment for the overland trip.

At Madison and Broadway, in the heart of the business district, the Ocean Wave saloon flourished. This saloon and gambling house was the most notorious den of iniquity between Chicago and the Pacific Coast, its fame having spread as far as the most obscure mining camp on the Sacramento River. For its day, it was a magnificent structure, with all the appointments and attractions in keeping. Day and night, it held forth, and crowds of men, young, old, middle-aged, thronged the place, belted, spurred, and armed. The Ocean Wave was struck by lightening and destroyed the night of September 9, 1861.

That was in the flash age of Council Bluffs, the river front days, in the harvest years of the gambler. One of the most famous of that ilk was Canada Bill, the most expert gambler in the West. With hat drawn down over his face and speaking the twang of a Texas cattle drover, this tall, ungainly, sallow stoop-shouldered gambling man could be seen on lower Broadway where his three-card Monte gang had its headquarters.

Travel to and from Council Bluffs in the early 1860s was by boat between that burgeoning city and St. Joseph, where the Hannibal & St. Joseph railroad made connections with the East. Or one could ride the stagecoach to Des Moines and there board a train. Stagecoaches also ran to St. Joseph and Sioux City. The many thousands of persons going west in search of homes passed through Council Bluffs in covered wagons drawn by oxen. They were taken across the river on the ferry, which connected Council Bluffs with Omaha. The Chicago & Northwestern railroad was completed to Council Bluffs January 17, 1867, giving an outlet to the East. On December 20 of that year, the St. Joseph & Council Bluffs railroad, the Kansas City line, gave outlet to the south. May 12, 1869 was a gala day, marking the arrival of the first train over the Rock Island. It also marked the laying of the cornerstone for the Ogden House, a magnificent hostelry with a marble-floored dining room capable of seating five hundred persons.

When the Union Pacific Bridge between the two cities was opened in 1872, the passenger station was a two-story frame building. The upper floor served as a hotel. The dining room was the main feature, the citizens going there on Sundays and holidays to dine in the grand manner for seventy-five cents. In connection with the depot was the Emigrant House, a fifty-room frame building where all the foreign emigrants, carrying their belongings in chests and sacks, were housed while waiting for the emigrant trains to be made up for continuing their journey into the West. Around this building ran a platform usually infested with gamblers, confidence men and cardsharps on the lookout for an unwary victim. All passengers going beyond Council Bluffs were compelled to detrain, purchase new tickets and recheck their baggage. The main building afforded a cosmopolitan touch – its hotel clerks and bartenders in full dress suits, glossy shirtfronts and diamond agleam. Here was a mixture of the high and the low, the rich and the poor, the good and the bad – all heading for the West. Through the center of the building was the famous corridor through which all incoming passengers had to travel. This corridor, and by extension, Council Bluffs itself, became known as "The place where the West begins."

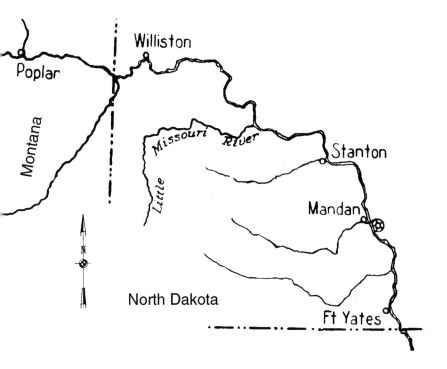

Chapter Twenty-Three

On the Far Nebraska Coast

Nebraska City, situated on one of a long line of hills which formed the beautiful coastline of Nebraska, could be seen for many miles, presenting, with the great Missouri River sweeping down its valley, a panorama both impressive and inspiring. To emigrants on the Eastern Shore, it was the visual manifestation of the West. When they had crossed the river to this frontier city, they were no longer were "going out West" –they actually were in the West. They were actually on that far Nebraska coast that had acted as a lodestone to draw from all parts of the East stouthearted men and women who sought new homes, new fortunes, and new adventures in the great new land beyond the Missouri.

In the spring of 1848, a Captain Wharton had moved upriver from Fort Leavenworth at the head of a troop of dragoons with orders to establish a post at Table Rock. This post consisted of log barracks for soldiers and officers, a two-story blockhouse, built of logs, and a hospital. Named for Colonel Stephen Kearny, it was considered important during the Mexican War, but thereafter the personnel was withdrawn, the buildings left to the supervision of Sergeant Hiram P. Downs, a native of Maine, a forthright character, the possessor of a strident nasal tone and many profane interjections. When his time was up, he pre-empted the one hundred sixty acres on which the fort had been located and in 1854 sold the acreage to the Nebraska City Townsite Company. He erected the Downs House, a large frame two-story building which was the town's only hotel for awhile. The Table Creek post office, with Downs as postmaster, was located in the store of Charles P. Cowles.

Then while Main Street was still a ravine, it was agreed to drop the old name of Table Rock and the newer name of Fort Kearney and call the place Nebraska City, that town having been founded by S.F. Nuckolls. The ferry right was owned by John B. Boulware and he was succeeded by William McLennan, who operated a steam ferry at the point, the landing itself becoming a part of the newly laid out Kearney City which was sandwiched in between Nebraska City and the river. The queenly Banner State is said to have been the first steamboat to land at the new town, though undoubtedly many had landed there since Captain Wharton had established old Fort Kearney on that ground.

The two towns were described as having "a good deal of enterprise," particularly Nebraska City. Prospects for a large emigration were promising, indeed, and one traveler noted that "Rents are about twenty-five per cent on investments. Carpentering two-fifty to three dollars a day. They have pushed their real estate up to the balloon prices already. It certainly seems as if they could not be pushed much higher."

In 1855, the Nebraska News was established in the second story of the old blockhouse, the editor being Shack Grayson. Also connected with the paper was a young reporter from Detroit, more recently from Bellevue, J. Sterling Morton, who was to become one of the state's most noted adopted sons and even then was constructing his first cottage at Arbor Lodge. Thomas Morton, who had set the first type for the upriver Bellevue Palladium, was setting the type.

When Martin Bouton and a Dr. Mathews brought back from the Cherry Creek diggings the first sample of gold dust to reach Nebraska City, the reaction was similar to what it had been in other river towns at the sight of gold. The rush to Pike's Peak in 1859 lined the south side of the Platte River with long trains of emigrants. The greater part of the outfitting business was done in Kearney, which lay between North Table Rock and the levee. This "wild and woolly" little town, with block after block of outfitting establishments, depended largely on the transportation business incident to the westward movement. Russell, Majors & Waddell sent out thousands of tons of freight to Utah and military camps of the West.

It was an era of wild and reckless speculation with everything on the boom. Drinking water was selling for five cents a quart. Men with revolvers and bowie knives in plain sight thronged the streets and local hostelries. Burglaries, rows and knockdowns were common occurrences, there were occasional murders and it was not considered safe to be on the streets alone at night. The bullwhackers thronged the stores of Kearny and Nebraska City, buying blankets, revolvers and clothing, without all three of which none would have been allowed to leave the Missouri River. The streets were full of bellowing oxen and braying mules, drawing the huge freight wagons – the Studebaker, the Murphy, and the Espenshied wagons, the latter two manufactured in St. Louis and frequently shipped up the Missouri River a boatload at a time.

These huge wagons lumbered out over the trail, which ran northwest from Nebraska City and struck the Platte River thirty miles west of its junction with the Missouri.

The bullwhacker, leading the life of fascinating adventure and romance, was in his glory as he pulled out over the long trail, popping his whip with its twenty-foot lash. He was considered the roughest and toughest thing in the uncurried West, red-shirted, big-booted, and longing for a fight, a footrace, or a frolic.

Many emigrants, intending to follow the South Platte route westward, crossed the Missouri River form Bethlehem, opposite the mouth of the Platte, to the little town called Wyoming. This crossing was a favorite with the Mormons and Wyoming Landing is said to have become a formidable rival, so that the Nebraska City Townsite Company bought it out. Old Wyoming did not die, however, and in 1866 had a population of three thousand. The town became known to a later generation as Dresden. Nebraska City continued as the principal freighting point on the Missouri River until the construction of the Union Pacific railroad gave Omaha a dominance of all Nebraska's coastline along the Missouri River.

Still older than Nebraska City or even the Fort Kearney which Captain Wharton had established, was Bellevue, sometimes called the cradle of Nebraska, it having had the first permanent settlement in what later became that state. In 1819 the American Fur Company established a trading post there and appointed Francis De Roin, a fearless and ambitious Frenchman, as Indian trader. He was succeeded by Joseph Robidoux, who later founded St. Joseph, and then came John B. Cabanne, who had a trading post a few miles above, just beyond Boyer's Creek. In 1823 and Indian agency was established at Bellevue which was used as a general deport of supplies and stopping place for trappers, traders, scouts and adventurers. This agency was removed from Fort Atkinson, a military post about thirty miles up the river. The American Fur Company in 1823 built a two-story log house on the bank of the river in which to keep its stores for the purpose of barter with the Indians.

Such famous frontiersmen as Major Andrew Drips, Lucien Fontanelle, Louis Vasquez and others frequently were in and about this post. One of the missionaries stationed there noted in his diary of June 3, 1837, that "Mr. Vasquez called on me today." This casual entry did not mention that Vasquez had walked in from the Cache le Poudre, several hundred miles to the west. About 1830, Drips and Fontanelle, who had working relations with the American Fur Company, erected a permanent building there to accommodate their Rocky Mountain trade.

In 1824 Peter A. Sarpy, who became the most important man in the whole area, succeeded Cabanne. He was below medium height and wore a heavy beard; "in stature, low sized, rather heavy, dark complexioned, full of energy, rather high tempered, generous and kind, ambitious and a hard drinker – a very determined and good looking man." He took a hand in all sorts of traffic. In 1855 he was keeping a store at St. Mary's, a lively town a few miles below Council Bluffs, and was proprietor of a newspaper there. He opened a branch of his fur company at Traders Point, across the river from and below Bellevue, to compete with Hamilton's trading post at that place. He also was proprietor of a ferry at Pull Point (Pont aux Pulles), approximately opposite Bellevue. In the first issue of the Palladium, in 1854, he advertised the Bluff City & St. Louis Packet Line on the Missouri River, declaring the steamers El Paso, Polar Star, and James H. Lucas to be "not excelled for safety, speed and comfort."

In the fall of 1835 a noted visitor, Albert Lea Miller, observed that; "At Bellevue we met a Mr. Fontanelle of New Orleans, a cultured gentleman, who had exchanged the luxury of city life for the wider and wilder enjoyments of trapping in the Rocky Mountains, where he had been three years, and had just come down to winter at this agency. He gave me my first knowledge of the Great Salt Lake." Fontanelle was born in southern Louisiana, some say of royal descent, where his parents perished in a hurricane when he was a baby. At fourteen he went to the Northwest country, as a protégé of Colonel Joshua Pilcher. He was employed by the American Fur Company, crossed the Rockies to the Pacific Coast, and later operated a traders post near Fort Laramie, probably in partnership with Major Drips. He married an Omaha Indian woman and spent a great deal of time at Bellevue, where he died and was buried.

Various missionaries were stationed at Bellevue, such as the Rev. John Dunbar and Samuel Allis. Samuel F. Merrill came when the mission house was completed in 1848. The old mission was turned into a hotel in 1856. With the opening of Nebraska Territory, Bellevue, as temporary state capital, was taking on new life. The territory's first newspaper, the Nebraska Palladium, was published at Bellevue on November 15, 1854. Despite its early show of promise, Bellevue sank into desuetude when Omaha became the territorial capital.

Town promoters appeared on the west bank of the Missouri River almost concurrently with the congressional act, which threw open to settlement by the white man the territory of Nebraska. Most of those towns long since have vanished from the scene, some in fact, hardly reached the point of making an impression on the scene.

Perhaps the first, considered geographically and not chronologically, beginning at the south border of the territory, would have been Rulo, named for a French trader named Ruleau. It and the next town, Falls City, still are thriving. But twelve miles above Falls City, Arago was a thriving town in the old steamboat days before Falls City existed. Edward Sachse was publishing the Southern Nebraskan there in 1867. The town long since has given way to the primeval woods. Above this, Richard Brown, who had been a resident of Oregon, Missouri, established Brownville in 1854. It became one of the most prosperous of river towns, but gradually withered, but only a shadow of its former self. Some distance above Brownsville, on an island was located Sumnerville in 1857, a small village with and extra wide levee for accommodation of the steamboats.

Next was Otoe City, or Bennett's Ferry, eight miles south of Nebraska City in 1857, it later became known as Minersville. Marietta was just south of Nebraska City. Another close neighbor of Nebraska City was Groveland, which had an extensive levee on the Missouri River.

Brooklyn on the Missouri River only a half-mile south of Old Wyoming, seems to have been in 1857 a rival but was smothered by the growth of Nebraska City.

Above Wyoming was Osage then came Cleveland, Liberty, Kanosha, and Bluffdale, almost treading on each other's toes, so closely were they grouped.

Two and a half miles above Bluffdale was Rock Bluff, which in 1856 stood well to become a city, being one of the leading points for equipping freight outfits to cross the plains. Kanosha was known as a steamboat town in 1856 and the traffic was very heavy on the ferry. The town had stores, saloons, and a blacksmith shop. Prof. Joseph Patterson conducted the Naomi Institute, an early day gesture toward education, there several years.

Some five miles above Rock Bluff, the towns of Williamsport, Summit City, Wheatland and Woodland, made up the town of Plattesmouth. Squeezed in between Plattesmouth and the mouth of the Platte was Oreapolis, and across the Missouri River from both was Pacific City, home of Hiram J. Graham, who became territorial delegate from the Territory of Jefferson and perhaps laid the groundwork for the creation of Colorado Territory.

La Platte was on the Missouri River between the Platte and the Papillon. The latter correctly was pronounced Pa-peel-yung, but more often was mispronounced and misspelled Papio, Pappio, or Pappeo. In the early days, Baptiste Roy kept a trading house and doggery at the mouth of the creek and Joseph La Barge was his clerk. In 1856, the site of La Platte was abandoned for higher ground to the west, where Larimer was founded. Then between Larimer and the river, Daniel Gantt platted Platona and still between Platona and the river Triaqua sprang up. The town of Hiawatha similarly was platted next to the river, between it and Cuming City but in 1857 the river took it away, so that in effect it went to join other ghost towns of the area, such as Hamilton, Fairview, Fredonia and Powhoco.

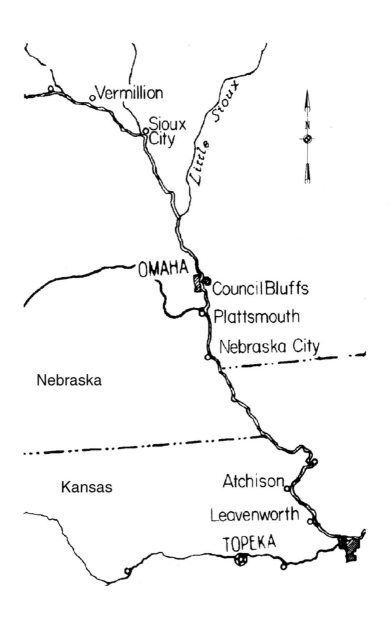

Chapter Twenty-Four

Proud Lords
of the River

In a day when the river was the life of the country through which it flowed and when steamboats were the life of the river, all personnel of the craft were of some importance, from the cocky pilots to the gay roustabouts. But it was the steamboat captains, the masters of the boats, who were indeed the proud lords of the river. With broad hat and white ruffled shirt, fine black broadcloth and fancy vest, booted elegantly, the distinguished captain gave dignity to the scene aboard ship. Standing in the glass-fronted cabin just beneath the twin eagles, and squarely between the towering smokestacks, he was symbolical of all the romance and glory of the river. He was, first of all, a gentleman, a social figure in his home, proverbial for kindness of heart and courteousness of disposition. He entertained his passengers, and always presided at the head of the table.

In the course of a season's run, the captain and his boat might have carried such a potpourri as "merchants, speculators, dandies, fine ladies, everything real, and everything affected, in the form of humanity, with pianos, and stacks of novels, cards and dice, flirting and love-making, drinking and champagne. On the deck, perhaps three hundred fellows who fear neither whisky nor gunpowder." He would have had Santa Fe traders, gamblers, adventurers, emigrants, mountain men, missionaries, and Indians.

Among the earliest was Captain Joseph W. Throckmorton, who was on the Mississippi River in the 1820s, running boats on the upper river out of St. Louis. A short, heavy-built man, he was described as looking "like Theirs, the little Frenchman who was bullied by Bismarck." Known up and down both rivers as a courageous man, he was at the Battle of Bad Axe (now Genoa, Wisconsin), in charge of the steamer Warrior with soldiers and artillery from Fort Crawford and Prairie du Chien. That contest, August 21, 1832, was the last between the United States and Black Hawk's warrior. With Captain Throckmorton then was seventeen-year-old Joseph La Barge, destined to become famous as a riverman and to spend more than fifty years of his life following the windings of the Missouri.

In the next thirty years Captain Throckmorton had the Red Rover, the Winnebago, the Burlington, the Malta, the General Brooke, the Cecilia, the Cora, the John Golong, the War Eagle, and the Florence. In the early sixties, it became difficult for the captain; a stanch Union man, to operate on the Missouri. After a career as full as that of any man on the river, he entered the insurance business in St. Louis and died in 1872, being seventy-two years old.

As colorful a figure as ever ran the river was Captain William C. "Dandy" Jewett. He built and ran the Lewis F. Linn, the Rowena, and the Martha C. Jewett; the latter named for his sister. Dressed always in the height of fashion, exceedingly polite and affable, he was a general favorite with the ladies of Boonville, Glasgow, Lexington and other river towns on the lower Missouri. The fact that he was a bachelor and considered a "good catch" accounted in some measure for this, but it was his innate courtesy that made him the most popular captain that ever ran the river. An old newspaper said of him:

"Captain Jewett was about five feet three inches tall, as dark complexioned as a Cuban, with an Aaron Burr cast of countenance. He wore curls, black as a raven's wing, down to the top of his black velvet collar, which was part of a blue pigeon-tail coat ornamented with brass buttons. Hat off, he met his lady passengers at the shore end of the stage plank and escorted them up the stairway and to the ladies' cabin. He was sincere in all he did and said. It was just the same if a woman showed up at a wood landing, dressed in calico, wearing a red pink sunbonnet with the brown pasteboard splits showing through the fringed edge of the bonnet – as if he were about to dance the Sir Roger de Coverly." The beloved little captain was stricken with cholera and died in Glasgow in 1854.

Captain John W. Keiser as early as 1837 was referred to as "Old Man Keiser" when he landed the St. Peter at Chouteau's Landing, a place soon to become the Town of Kanzas. He had gone to Missouri at an early date, locating at Rocheport, where his mechanical ability attracted the attention of Pierre Chouteau of the American Fur Company who took him to St. Louis to superintend the building of that company's boats. He afterwards went on the river as a captain, commanding the Iatan, the Trapper, and the St. Peter. His three sons, John P., Charles W. and David, all became steamboat pilots. Captain John P. Keiser commanded the J.M. Cledenin, the Isabel, the Clara, the Sam Cloon and the Isabella.

On the river at fifteen, Captain David Massie in sixty-five years was on nearly as many boats, in his later years usually as master. His activities in the fifteen years prior to the outbreak of the Civil War were many and varied. In 1861 he took the Spread Eagle to the mountains for the American Fur Company, accompanying the Chippewa. The next year he was on the Fannie Ogden, owned by Captain Kinney, and the year after that was on the Nellie Rogers. Then he took the Yellowstone to the mountains for the American Fur Company. In 1865 he was on the Twilight and the following year was again in the employ of Captain Kinney, this time on the Cora. He was on the Antelope, which burned in 1869, after which he went to Utah. The following year he bought the Ida Stockdale which he ran for two years: then the E.H. Durfee, the Silver Lake, the Western, the Carroll, and the Josephine, the Red Cloud, the

Bright Light, the Benton, the Dakota, the Montana and the Wyoming. About 1890 he went up the Mississippi. He died in 1910.

A master of the steamboats whose activities were close to St. Louis in the days before the war was Captain James Dozier, a picturesque figure having an adventurous spirit of leadership. Born in Nash County, North Carolina, in 1806, he left home at eighteen and four years later was in St. Louis. But it was not until 1844 that he began to acquire fame as a steamboat owner, at a time when the river trade was entering the palmy days of its prosperity. He owned and operated such steamboats as Lake of the Woods, St. Louis Oak, Cora, and Mary Blane and later with his sons, the Thomas E. Tutt, the Elvira and the Mollie Dozier. The two latter were named for his daughters. He built a beautiful home at Dozier's Landing on the banks of the Missouri in St. Charles County – an estate that was a counterpart of the plantation of his earliest remembrance. Slaves cultivated this farm. Retiring to this estate in 1854, the captain and Mrs. Dozier made it the center of social life in the carefree days before the war. Dozier's Landing was known far up and down the Missouri River for its lavish entertainment, good cheer and charming hospitality. The high spirits of the ten Dozier children gladdened the place. Captain Dozier's contemporaries in those flourishing days of the river trade were Captains Roe, Throckmorton, La Barge, Brown, Eaton, Keiser, and others equally well known in the history of the river's day of greatness. The captain lost his slaves during the Civil War and his fortunes suffered otherwise. At the close of the war, he moved to St. Louis and made another fortune in a commercial venture. He died in 1878.

Captain Joseph Kinney had been a pioneer steamboat man on the Mississippi before 1844, in which year he went to Boonville on the Missouri and thereafter his fortunes were cast with Big Muddy. He built and operated steamboats, extended his power on the river and waited for the time when he would build a home suitable for his wife and eleven children. He had selected the spot, four hundred and sixty acres of rich bottomland opposite Boonville. The masters and pilots of his boats had standing orders to buy and fine walnut log and carry it to St. Louis. In 1869 he built "Rivercene" on those broad acres and the walnut logs were brought up from St. Louis in the form of finished lumber to go into the fifty-thousand-dollar mansion, "the costliest, finest mansion along the whole length of the Missouri River." Captain Kinney built or bought and operated such boats as the W. H. Russell, named for a friend, the Alice, the Cora, and the Margaret, named for his daughters, the R.W. Dugan, the Fannie Ogden, the Joseph Kinney, the Kate Kinney, and the St. Luke. Having seen the river trade die, Captain Kinney passed away in 1890.

Captains Yore, Gunsollis, Baker, Kercheval, Wineland, Brierly, Shaw, Hanson, Bart, Able, Barker, Bissell, Terrill, and Boyd were noted river men and pioneer commanders. Captain William C. Postal was an experienced river man in 1879 when he bought the Headlight from Captain Keiser and Captain McPherson. The latter was on the Rob Roy in 1883. In that year Captain Henry Keith was on the Bright Light which had been the Alice until purchased by Captain D.H. Silver. In 1885 Captain Keith was on the Dakota. Captain A.J. Spahr of Boonville went on the river in 1865. He was a big man, more than six feet high, weighing two hundred and forty pounds. In the later days of steamboating he was commander of the Mason. Captain Barns for many years after the war ran the Columbian between St. Louis and Omaha. The wreck of his boat now is covered with sand and undergrowth of willows at Buckhorn Point near Brunswick.

Captain Charles K. Baker had the Admiral, the Minnehaha, and the Sioux City. At one time he was paid sixteen hundred dollars a month for piloting the Mepham. He was said to have been one of the most skillful pilots that ever turned a wheel. He died about 1891 near Westport at the home of his son, Charles K. Baker, Jr.

Captain John Gunsollis made eleven hundred dollars a month. He was killed in a steamboat explosion about 1890. Captain Willoughby, "Old Willoughby," the river men called him, has left behind a record, even among blasphemous deck officers who swore with every breath, of being the most shockingly profane man on the river. He drifted to Memphis and out of the ken of riverains. The list of river captains was a long one.

Captain Alexander Gillham, owner of the A.B. Chambers, died in Kansas City and was buried in his front yard on McGee Street in what now would be the heart of the city, though his body was afterwards removed to a cemetery. Another Kansas Citian, Captain Pierre M. Chouteau, was born in St. Louis in 1823 and was taken to Chouteau's Landing when he was three months old by his father, Francois Gesseau Chouteau, one of three brothers operating a fur depot at that point. Pierre grew up with the town of Kansas City and held a number of civic offices. He was captain and owner of the Amazon and other boats. He died in Kansas City August 28, 1885, several days after having been struck by a train.

James A. Yore was master of the H.S. Turner in 1867. He was a St. Joseph man. Captain McCord frequently employed Captain Martin Anderson, son of the Judge Anderson, who sat on the first court in Old Bluffton and maintained a notable tavern in that town. McCord, whose home was in East Leavenworth, or McCord's Landing as it was known before the city of Leavenworth was laid out. Captain Anderson's home was in Lexington. He died November 16, 1853, at the store of Bray & Brother in Maryville, California.

On May 4, 1885, word was flashed up and down the river that Captain John B. La Barge had dropped dead of a heart attack in the pilothouse of the steamer Benton No.2 at Bismarck, North Dakota. One of the oldest pilots on the river, his experience had almost spanned the life of the steamboat trade on the Missouri.

One of the best-known captains and pilots, particularly on the upper Missouri, was Grant Prince Marsh, a Western Pennsylvanian, who at the age of twelve became cabin boy on the Dover, an Allegheny River steamboat. IN 1852, he was a deck hand on the Beaver, bound for St.

Louis. He was on the Missouri River in 18544, a deck hand on the F.X. Aubrey. Later he was on the A.B. Chambers, the Alonzo Child and the Hesperian. In the winter on 1858-9 he was on the lower Mississippi on the Chambers No.2. As mate of the John J. Roe he was at the Battle of Pittsburg Landing on the Tennessee River.

In 1864 Marsh made his first trip to the upper Missouri, on the Marcella, and two years later had his boat, the Luella, in the Fort Benton trade. The next year he had the Ida Stockdale that paid for itself twice over on a single trip. In 1868-9 he had the Nile in the Fort Benton trade. In 1870 he was on the Ida Reese No. 2, working out of Sioux City. He was on the Nellie Peck in 1871-2. He was operating the Josephine in 1874-5 between Yankton and Fort Benton.

In 1876 he was the captain of the Key West. It was on this boat that Generals Gibbon, Terry and Custer planned their strategy before the latter went out to annihilation and glory. Wounded soldiers from other parts of the battlefield were taken swiftly on the Key West down to Bismarck, where the first news of the Custer massacre was flashed to the world. Though Captain Marsh continued actively in steamboating virtually until his death forty years later, this was his most celebrated feat.

Chapter Twenty-Five

To the Edge
of the Frontier

Omaha became not only the political capital of the new territory of Nebraska, an honor it soon lost to Lincoln, but the commercial capital of the whole Nebraska coast and its hinterlands. Founded in 1854 as a speculative venture by the businessmen of the older town of Council Bluffs across the river, it grew largely at the expense of the latter. The Omaha Arrow appeared October 18, 1854, with J.W. Patterson as editor, being printed at Council Bluffs. J.E. Johnson, the business manager, was a Mormon with three or four wives. The Nebraskian succeeded the Arrow late in 1854.

By 1856 the town was claiming a population of one thousand, an able and brilliant lot, one local hostelry having housed at one time eight young men whom later became United States senators. There were but few women among the students, scholars, lawyers, surveyors, speculators and lot owners who spent their time "talking lots and lands and boasting to newcomers." Their motto was buy today, sell tomorrow, and they didn't always wait until the next day to sell.

That the town was experiencing a real estate boom was evidenced by the actual sales of land which took place on the steamer Omaha, upbound. Passengers were flooded with circulars and pamphlets boosting townsites for cities now long forgotten. But then they loomed up in all the magnificence of coloring and print. Passengers carried an abundance of money, expecting to invest in Omaha real estate.

Omaha's first great boom was beginning and the prices of property rapidly were rising. The very greatest enterprise was manifested, and in some cases, such was the haste to build, that houses were shingled at night. Great schemes were afoot and new plans were created every day. Money was never so abundant. The territorial legislature was in session, every member armed to the teeth, each provided with a brace of Colt revolvers and a bowie knife.

It was January 5, 1859, that Al Steinberger and Colonel Wynkoop came into Omaha from the Rocky Mountains bringing the first gold from Cherry Creek. The precious metal was in goose quills, not more than six quills altogether, but enough to start a stampede of fortune hunters. When the Omaha arrived March 10, first boat up the river that spring, the wharf was thronged with men, women, children, horses, mules, oxen, wagons, carriages and Pawnee Indians. Omaha as a thriving river town intended to get her share of the trade incident to the gold rush. Passengers were given handbills announcing the discovery of gold and the prices of transportation from Omaha to Cherry Creek.

In another decade, Omaha was a busy town, the liveliest town in the country. It had outgrown its status as outfitting post for wagons and had become supply depot for the railroad. Nor had it ever enjoyed a richer river trade. Steamboats puffed upstream and emptied their cargoes of freight, horses and mules – packet boats from St. Louis and St. Joseph, and "mountain boats," hell-bent for Montana and its gold fields. The city was boasting a population of five thousand, and was said to have had as many saloons as stores.

From Omaha to Sioux City, the land boom was in full vigor by 1857, and there were many platted towns and still more lithographed cities. Land claim clubs were bold, frequently resorting to outlawry, and respecting nothing but the force of arms. It was said that a good six-shooter was the best title to land. There was a scarcity of farmers and an abundance of land sharks, with every townsite along the Missouri River being in possession of some land claim club. It was complained that the man who came to honestly homestead a piece of land was compelled to go inland five or six miles.

The earliest settlement in that section of the river had been made at the Council Bluffs, on a straight line sixteen miles above Omaha, or forty miles by river, where Lewis and Clark had held a council with the Indians in 1804. Prior to that, it had been an Indian village. In 1819, Camp Missouri was established there, named by the engineers of Major Long and the army of General Henry Atkinson. In 1821, the name was changed to Fort Atkinson, which with its twelve hundred men of the regular army was the nation's greatest western outpost. Later the name of the post was changed to Fort Calhoun.

Major O'Fallon's trading post was immediately south of the barracks, on a road leading to the mouth of Hook's Hollow and to the steamboat landing. Manuel Lisa had a trading post some five miles below this, and Cabanne's post, consisting of six large buildings, was another mile south, though Lisa's trading post was known afterwards as Cabanne's Fort.

Florence, six miles above Omaha, on the site where the Mormons camped in 1846, had been incorporated in 1853. The Saints had built a town called Winter Quarters on the plateau overlooking the river, a mushroom town of thirty-five hundred persons.

Decatur had its origin when Peter A. Sarpy, Henry Fontanelle and Clement Lambert built log houses and established stores or posts there to serve the Indian trade. Half a dozen or so temporary traders would come over from Council Bluffs at Indian payment time and pitch tents. Then the Indians would engage in a brief spending spree. The town was incorporated in 1856 and its high riverbanks gave it one of the best steamboat landings on the river.

The town of Fort Calhoun, immediately west of Fort Calhoun, was surveyed in 1856. Omada, in Dakota County, in 1857 had a population of four hundred. In 1862 the river washed away part of the town and eventually ate away the balance of the townsite. The citizens sidestepped the river and Omada now is on the Iowa side.

Tekami was halfway between Omaha and Dakota City – a clean little town, half frame, half log houses, situated on the river at the foot of a bluff. Dakota City and Harny City, adjacent towns opposite Sioux City, were filed for record in 1856. The name of Harny City was changed to Newport and finally to Covington. The land offices, established in 1857, were located at Dakota city, giving that town local importance. But it soon yielded first place to Sioux City.

The latter was on the edge of the frontier, where one could look a thousand miles into Indian country. William Thompson, first white man to settle, took up a claim just south of Floyd's Bluff in 1848. He laid out a town and called it Thompsonville, which became a post for Indian traders. But the site was so steep there was no landing for the steamboats and the town's decline was inevitable. Theophile Bruguier settled at the mouth of the Big Sioux in 1849, bringing his band of Indians with him. His establishment has been described as a feudal set-up.

Near the bluff and crossing War Eagle Park is a section of the old Missouri River Trail, which was well marked and traveled by traders prior to 1854 when General Harny established the Military Road. In that year, several French traders and trappers were living in log houses along the Missouri River and others were living at the mouth of the Floyd and in the vicinity which later was to become Sioux City. Joe Leonais cultivated his cornfield where the business district of Sioux City now stands. A dozen of these Frenchmen had come down the Missouri River two years before when some difficulty had arisen with the Indians at Fort Vermillion in Dakota, and had established themselves in log houses in the safer territory below the Big Sioux. They had been in the employ of fur companies on the upper river for many years, many of them marrying Indian women and becoming independent trappers. They kept large stores of goods to trade to the Indians for furs. Louis Letellier operated one of these posts at the mouth of the Floyd. Several times a year these traders had to make the journey downriver to Council Bluffs to dispose of their furs and to restock with provisions and trading goods.

It was a case of "everything happens at once" to the site of Sioux City. In 1855 General William S. Harny in command of the Sioux expedition, had been sent to occupy old Fort Pierre, the war department having bought it from Pierre Chouteau & Company for use as an army post. Deciding the location was bad and the buildings unfit for a garrison, he divided his command, sending one detachment to Fort Lookout. With the other, a part of the Second Dragoons, he proceeded downstream, investigating locations for a permanent military post. Being so favorably impressed with the site at the junction of Big Sioux and the Missouri, he established a military camp on the west bank of the Big Sioux.

Thus, the time was propitious and the contributing elements had come together to presage a sound growth for the new town, which had far more sound reasons for being brought into existence than many another on the Missouri River. The combination of the river trade and the fur trade had made possible Sioux City's founding. The boats of the fur companies always stopped there and sometimes rough encounters took place at the mouth of the Big Sioux between engagees of different outfits.

In 1856 the Omaha arrived with seventy thousand dollars worth of merchandise for the new store of Jackson & Tootle. For long afterwards the Omaha was the favorite boat at Sioux City, her arrival being the signal for a general holiday and a dance on board with the captain playing host.

One of the first to come to the new town in 1856 was a slender young printer named Henry Clay Work, but as there was not a print shop nearer than Council Bluffs, he did not stay. He built a cabin, but soon sold out at fifteen hundred dollars profit. He went back to Chicago to set type and became famous as the composer of such songs as "Grandfather's Clock," "Wake, Nicodemus," "Land of Jubilo" and others.

The Sioux City Eagle was in existence by July 4, 1857, when it reported that the steamer Emma had passed down with soldiers on board from the abandoned Fort Pierre. That same July 4, Sioux City celebrated its first Independence Day in the grove to the west, which was the town's first common meeting place.

Stage and steamboats from downriver were bringing young wives and mothers with families and household treasures to enter upon the making of homes. The Sioux City House and the Western Exchange were serving the transients. Cassady's Hall was being used for social festivities.

The Civil War in 1861 was taking many of the little frontier town's able-bodied men, so its first local military organization, known as the Frontier Guards, was formed, ostensibly to protect the outpost against Indian raids. In August of 1862 news of the New Ulm massacre in Minnesota sent settlers pouring into Sioux City and a courier came baring the dread tidings that the Strike-the-Ree had joined forces with Smutty Bear and the Sioux were about to descend upon the town. The steamboat Lewis Burns brought logs and the men of the town built a stockade on the levee. "Old Strike," however, had given his word to Father De Smet, the blackrobe, that he would not make war, and without his assistance Smutty Bear dared not strike.

The fur industry still was important that far up the river in 1864, as the following from the Sioux City Journal of August 20 indicates; "The fur company's boat, the Yellowstone, passed down yesterday. Pierre Chouteau was on board, the leading man in the company. The Yellowstone had on board over two thousand bales of buffalo robes; her deck was covered with immense elk antlers, which with the fresh buffalo meat, the half-breed crew, and buckskin dressed passengers, presented a fine picture of an upper Missouri steamer.

A tremendous volume of freight was being transported from Sioux City in the mid-sixties, going for the maintenance of military posts and Indian reservations. Government warehouses were built near the levee and goods brought by steamboat were stored to be hauled into the upper river country by bull train. One of the largest contractors for supplies and freighting was Theophile Bruguier, assisted by his sons John and Bill. Their wagon trains, drawn by long strings of double-yoked cattle, went out along the Military Road to Bruguier's, beyond to Paul Paquette's ferry across the Big Sioux and on into Dakota.

Discovery of gold in Montana added to the volume of goods sent upriver by steamboats. In 1867 forty steamboats passed Sioux City before June 1 on their way upriver.

The population of Sioux City doubled. The frontier town became a thriving city, a status that was not changed when, within a few years, the railroad was built to Yankton, South Dakota, and Sioux City was no longer the gateway to the Northwest. When the Northern Pacific railroad built into Bismarck, North Dakota, the business of steam packets declined. Yankton and Bismarck were rowdy capitals of the Northwest. Men were seeking gold and adventure in the Black Hills and Montana. Sioux City continued to prosper, but the frontier had move on.

As the area along the upper Missouri River grew in population, wealth, and importance, the steamboat trade was entering its twilight.

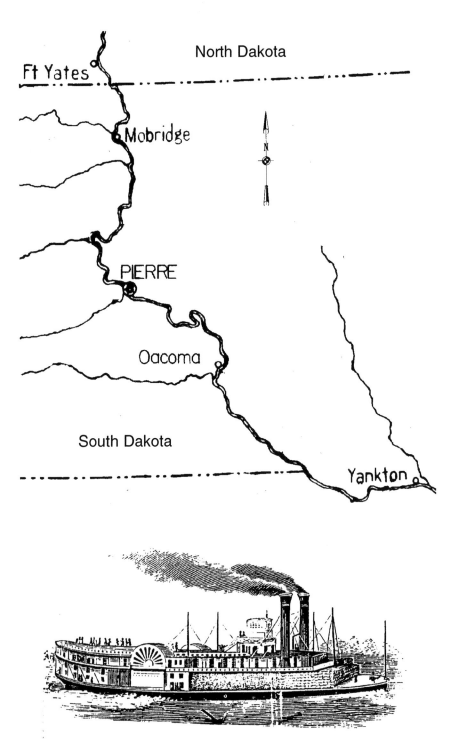

North Dakota

Ft Yates

Mobridge

N

PIERRE

Oacoma

South Dakota

Yankton

Chapter Twenty-Six

Twilight of the Steamboats

By the 1870s railroads paralleling and crossing the Missouri River were making deep inroads into the steamboat tonnage. The last big fight of the riverains was made in the latter part of that decade when Colonel Hunter Ben Jenkins, Captain George Keith and others formed a company to buy and operate the Wyoming, Dakota and Montana. This precipitated a rate war with the railroads in which the boatmen carried fourth-class freight upstream for as low as six cents per hundred in order to get a cargo. They put up a gallant fight for a few seasons before the railroads scored an inevitable victory. It was the twilight of the steamboats.

The once famous Star line had in operation the David R. Powell, the Kate Kinney, the Joe Kinney, the Fanny Lewis, the William J. Lewis, the Mattie Bell, the Bright Light, and the Mollie Dozier. Captains and pilots on the line included Ralph Whitledge, George and Henry Keith, Bill and John Massie, Jim and John Gonsaullis, Ed Baldwin, Tony Swope, Tony Burbank, and Bill Lingo, most of who had served as "mountain pilots."

Operating on the river in 1870 were the A.C. Bird, Dallas, Last Chance, Mollie Moore, and the Far West No.3. Captain Grant Marsh ran this boat to fame and glory in bringing out news of the Custer fight in the shortest possible time. The boat later ran in the lower river trade under Captain Henry N. (Hal) Dodd. It was snagged and wrecked October 20, 1883, at Mullanphy's Island, seven miles below St. Charles. The Fannie Lewis took off most of the cargo.

Captain Dodd, a huge man, was known up and down the river. He was born in 1844 on Dodd's Island at the mouth of the Osage, the son of Captain James Dodd, who operated the Maid of Orleans and other steamboats before the Civil War. Captain Hal had owned an interest in the Regulator, Last Chance, Umpire, Belfast, Morning Star, Far West, and John L. Ferguson. He was one of the crew in 1868 when the St. John was first that year to reach Fort Benton after a race with the Deer Lodge. He died in Kansas City in 1910.

The Gold Dust, on the river in 1870, blew up near Hickman, Kentucky, August 7, 1875, killing seventeen, Captain John T. McCord being one of the victims. The Susie Silver was another on the river in 1870, Captain David Silver having named it for his wife, who always traveled with him. The boat was said to be worth a hundred thousand dollars.

In the autumn of 1871, a powerful syndicate was formed to secure control of business on the upper river, the new concern being the Coulson Packet Company, which became famous in river history. Sanford B. Coulson headed the company, other members of the syndicate being his brothers, Captain Martin Coulson and Captain John Coulson; Captain James C. McVay, Captain John Todd, Captain Grant P. Marsh, and Messrs, Durfee & Peck. This syndicate owned the Nellie Peck, Far West, Key West, E.H. Durfee, Sioux City, and Mary McDonald. That year also saw on the river the Flirt, Katy P. Kountz, Lady Lee, Matamora, Capital City, and Selkirk.

In 1872 the Big Horn was on the river, along with the C.P. Huntington, Nadine, Platte Valley, Vice-President, Western, Dora, and the Esperanza, which burned at Prophet's Island, Dakota, October 23, 1874. The De Smet, built in 1872 for the mountain trade by Captain Joseph La

Barge, was named for Father De Smet, famous missionary to the Indians. The father made his last public appearance in order to bless the boat on May 13, just ten days before his death.

In the next three years there were operating on the river such boats as the Governor Allen, W.J. Behan, Belle of Jefferson, Belle of St. Louis, Benton No. 2, May Bryan, Carroll No. 2, Charles P. Carroll, De Bussy, Gate City, T.T. Hilman, J.F. Jay, W.J. Lewis No. 2, Mary Lowry, Mattie Belle, C.W. Mead, General Meade, Osceola, Perry Belle, Petrel, Plow Boy No. 2, Red Cloud, Silver Wave, George Spangler, George C. Wolf, and the Elkhorn No. 2. The Josephine, named for the daughter of General David S. Stanley, was on the upper river in 1873 and on the Yellowstone for years, going as high as ten miles above Powder River, highest point reached by a steamboat. Still going in 1907, it was one of the last of the boats.

Daniel Rice's showboat, the Damsel, was on the Missouri in 1873. It had been in the St. Paul trade on the Mississippi in the 1860s. Rice chartered it and engaged Captain Charles Davis as pilot. Rice's name as a funnyman was a household word in America. P.T. Barnum had paid him as high as a thousand dollars a week. At one time he essayed to run for president, either in earnest or as a publicity gag, and was taken seriously by many newspapers.

According to some authorities, the Damsel struck a snag at the head of Onawa Bend, near Onawa, Iowa in 1876 and sank without loss of life, members of the circus company being taken off by Captain Joseph La Barge of the John M. Chambers.

A different version has it that in 1878 "with the encouraging addition of the marvel milk-white horse, Excelsior, the one horse show and the Damsel again took to the rivers. The boat was snagged and burned near Decatur, Nebraska, on the Missouri River. The Damsel was a total loss, but local inhabitants saved Excelsior and some of the boat's circus paraphernalia. Rice presented the boat's bell to the village church as a token of gratitude." Decatur and Onawa were in the same stretch of the river, but on opposite sides.

The F.Y. Batchelor, with Captain Grant Marsh, made a record run from Bismarck to Fort Buford, three hundred and seven miles, in fifty-five hours and twenty-five minutes, in August 1879. In 1885 the boat was sold to the Benton Packet Company, which operated it between Sioux City and Fort Benton. Captain Joseph La Barge built the Big Horn No. 3 for the mountain trade in 1872. Phil E. Chappell, a Jefferson City banker, who wrote a book on the history of steamboating on the Missouri River, owned the Phil E. Chappell, J.A. Ware, master. In 1883 the Chappell was converted to a cotton boat and taken to the Red River where she burned in 1886.

The Carroll No. 2 was in the Sioux campaign and took Colonel Elwell S. Otis and six companies of the Twenty-second infantry up the Yellowstone. After passing the mouth of Powder River, it was vigorously attacked by a considerable body of Indians who were driven off by soldiers from the boat. The John M. Chambers was built by Captain La Barge and named for the infant son of B.M. Chambers of St. Louis. In the Sioux campaign, it ascended the Yellowstone to the mouth of the Tongue River. The E.H. Durfee, G.W. Keith, master, which had been taken over by the Coulson Packet Company in 1871, and was named for a member of the firm of Durfee & Peck, steamboat operators, took Colonel Nelson A. Miles and six companies of United States infantry up the river in August, 1876.

The Don Cameron was built by the government for the Yellowstone trade and was transporting the Fifth Infantry from Fort Leavenworth to Fort Keogh on the Yellowstone on May 19, 1877, when it struck a snag and sank at the Omaha and Winnebago agency, forty miles below Sioux City. Its seventy-five passengers, who were rescued by the W.T. Sherman, included the wife of Colonel Nelson A. Miles and her sister, Miss Lizzie Sherman, niece of General Sherman. The boat was being operated without a regular licensed pilot.

(chart here)

The Benton No.2 was one of Custer's Fleet in his expedition against the Sioux in 1876. It was a popular mountain boat that ran for a number of years in the St. Louis and Rocheport trade. As late as 1885 it would go to Rocheport, deliver its cargo, and on the way back would go up Linn Creek, on hundred and ten miles up the Osage River. A small sternwheeler, it ran on the upper river from Yankton to Fort Benton until the railroads came. T.C. Power & Company and Isaac G. Baker of Fort Benton owned it. It was on this boat Captain John La Barge died at the wheel at Bismarck. He was backing out of the Bismarck landing for an upriver trip. John C. Barr, master, was on the roof and as La Barge got the Benton straightened out and rang his go-ahead bell, Barr noticed that the boat had swung in and was heading for the bank and in line with some other boats lying at the warehouse, one of which was the Helena. Barr quickly ran to the pilothouse where La Barge's body was blocking the door. Barr stopped the boat quickly, avoiding a collision with the Helena.

In the seventies the roustabouts began to learn the power of concerted action in the matter of wages and by striking could force an owner to raise the rate paid them. Twenty-five to fifty dollars a month and board was standard. The roustabouts, or roosters as they were called, struck the steamer Meade at Yankton and the owner was compelled to pay seventy-five before the boat could move. In 1881, the crew of the C.K. Peck, receiving twenty-four dollars when they left Sioux City, struck for thirty at Yankton, thirty-five after leaving there and for fifty at Bismarck. When boat owners at Bismarck combined to resist wage demands a riot ensued, twenty-seven roosters were thrown in jail and soldiers came from nearby Fort Lincoln to preserve the peace.

Boats coming on the river in the 1880s were the Aggie, Mary E. Bennett, Capitola, Robert Campbell No.3, Harry Clyde, Gus Fowler, Frederick, J.P. Gage, Glencoe No. 2, Hope, Dan B. Hulbert, Judith, Ella Kimbrough, Kate Kinney No. 2, Mattie Lee, Lilly Maud, Little Livingstone, James Lyons, A.L. Mason, Messenger Boy, Onawa, Abner O'Neal, General Perry, Pin Oak, Plattsmouth, Plow Boy No. 3, John L. Roach and the Tom Rogers.

The spring of 1881 was unusually severe and nine boats wintering at Yankton were in difficulties as the result of ice gorges, two of them being completely wrecked. These were the Western of the Coulson line and the Fontanelle of the Peck line. Others caught in the jam were the Peninah, Nellie Peck, Black Hills, Butte, Helena and Big Horser. There were two stages of high water caused by the gorges and all boats were saved but the Western and Fontanelle, being floated up to various points back from the water. The Black Hills and Peninah were floated over the railroad track by the first gorge and the second took the Peninah on east to a point in the James River lowlands. It was July 26 before the Nellie Peck could be returned to the river.

Captain Isaac P. Baker said that in 1881-2 he carried more than two hundred and fifty thousand buffalo hides on his boats. On one trip the Rosebud, of which he was captain, carried more than ten thousand hides bought from buffalo hunters in the upper Missouri region. He was born at Weston, Missouri, in 1855 when the steamboating there was at its highest point. He went to Dakota in 1882 and took charge of the Kendall line of steamers that operated on the Missouri and Yellowstone rivers. Principal cargoes of his boats were beef, hides, robes, pemmican, and tanned furs and gold dust and minerals. He died at Bismarck in 1938, one of the oldest veterans of the river.

The great rival of the steamboat was the railroad and the struggle between the two lasted from 1859 when the Hannibal & St. Joseph reached St. Joseph, Missouri, until 1887 when the Great Northern reached Helena, Montana. The base of the river trade had been gradually moving up the Missouri. The Union Pacific was at Omaha in 1867; the Sioux City & Pacific reached Sioux City in 1868; and the Northern Pacific was at Bismarck in 1872. Discovery of gold in the Black Hills helped bolster a waning river trade, but the respite was only too brief.

The days of the old river traffic have long since passed away and been lost in the ocean of the past. The wharves are weed-grown, razed or rotted away, the channels changed, the old race of courteous captains and proud pilots has passed into a port marked "Elysium," while the stately floating palaces have been all but forgotten.

The benediction on the steamboats and the steamboat traffic on the Missouri River were pronounced by the Jefferson City Tribune in its issue of September 23, 1888. This was a message not only nostalgic, but which in the light of later events might be considered prophetic:

"When navigation on the Missouri River closes this winter, the probabilities are it will close forever. Had anyone predicted thirty years ago, when one hundred twenty-five majestic steamboats were engaged in traffic between St. Louis and Kansas City, that all boats would be withdrawn, in the fall of 1888, he wold have been looked upon as insane. But such an event is about to happen, nevertheless… The refusal of the underwriters to any longer assume risks on the Missouri River steamboats removes the last obstacle in the road of a complete abandonment of the river… It is a pity that such a grand stream of water must be abandoned… What the future may have in store for the Missouri River is a matter of conjecture… Farewell to the beautiful steamboats which one floated so proudly upon the great Missouri River. They have departed, never more to return."

Chapter Twenty-Seven

The Upper Missouri, Fur Empire

The wild and rugged area comprising the upper Missouri River territory was a fur empire where titans of the industry contended for control of its valuable output of peltries. In this early race for empire none except fur seekers entered. These were the true pathfinders, the true explorers, and the heralds of empire. Their fur-laden vessels floating down the Missouri and its tributaries represented the wealth, the adventure, and the romance of the Northwest.

It was distinctly Indian country, its only permanent abodes being the forts and fur trading posts that in retrospect seemed to have lined the river.

It would be difficult to even name all the fur companies, strong and weak; all the forts and their builders, bourgeois, clerks, and engagees: to mention the scores of steamboats, their captains and their pilots; to list the hundreds of explorers, traders, hunters, trappers, and voyageurs. Each category would be entitled to a book at least, and some forts and individuals have rated a volume.

One whom the Indians might have called "the fort builder" was Captain James Kipp, a power on the upper river in the days of the fur trade, whose name recurs in the journals of western explorers and travelers and in the annals of the fur trade. He came from a long line of New

York City Dutch, tracing back to Jesse De Forest, reputed founder of New Amsterdam. The Kype (Kip, Kipp) family probably arrived there about 1645. His father, Samuel Kipp, was an officer in the Westchester Loyalists (DeLancy's "Cowboys") and was wounded at the battle of Harrison, Westchester County, in 1781. He married Mary Knapp, also a loyalist, and they sought refuge in Quebec, where the records of the Anglican Church show James Kipp baptized August 30, 1789.

The family moved to Montreal about 1795. James Kipp married Elizabeth Rocheleau in 1813 at St. George's Anglican Church in Kingston, Upper Canada. In 1816 and 1818 he is shown in Montreal lists as a resident of that city, a master carpenter and joiner by trade, but thereafter is always "absent from the province." He probably entered the fur trade then and went to the Red River of the North, where he was employed as a trapper and hunter, though his skill as a carpenter may have been a factor in his employment. He had two Mandan wives on the upper Missouri, one of whom was the daughter of Mandeek-Suck-Choppenik (Medicine Bird). The other was Earth Woman, daughter of Four Bears, famous Mandan chief, and mother of Joseph Kipp, noted hunter and trader in the vicinity of Fort Benton and the Bear Paw Mountains. In 1844 Captain Kipp married in New York Mary Bloodgood, probably of French descent, who attended his farm at Barry during his long absences upriver.

In 1822 he built for the Columbia Fur Company a trading post among the Mandan Indians sixty miles above the present Bismarck, North Dakota. Three years later he built for the Assiniboine trade a fort near the mouth of White Earth River, the place being abandoned four years later. There is reason to believe Kipp helped Francis A. Chardon build Fort Berthold, which at first was called Fort James in Kipp's honor. There is authority for believing he built Fort Floyd in 1829 at the mouth of the Yellowstone. This was the forerunner of Fort Union, which became the most important in the chain of forts erected and maintained along the Missouri by the Columbia Fur Company and its successor, the American Fur Company. In 1831 he built Fort Clark at the mouth of Knife River, where for a number of years he was Mandan trader and supervisor of the fort.

While commandant at Fort Clark, Kipp entertained for part of one summer, the celebrated artist, George Catlin, and was authority for much of what the latter had to say about the Mandans. Shortly after, in the winter of 1833-4, Captain Kipp had the honor of playing host to Maximilian, prince of Wied, botanist, zoologist, and ethnologist, who was accompanied by Charles Bodmer, young Swiss artist.

In 1831, Kipp built Fort Piegan, near the mouth of the Marais River, deep in the heart of the dangerous Blackfoot country. This soon was abandoned in favor of Fort McKenzie, only a few miles away. Kipp for a time had charge of this fort, too, considered one of the most dangerous posts of duty on the entire river.

Father Pierre-Jean de Smet met Captain Kipp at Fort Union in 1841, and John James Audubon, the naturalist, met him at Fort Alexander on the Yellowstone. Although temporarily retired to his farm near Barry, in Clay County, Missouri, in 1847, Kipp accompanied his friend, John Palliser, traveler and author of Solitary Rambles and Adventures of a Hunter in the Prairie, on a trip to the Yellowstone.

Kipp kept up a running feud for several years with Charles Larpenteur, author of Forty Years a Fur Trader on the Upper Missouri, the latter charging Kipp showed partiality in dealing with one of the captain's nephews, Jacques Bruguier. Another of Kipp's nephews was Joseph Desautel, trader at Fort Clark. A third nephew was Theophile Bruguier, whose fur-trading establishment was at the mouth of Big Sioux River, near the site of Sioux City.

Kipp was in charge at Fort Berthold in the summer of 1851 when he assisted Rudolph Friedrich Kurz, artist-explorer, in compiling a Mandan dictionary of some six hundred words.

Among the earliest forts on the river was Fort Mandan, where the Knife River joins the Missouri, built by

Lewis and Clark as their winter quarters in 1804-5. Another of the upper river's earlier outposts was Cedar Fort (Fort Recovery) on the west bank of the Missouri ten miles above the mouth of the White River. Fort Brasseaux was nearby. Another pioneer trading post on the Missouri was that kept by Joseph Bijou, whose real name was Bissonet. This was at the foot of the Bijou Hills, named for him. He had been with the Long expedition and was a well known frontier character. Eventually, the Indians got him.

Fort Pierre, one hundred eighty-five miles above Yankton, was occupied in 1832 and named for Pierre Chouteau, junior, leading member of Pratte, Chouteau & Company. A mile below, but on the east bank, Fort Tecumseh had been built by the Columbia Fur Company in 1822 and relinquished to the American Fur Company in 1827, the latter abandoning it for the newer Fort Pierre. William Laidlaw and Honore Picotte respectively served as superintendent at this post. Laidlaw was an able trader, but of quick irascible temper, and unpopular with his associates. He retired to a mansion near Liberty, Missouri. Picotte entered the Upper Missouri Outfit in1830 after earlier connections with the Columbia Fur Company and the French Fur Company. In 1851 he was in charge of the Lower Missouri Outfit, which included Forts Pierre, Lookout, Vermillion, Clark, and Berthold.

Joseph La Framboise, fur trader, had in 1817 built a trading post a mile below the site of Fort Tecumseh, naming it Fort La Framboise. This was directly opposite the mouth of the Teton or Little Missouri (Now called the Bad River).

Fort Pierre was for twenty years close to Fort Union as the chief fur-trading post of the upper Missouri country. The site was purchased in 1855 for a military reservation. It was abandoned in 1857 and became the site of Pierre, laid out in 1880.

Fort Union, opposite the mouth of the Yellowstone, was established in 1829 and served as a bastion of the fur trade for thirty-seven years. It became the greatest of trading posts within the boundaries of the United States, and a center of much commercial importance. Most powerful tribes congregated there to trade and voyageurs came from as far away as the Great Slave Lake, the Red River of the North, and the Rocky Mountains. North Dakota's first newspaper, the Frontier Scout, was published at Fort Union in 1864. For a number of years the factor at the fort was David Dawson Mitchell.

This handsome Virginian was also the factor at Fort McKenzie at one time. A great man in the fur trade, a stalwart of the American Fur Company, he later was to serve as an Indian agent and to become a distinguished lieutenant-colonel under General Sterling Price in the Second Missouri Cavalry and in General Doniphan's First Missouri in the Mexican War. His job at McKenzie was precarious and delicate, requiring poise, judgment, and nerve. Fort Mitchell, at the mouth of the Niobrara, built in 1833 by Narcisse Le Clerc and abandoned in 1837, was named for him.

Fort Lewis stood farthest up the river of all the American Fur Company's early trading posts. It was the successor to Fort Chardon, but on a different site. The latter had been built at the mouth of the Judith River about 1843. After a year, Alexander Culbertson moved it and named it for Meriwether Lewis. It was torn down and moved downstream where it was rebuilt and in 1850 named Fort Benton to honor Missouri's great senator, Thomas Hart Benton. Culbertson, after McKenzie the most important trader on the upper Missouri, entered the American Fur Company in 1829. In 1840 he succeeded McKenzie in command at Fort Union and in 1848 was in charge of all the upper Missouri and Yellowstone posts. His assistant at Fort Benton was Malcolm Clarke who went to the Northwest in 1841 and for many years was with the company at Fort Benton, where he was occasionally in charge. He was called Four Bears and was killed by Indians. Charles Larpenteur relieved Culbertson for a while and entertained Fathers Point and De Smet there in the autumn of 1846. He came from Baltimore but was a native of France. At twenty he went to St. Louis and signed up with the Rocky Mountain Fur Company. His Forty Years a Fur Trader on the Upper Missouri has become a classic on the subject.

In May of 1847 Culbertson closed the post, transferring it to a point about three miles below on the opposite bank of the river. The new place was called Fort Clay.

William Sublette, having with Robert Campbell formed a fur-trading company, went upriver in 1833 on the Otoe, under Captain James Hill. At the mouth of the Yellowstone he met Campbell, N.J. Wyeth, and others including his brother, Milton Sublette, called "the thunderbolt of the Rockies." On the north bank of the Yellowstone they built Fort William, honoring Sublette. This was about six miles below Fort Union. It was the purpose of this new firm to contend with the colossus of the fur trade, the American Fur Company, for control of the industry along the upper Missouri. This may have been a bluff. At any rate they sold out in 1842 to Fox, Livingstone & Company and the name of Fort William was changed to Fort Mortimer, with John Collins, a Kentuckian, in charge. This was the site later of Fort Buford.

Fort McKenzie was named for Kenneth McKenzie, called "King of the Missouri," whose headquarters were at Fort Union. Native of Scotland, he went to Canada at nineteen and worked for the North West Fur Company. In 1822 at St. Louis he organized the Columbia Fur Company. He built Fort Union. In later life, he retired to St. Louis where he became a wealthy importer of liquor.

John N. Ebbetts and F. Cutting built Fort George, about twenty-one miles below Fort Pierre, in 1842 for Fox, Livingstone & Company (the Union Fur Company). James Illingsworth, a young Englishman, was in charge. Chouteau & Company bought out this company in 1845.

In 1859 the Chouteaus contracted to carry annuity goods by steamboat to Fort Benton, and, although they did not reach the fort that year, they came close enough that thereafter steamboating to that point was regarded as feasible.

In 1866 Smith, Hubbell & Hawley purchased all interests of the American Fur Company in Fort Union and a decision was reached by that firm to abandon it. In that decision passed the last vestige of the commercial fur trade on the upper Missouri and an epoch was brought to a close.

Chapter Twenty-Eight

In Graves of Water and Sand

The Missouri River was notorious as a graveyard for steamboats. Its treacherous snags were the most prolific source of destruction, with fires, explosions and collisions accounting for by far the smaller number of steamboats that went down was set at two hundred and ninety-five by a government bulletin issued in 1897. This perhaps is as accurate as any of the estimates as to the number of steamboats that lie buried in graves of water and sand.

The first boat to sink was not the Jefferson, as so many have believed; and for the very good reason that it did not sink at all. It was reported in difficulties August 19, 1819, near the mouth of the Petit Bonne Femme, some thirty miles below Old Franklin. Jacob H. Holt as a boy of fifteen was on the R.M. Johnson, one of the boats of that expedition. He afterwards worked for the Johnson family in Kentucky, running on the Calhoun between Louisville and St. Louis. In a statement written in 1874 he said: "In 1823 I had charge the Johnson and the Jefferson, which were laid up at Shippingport."

W.L. Scott of Jefferson City reported in the Daily Tribune of October 12, 1875, that he saw in July 1819, "the second boat up the river" strike a snag and sink at the head of Hardeman's Island. Just what he meant by "second boat" is a matter of conjecture. If any boat had sunk, the

Missouri Intelligencer, published five miles away, should have had an item. But its old files disclose no such piece of news.

A similar story appeared in the Glasgow Journal for March 12, 1880 that said the John Golong No. 1 sank at the spot mentioned by Scott, but the year was 1821. The John Golong No.1 had not been built, although the John Golong No. 2 did sink at approximately the spot named. A boat did sink at that spot in 1820. The Intelligencer reported the Missouri Packet as having sunk after striking a snag. This probably was the first boat to sink in the Missouri River. The George Washington is listed as having gone down near the head of Hardeman Island in 1826.

A writer on river topics in the St. Louis Globe-Democrat in 1893 said: "The oldest wreck of which there is any knowledge, is that of the government steamer which sank in the early thirties at Arrow Rock Island, near Boonville." One may wonder as to what boat is being described, as he records do not indicated any as having sank in that stretch of water "in the early thirties." The Shoal Water sank at the Brick House Bend near the mouth of the Missouri in 1828 it is said; though both the place and the date are open to doubt.

In 1830, the General W.H. Ashley, of which Captain James Sweeney was owner and master, sank at the mouth of Femme Osage. The Car of Commerce, under Captain Reed, struck a snag at Musick's Ferry and sank May 8, 1832. The Liberty, owned and commanded by Captain J.M. Mousette, went down October 24, 1831, at the Brick House Bend. The Trenton sank a few miles below St. Charles, April 3, 1833. The Halcyon, under Captain Shepherd, sank at the Charbonnier Island, November 14, 1834.

The Assiniboine, an American Fur Company boat under Captain John Carlisle, burned at Sibley Island, in what now is North Dakota, on June 1, 1835. Another fur boat, the Diana, went down in the Diana Bend below Rocheport, and a third fur boat, the Chian, sank March 20, 1836, in the Euphrasie Bend. The veteran Captain John Shallcross commanded the Diana. The St. Charles burned at the Richmond Landing opposite Lexington, July 21.

In 1838 the Boonville hit a snag in the bend above the mouth of the Kaw and went down. The Elk sank five miles below Hermann. Captain Joseph La Barge came along on the Kansas and took the passengers off. The Howard sank at the mouth of the Auxvasse River. The following year the Camden struck a snag and sank at Patton's Point.

The steamboat Bedford struck a snag about a mile above the mouth of the Missouri on the evening of April 25, 1840. Five passengers and four Negro employees of the boat lost their lives. On the same day the Naomi sank at the mouth of the Grand River. The Euphrasie sank September 17, 1840, in the Euphrasie Bend, four miles below Glasgow. The John Hancock, a veteran boat, sank in 1840 at the Brick House Bend, and in that year the Little Red, named for Senator Barton, sank at Loutre Island, opposite Hermann. Captain McCord's Pocahontas No.1 sank a half-mile below Rock Bluff on August 11, 1840, while the Astoria, which went down opposite the mouth of the Blue River, completed that year's casualties.

Captain Joseph Throckmorton was the only unfortunate owner in 1841, his steamer Malta, which he had been running successfully on the upper Mississippi, sank in August at the bend which now bears its name. But 1842 was a devastating year for the steamboats.

In that year, the Bowling Green, owned by the wealthy St. Louis operator, John J. Roe, struck rocks at the head of the Osage Chute and sank December 12, while the Corvette sank twelve miles below Eureka Landing. When the boiler of the Edna burst at Green Island in the mouth of the Missouri July 3, about fifty-five German immigrants are said to have lost their lives. The boat was owned by Captain McCord of McCord's Landing (later East Leavenworth) and named for one of his daughters. The Emilie No.1, belonging to P. Chouteau & Company, under Captain Keiser, sank at Emilie Bend. The Lynchburg sank at Pittman's Bend, near the mouth of the Osage, March 27, the passengers being taken off by the steamer Thomas. The Pirate went down three miles below Belvue, in what is now

Nebraska. The following year was easier; the two casualties being the General Brady, under Captain J. Gunsaullis, which sank opposite Hermann, and Captain Littleton's Weston, which burned at St. Charles Island.

There were no sinkings reported in 1844, but the year 1845 came in for a full share. The most spectacular accident of the decade was the explosion of the Big Hatchie, as it left the landing at Hermann on the night of July 25. A number of passengers were killed, but the boat itself was floated to St. Louis for repairs. The Columbian sank September 27 at Lexington Bar. The Lexington, under the popular Captain William Littleton, sank in September at Frankfort, but was raised, and the Little Mail was lost at Mount Vernon. Sinkings increased in the following year.

An interesting case, giving rise to many legends, was the burning of the Boreas No.2, a new boat, at Hermann. It had on board a large amount of silver bullion and Mexican money, and many stories have been told to the effect that the boat was set on fire and the money stolen. The Haidee went down at Mount Vernon, just above the mouth of the Saline River, and the John Golong No.1 sank at the Malta Bend. The Radnor, Captain J.T. Douglas, sank just above the mouth of the La Mine River and the Wakendah, under Captain J.M. Converse, struck the chain of rocks at Sibley, April 2, and sank across the stream at the mouth of Fishing River. The Warsaw, while towing the Lexington in March, struck a snag and sank at the Lower Bonhomme Island.

The St. Louis Oak, Captain Jim Dozier, sank in 1847 at the head of Howard's Bend. The next year the Tamerlane sank at the foot of Wakendah Prairie; the Balloon, Captain John McCloy, owner and master, struck a snag and sank below Augusta; the Louis F. Linn went down at the head of St. Charles Island. Captain W.C. "Dandy" Jewett commanded it. A decade of sinkings was rounded out by the Algoma, a tramp, which ran on the rocks and sank a mile below Lexington, and the Julia, Captain Keiser"s boat, which sank at Bellefontaine Bend.

Rather prosaically, the Parkville Democrat of September 19, 1856 noted that; "On last Friday evening, just before nightfall, the Missouri River passenger steamer Arabia, while in sight and nearing our city, struck a snag. This perforated her hull in such a manner that she sank in the short space of ten minutes in twelve feet of water. No lives were lost, but the boat and cargo, which was a large one, bound for points above and Council Bluffs, is a total loss. Water now is running over her hurricane deck in one or two places where the vessel has broken in two."

The Arabia was reputed to have on board four hundred and eight barrels of fine aged whisky and "a considerable amount of gold." One Robert Treadway noted the location of the wreck and for more than a score of years noted the changing currents and curving channels of the river, believing he could immediately put his hands on the treasure-trove when the statute of limitations had run. Having interested the Toebner brothers, tobacco merchants of Kansas City, they set to work in 1877 with pump and derrick to unearth the treasure which it was estimated would be worth seventy thousand dollars after all expenses had been paid. But all they recovered was a cargo of old wool hats! Finally, in the fall of 1988, and old river map helped lead the way to the lost treasure. Over time the river's course moved, leaving the Arabia and her treasure buried 45 feet deep beneath a Kansas cornfield...... one half mile from the river's edge.

According to Kenneth Weyand, Editor of Explore Kansas City, "The recovery team of River Salvage, Inc. (the Hawley family) based in Independence, Missouri used modern drilling and testing equipment to pinpoint the steamer's location. For weeks, the team dug into the bottom-land, using a series of pumps to hold back the ground water. The team first discovered the coffer dam erected by the 1897 salvagers. More weeks went by, the team uncovered a single weathered plank, later identified as one of the spokes of the sidewheeler's left paddle wheel.

The first genuine artifact uncovered was a rubber overshoe, still bearing the Goodyear Shoe Company's patent for the year 1844. After tons of sand were removed from the excavation, both paddle wheels began to take shape, and then the giant steel boilers. As more sand was removed, the team was able to walk about on the steamer's deck, then map it. Then they excitedly went to work removing artifacts of all description..... barrels of fine china, door knobs and locks, saw blades, weight scales, wagon parts, sacks of buckshot, flintlock rifles, hand-made boots and shoes, clay pipes, tobacco, spectacles, mirrors, and thousands of other items. The recovered artifacts were taken to a laboratory facility in Independence where the storage and reconstruction process was begun.

As the recovery team worked, they discovered the Arabia's sinking had caused one fatality. The skeleton of a horse was found, fully saddled and bridled. Old newspaper accounts had quoted the owner, a carpenter, as saying he had tried to free the animal, but it had refused to leave the steamer. The evidence proved otherwise: the horse was still tied to a heavy wood-press. The recovery team named the horse 'Lawrence' (of Arabia).

Unlike the Bertrand, major parts of the Arabia were salvaged and restored: the paddle wheel structure, engine and boilers, and the stern section of the boat, including the steering rudder. Along with the artifacts, they have been assembled for public display in a museum located in the City Market area of Kansas City, Missouri."

In September 1859, the Ogden, Captain Hamilton Lee, owner and master, struck a snag and sank at the Claysville bend, a few miles above Jefferson City. Captain Jim Bissell was in charge. This boat, too, was reputed to have had on board a considerable cargo of old whisky and a "large amount of gold." It was impossible to recover any of the cargo and in time the location of the boat was lost.

Ten years later, a boat whose name is not learned sank at the Murray Bend near Claysville. It was said to have had five hundred barrels of whisky in its cargo. Only the pilot-house of the boat remained in sight after the wreck, and it was torn away and the doors and windows used by a near-by resident in the construction of a house. A few years later an unsuccessful effort was made to recover the cargo of this boat.

According to the River Column of the St. Louis Globe in 1863: "The John Golong sank near the mouth of the La Mine River loaded with whisky – she had three hundred barrels in freight – and agricultural implements for upriver parts. There also was the sum of sixty-two thousand dollars in specie on the Golong, which was to be taken to Leavenworth for the payment of troops on the border. Captain Jim Lanphier was drowned when the Golong went down. As had been his custom in similar trying cases, he remained on his boat to the last. As he was preparing to leave, the Golong suddenly settled on her side, and a rolling barrel knocked Lanphier through the gangway into the river."

A writer in the Chicago Times of September 7, 1894, reminisced further of the wreck of the Golong: "The channel is a mile away and the young cottonwoods grow where thirty years ago were five fathoms of the yellowest and most uncertain current that ever drove pilots to drink and converted roustabouts into food for catfish. The Golong was not raised. The sands settled around her and about her – and over her. After the war when quiet came, a small flat came, and no man was able to locate the place of the wreck. It might be here and it might be there. The honest Missourian would contemplate the spot and become sad. Three hundred barrels of good drinking whisky buried in the sand! Fifteen thousand gallons of the necessities of life perished from off the face of the earth! But as the years wore on, the Golong became a regret, a sad memory only."

One of the best known of the lost vessels was the Twilight, which sank in September 1865, near Sibley, opposite the mouth of the Fishing River. It had left the channel in the fog and struck a submerged sycamore tree. The boat went down, leaving the pilothouse and the texas above the water. The passengers escaped to the shore and were cared for by farmers. The boat was heavily loaded, having three hundred barrels of whisky in addition to oil, white lead, pig iron, stoves, stamp mills and engines. For several years, during low water, parts of the boat remained in sight, and numerous attempts were made to recover a portion of its cargo. As the years rolled on, according to the Lexington Intelligencer of November 22, 1895, the steamer became buried in sand, and after the flood of 1881, it was estimated the Twilight was beneath thirty-nine feet of silt and was half a mile from shore at low water. In 1895 a company was formed in Kansas City to probe for the hulk. Workers probed with long steel rods and after days of work, one of the rods located the old engine of the Twilight. Several bottles of "Old London Gin, 1860," were the total of the treasure recovered however. "The bottles are square-faced, of dark green glass, and hold an honest quart. It was the old London 'square face' that Dickens wrote about and smacked his lips over."

The foregoing list may well be incomplete, so many disasters having faded into shadow and passed from the memory of man, their stories having become folk tales seldom told.

And so they lay, the proud river beauties, only at times of low water giving glimpses that roused romantic nostalgia; others, unseen, whose legendary manifest of gold, whisky, or other treasure, aroused the cupidity of men for generations. Now even the generation that forgot them has been forgotten, and there remains nothing but a faint tradition of romance and treasure-trove.

Courtesy ARABIA MUSEUM, K. C. MO.

Just a portion of the vast amount salvaged from the Arabia.
Courtesy ARABIA MUSEUM, K. C. MO.

The Arabia was buried 45 feet deep beneath a Kansas cornfield…one half mile from the river's edge. *Courtesy ARABIA MUSEUM, K. C. MO.*

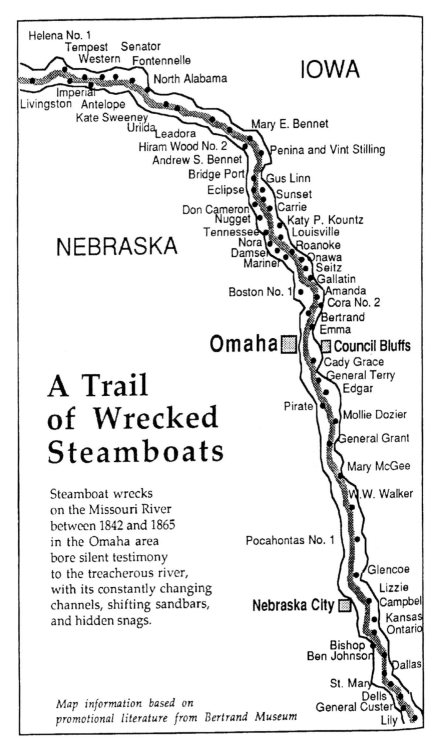

Helena No. 1
Tempest   Senator
Western   Fontennelle
IOWA
North Alabama
Imperial
Livingston   Antelope
Kate Sweeney
Urilda
Leadora
Mary E. Bennet
Hiram Wood No. 2
Penina and Vint Stilling
Andrew S. Bennet
Bridge Port
Gus Linn
Eclipse
Sunset
Don Cameron
Carrie
NEBRASKA
Nugget
Katy P. Kountz
Tennessee
Louisville
Nora
Roanoke
Damsel
Onawa
Mariner
Seitz
Gallatin
Boston No. 1
Amanda
Cora No. 2
Bertrand
Emma
Omaha
Council Bluffs
Cady Grace
General Terry
Edgar
Pirate
Mollie Dozier
General Grant
Mary McGee
W.W. Walker
Pocahontas No. 1
Glencoe
Lizzie
Campbel
Nebraska City
Kansas
Ontario
Bishop
Ben Johnson
Dallas
St. Mary
Dells
General Custer
Lily

A Trail of Wrecked Steamboats

Steamboat wrecks
on the Missouri River
between 1842 and 1865
in the Omaha area
bore silent testimony
to the treacherous river,
with its constantly changing
channels, shifting sandbars,
and hidden snags.

*Map information based on
promotional literature from Bertrand Museum*

Chapter Twenty-Nine

Fort Benton, Top of the River

Farming succeeded furs on the upper Missouri River, but before this could be brought about there were to be sanguinary years given over to a test of strength between the military forces and those Indians who claimed the land by right of heredity and tradition. A number of forts were established along the river to serve as bases for the soldiers and the latter proved to be the forerunners of the settlers who were ever eager to press forward into new areas as soon as, or even before, they appeared safe from Indian attack.

Dakota's first settlement in the Missouri Valley was at Yankton, sixty miles above Sioux City. A trading post had been established there as early as 1838 and the town was laid out in 1850. Dr. William Jayne of Indiana, who had been appointed territorial governor, named it. The Weekly Dakotian was established the same year by Frank M. Ziebach, who sold it the next year to J.C. Trask, first public printer.

When Dakota's first legislature assembled at Yankton it was made up in part of such colorful characters as Jim Somers, daredevil frontiersman from Chamberlain, "armed like an arsenal," who was appointed sergeant-at-arms. Men like John W. "Father" Turner of New York; George W. Kingsbury, newspaperman, who for many years published the Press and Dakotian at Yankton; Dr. Walter Burleigh, and General T.C. Campbell.

At the 1863 session, after Newton Edmunds of Yankton had been appointed territorial governor, there was a rift in the state assembly during which one house met on the levee by the Missouri River while the other held its sessions on a hill above the river. However, the differences were patched up, and the legislature proceeded with its business.

Fort Randall, situated just above where the south boundary of South Dakota touches the west bank of the Missouri, became first of a line of military forts. These included Crow Creek (Fort Thompson), Fort Sully, Fort Rice, Fort Stephenson, Fort Buford, Fort Hawley, and Camp Cooke, the latter near the mouth of the Judith River in Montana.

All these forts were meant to defend the frontier settlements from hostile Indians. Most of them were at one time or another subjected to Indian attacks. Fort Sully, four miles below the site of Pierre, was established in 1862 by General Alfred H. Sully, succeeding Fort Randall as the most advanced post in the valley.

Steamboats assigned to carry supplies for his expedition of 1864 included the Marcella, Captain Sousley, the Sam Gaty, Captain Silver, the Chippewa Falls, Captain Hutchinson, the General Grant, Captain Packard, the Isabelle, Captain Dozier, the Alone, Captain Rea, the Island City, Captain Lamont, and the Tempest.

Fort Rice, on the west bank of the Missouri, above the Cannonball River, was established by General Sully in 1864 and garrisoned by the First United States Volunteers. Its members were called "galvanized Yankees" for the reason that they were captured Confederate soldiers who had been given a choice of fighting Indians on the frontier. It was to this fort that General Sully brought a caravan of Minnesotans, which, under the leadership of Captain James L. Fiske, had been heading for the Montana gold fields when set upon by the Sioux. It was also here that the soldiers published North Dakota's Second newspaper, the

Pioneer Scout, in 1865. Fort Rice was dismantled in 1875.

General George A. Custer's Seventh Cavalry had been stationed at Fort Rice and Fort Abraham Lincoln during the winter of 1875-6. It was from Fort Abraham Lincoln that Custer's troops marched away on May 17, 1876, to the strains of "Garryowen," bound, eventually, for the Little Big Horn and a rendezvous with destiny that was to bring them undying glory. Fort Abraham Lincoln was the successor of Fort McKeen, which had been built on the site in 1872.

Fort Buford, on the north bank of the Missouri River, opposite the mouth of the Yellowstone, was established in 1866, having been named for General John Buford.

Chief Joseph of the Nez Perces was there in 1877, a prisoner on the way to Leavenworth. It was there Chief Sitting Bull surrendered after coming down out of Canada with one hundred eighty-seven men, women, and children, a remnant of the once proud Sioux race. He was taken to Fort Randall to spend the winter and then on the W.J. Behen to Fort Yates where he was transferred to the Standing Rock reservation.

Bartholomew Berthold traded in the river country for many years and established a trading post in 1845. Sully's men were there twenty years later when the place was turned into a fort and named for Berthold. It was abandoned in 1867 to be replaced by Fort Stephenson, twelve miles east.

Persons going up or down the river frequently were subjected to attack by the Indians. The pilothouse of every steamboat was sheathed with boiler iron as protection against their bullets. In 1863 tribesmen, angered at what they considered an arrogantly unfair distribution of their annuity goods at Fort Pierre, followed the Robert Campbell, of which Joseph La Barge was captain, six hundred miles upstream, harassing it all the way. Near the mouth of Tobacco Garden Creek, a concerted attack was made in which three of the boat's crew and eighteen Indians were killed.

Gold, that most potent magnet to the adventurers of

all times and lands, had been found in Montana and a ceaseless stream of emigrants was being poured into the area.

The greater profits to be derived from the "mountain trade" caused the owners of many deep-draft steamboats to enter the trade, though shoal water and impediments of the upper river were ill suited to that type of boat. It usually was a two-month trip from St. Louis to Fort Benton and only one round-trip was permitted the larger boats, though some of the smaller ones were able to make two trips in a season. With cargoes often amounting to hundreds of thousands of dollars, officers and owners of all river craft found the lure difficult to resist. Freight was piled high and every boat was jammed with passengers.

Many of the prospective miners came by boat up the Missouri River to various points of debarkation where they purchased supplies and employed means of transportation varying from handcarts and wheelbarrows to ox teams for the overland journey. The importance of this river highway to the gold mines was enhanced in 1866 by the closing of the Bozeman Trail in Wyoming that had carried many gold seekers. The impetus given to river traffic by the discovery of gold in Montana is well illustrated by the increase in the number of steamboat arrivals in the vicinity of Fort Benton. Out of a total of one hundred fifty arrivals in the decade of 1860-70, all except twelve are recorded for the last five years. The years 1866-1869 marked the high tide of Missouri River traffic with thirty-one arrivals at Fort Benton in 1866, thirty-nine in 1867, twenty-eight in 1868 and twenty-four in 1869. In 1865, a thousand passengers arrived at Fort Benton by steamboat. In 1867 the number of passengers had increased to ten thousand.

The veteran Captain Abe Wolf was able to take his heavy-draft Marion through to Fort Benton, but in returning downstream his boat became stranded at Pablo Rapids.

Captain Jim Moore was unable to reach Fort Benton, but arrived at the mouth of the Marias River with his stern-wheeler, the Cutler, on July 14, 1864. She was loaded with miners and passengers whose destination were the gold fields of Montana. They were compelled to proceed over-land the twelve miles to Fort Benton. It would have been thirty miles by the tortuous river. Captain Moore conceived the idea of building a town at the mouth of the Marias, at least a day nearer the gold fields, which should rival or even surpass Fort Benton. Going to Virginia City, he got a score of men to return with him to Ophir, as he had named his embryo seat of commerce. He was quick to point out that it was only two hundred and forty miles from Virginia City, "with a good road passing through Prickly Pear and Last Chance Gulch." However, the hostile and ever-watch-ful Indians attacked the party and killed eleven men. The project was abandoned.

Not all the steamboats plying the perilous upper Missouri made it safely through. The Kate Swinney sank at Kate Swinney Bend, between Vermillion and Elk Point, in 1865, when she was returning from St. Louis to Fort Benton; the Urilda at the same bend, 1869. The Peoria Belle sank in 1864, five miles above the mouth of the Cheyenne. Others lost included; The Pocohontas No. 2 at Pocohontas Island in 1866; the Imperial at Bon Homme Island, 1867, and the Antelope burned at the same island two years later. The North Alabama sank near Vermillion, 1870; the Ida Reese, south of the White River, 1871; the Western, the General Meade, the Mollie Moore, and the Minnie Harmon.

In 1862, La Barge, Harkness & Company was formed in St. Louis to trade on the upper Missouri River. The part-ners were Eugene Jaccard, James Harkness, Joseph La Barge and John La Barge, and William Galpin. They acquired the steamboats, the Shreveport and the Emilie. The latter, named for Captain La Barge's daughter, was a side-wheeler, an exceptionally beautiful craft which had the honor in 1859 of carrying Abraham Lincoln. Nicholas Wall was in charge of the Emilie upstream in 1862. He later became co-owner with John J. Roe of the Diamond R, largest freighting outfit in Montana.

By 1872 the Northern Pacific Railroad had reached the Missouri River at Bismarck, which at first was called

Edwinton. It was a long row of shanties and tents on the street facing the railroad track, most of them saloons and gambling resorts. Bismarck, or Edwinton, was wide-awake and wicked, as rough and disreputable a community as could be found in the Northwest. In a few years it became headquarters for parties going by stage to the Black Hills gold fields. Colonel Clement A. Lounsberry on July 6, 1873 established the Bismarck Tribune, the first issue containing an advertisement from every business establishment in town. In the fall of that year it was forced to print on wall-paper, due to snow blockade. The editor frequently heard gunshots.

When the "Dakota boom" began in 1878, settlers came by the thousands, filled the river bottoms and pushed out across the plains. In Bismarck, all was bustle and excite-ment; the streets jammed with homesteaders and wagons loaded with immigrants' goods. Every stage going west was filled with adventurers going to the gold fields of Deadwood; and all roads leading to that land of opportu-nity were filled with lumbering freight wagons and resounding to the profane shouts of the bullwhackers. By 1880, Bismarck had a population of nearly two thousand, with its chief hostelries being the Sheridan House, the Custer Hotel, and the Merchants Hotel. But the boom the railroad was bringing was a railroad boom and spelled fur-ther decline for the steamboat trade.

Fort Benton, at the top of the river, was a crude little frontier town, a lusty, brawling river town, with adobe and log huts scattered along its single street. A row of disrep-utable saloons or hurdy-gurdy houses stood, boisterous and wicked...a squaw town, a scalp market, home of horsethieves and cutthroats. In the 1860s it had men who knew every river and stream between the Missouri and the South Saskatchewan; a restless population from along the Missouri River made up of gold seekers and free traders gathered to invade the last frontier.

With the advent of the gold seekers, the town became the commercial center of a widespread trading area, but still a place where all and sundry, out at night, were told to mind their own business and walk in the middle of the street.

Montana's territorial governor, a soldier of fortune, came to Fort Benton one day intent on a downriver errand. He had been feuding with the vigilantes of the gold camps. Boarding a steamboat that was scheduled to leave the next morning, the governor disappeared and never was seen again. Foul play was hinted, but the mystery has never been solved.

To Fort Benton's mile-long levee came supplies for an inland empire. It was the trade center from which the supplies went out over the Whoop-Up Trail to Fort McLeod in Saskatchewan and over the Mullan Road to the gold diggings of Montana and Idaho.

The town's merchant princes were Isaac G. Baker, Thomas C. Power, and William C. Conrad. Power organized the Fort Benton Transportation Company, the famous Benton "Block P" Line, whose little steamers, the Helena, Butte, Benton, and Black Hills, were familiar names on the upper river. Baker, too, was interested in steamboats, but the interest died with the sinking of the Red Cloud in 1882.

When the Great Northern and the Canadian Pacific built west, the fortunes of Fort Benton began to recede. Steamboating on the Missouri as a way of life faded as a dream. Only a few boats remained, perhaps carrying coal or other commodities between railroad points on the river. The Benton Packet Company owned the Washburn, the Expansion, the Bismarck, the Weston, and the Imelda. But the rich rewards, the romance, and the high adventure had gone out of steamboating, never to return.

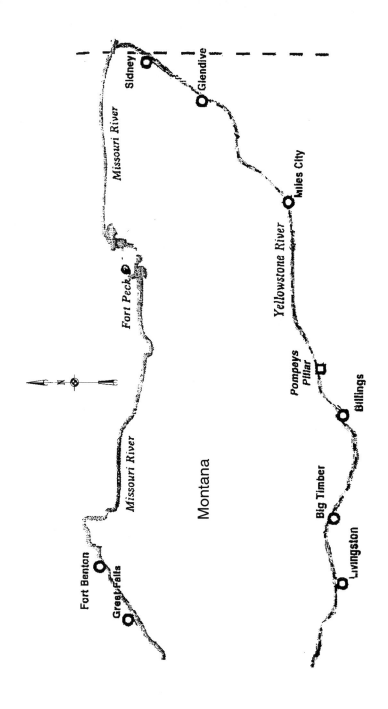

Chapter Thirty

The River's
Old Ghost Towns

From the chronological point of view, Charette was the first ghost town of the Missouri River. Located not far from the present town of Washington, it was the last settlement passed by Lewis and Clark as they ascended the river in 1804, being then only a huddle of huts established but a few years. In a few more years, some say by 1811, it had passed out of existence. But, geographically, none could be ahead of the "city of Missouri," in which town lots were advertised in the Missouri Gazette of January 16, 1818, by Abraham and William Musick as "at the junction of the Missouri and Mississippi rivers."

Daniel Boone was advertising in the February 13 issue of the Gazette lots for sale in "the town of Missouri, twenty-five miles above St. Charles in the heart of the Femme Osage settlement." And he was describing it as "the most convenient point on the Missouri River for a great proportion of the inhabitants of St. Charles County." It was more than a year later that lots in Missouriton were offered for sale by H. Carroll and Robert Wallace promoters. This town was far up the Missouri, on the north bank, "equally distant from Grand River and Crooked River Bluff, in the Sugar Tree Bottoms."

A traveler up the river in 1839 mentioned the town of Cavern Rock, twelve miles above St. Charles, and an unnamed town adjoining it; also the town of Formosa, situated at the mouth of the Osage, and New Baltimore, a sign, a few miles below Dover Landing.

No other town on the river, among those destined to become ghost towns, had the heart to live and become great as did Cote sans Dessein, however it might have been matched in ambition or physical vigor. But even in 1860, while in one paragraph the local newspaper was boasting of the town's physical progress, there was in another paragraph a note of decadence; "Where is there one who has ever visited this beautiful and picturesque place that has not left it with regret? Still, in its desolation, it possesses unrivaled charms. It was first settled by a company of French immigrants, attracted no doubt by its romantic situation and its easy access to the neighboring cities and towns. It stands on an eminent tract on the north bank of the mighty Missouri, and commands a fine view of the surrounding forest, lofty hills and the many steamers with which the river is thronged. The French, who so appropriately named it 'a hill without design,' have deserted it; almost entirely nothing remains of them save the inanimate forms of those who are quietly resting in the silent city of the dead. In 1889 it was written; "Cote sans Dessein now consists of a post office and general merchandising store, a blacksmith shop and three or four scattering houses. It is about two or three miles below Barkersville."

Other ghost towns between the mouth of the Missouri River and Old Franklin were Nashville, Pinckney, and Griswold City. Among the later ghost towns was Brotherton, opposite St. Charles, which had disappeared by 1883, the ground gone into the channel of the Big Muddy.

Old Franklin was the most important town on the Missouri River to become a ghost town and this despite the fact that the span of its life was not more than fifteen years. From its founding, in 1816, it was the head of the Boone's Lick Trail and population poured into it. It was the mecca of all the emigrants from the old Southwest and for many from the Old Northwest. It was the birthplace of the Santa

Fe Trail and on the receiving end of the vast stores of wealth brought into this country in exchange for the goods carried out over the deserts by the intrepid Santa Fe traders. From the very beginning of steamboat transportation, it was an important steamboat town, receiving and sending great cargoes of merchandise and produce until the river swallowed up Old Franklin and compelled the citizens to move to New Franklin on higher ground.

Soon after its founding, Franklin was experiencing a boom. It teemed with activity and was thronged with men, eyes bright with eagerness to be out and along the high road to adventure and perhaps to wealth. Major Elijah Iles, employed in the land office, said lots were as valuable in Franklin as they were in St. Louis. On one occasion he kept more than one hundred thousand dollars in the barrel that served as his "safe." Citizens of this "first American town in Missouri" included such men as Hamilton R. Gamble, Abiel Leonard, Lilburn W. Boggs, Benjamin Reeves, Claiborne F. Jackson, John F. Ryland, Duff Green, Ben Holladay and David Todd. The town had its Masonic lodge, academies for boys and girls, tobacco warehouses and factory, two schools, a public library, three taverns, five stores, a carding mill, a fire company, a company of militia, a rope walk and a cordage factory. The Franklin Dragoons met at the home of William V. Rector. William L. Scott kept a nail factory near Ludlow's mill. John J. Lowery, one of the town's early doctors, was librarian of the Franklin Library Company. John Mines kept a blacksmith-plumber-mechanic shop and J.B. Bolton opened a barbershop in Messrs. Ward & Parker's house.

Above Old Franklin, the town of Chariton had been a place of importance; having been founded two years before the first steamboat ascended the river. It died a lingering death after most of its business houses and residents removed to the newer town of Glasgow, two miles downriver, which had been laid out in 1836. Still farther up were Victoria, Grand River City, Doyleston, and towns leaving little impress. Carroll City had only a brief existence. Alderson was an early town located near the river.

Winsor City did not become a ghost town, but changed its name to De Witt and by that name still exists. Near it were Miles Point, Coloma, San Francisco and Hill's Landing, all now vanished.

Mount Vernon, a sprightly place, was first county seat of Lillard County, the name of the county being changed to Lafayette in 1826. County court was held in Adam Lightner's tavern. When the county seat was removed to the newer town of Lexington in 1822, Mount Vernon began to go downhill. In 1899, the Independence Progress reported; "Sixty years ago, at the mouth of Tabo River, Mount Vernon lay at the foot of the bluff and watched the stately river steamboats glide on their journeys to the sea. There the pioneers held county court in the old convivial days and dealt out justice in a slow but effective manner. But now weeds and woods have obliterated every mark of habitation, and reptiles crawl undisturbed down the streets. Only a short distance east of this point lie the landmarks of Berlin, a town which General Joe Shelby and his brothers-in-law built, but now it, too, is mouldered into ruin."

Across the river, on the north bank, and up a few miles, Bluffton had been established even before Mount Vernon came into existence. As farthest west town on the river, it was important for a few years, but seemed to have succumbed to three-way pressure of competition from the energetic towns of Lexington, Richmond and Liberty. The little town of Gallatin was on the Missouri River, about three or four miles from the new inland town of Liberty. It was there but not thriving in 1823, but history throws no light on its beginning or its demise.

To the west a few miles, Randolph Bluffs became neither a big town nor an important town, and its passing is without note. The next ghost town was the short-lived Winston, neighbor in 1840 to the new town of Parkville. But it soon disappeared or became part of Parkville. On a site across the river, one of the more important towns sprang up.

This was Quindaro, which had an interesting history

from 1857 until the outbreak of the Civil War. Abelard Guthrie was the moving spirit in founding this town and New Englanders made up the greater part of its inhabitants. When the war came on, most of the men joined the Union army and sent their wives and children back to their old homes in the East. Business stood still and then declined. The boom was over. Through four years of war grass grew in the streets; some of the buildings were torn down, others collapsed from neglect. Vines and shrubbery spread over its crumbling walls and its once busy thoroughfare became covered with brush and trees and foliage.

When the Rev. Pardee Butler was given a coat of tar and feathers by an Atchison mob and set afloat on the Missouri River amid great eclat, he had only three miles to float until the sympathetic citizens of the thriving town of Sumner rescued him. He lifted up his hands and blessed the town and prophesied it would wax fat when the "upper landing" as some called Atchison, would sleep in a dishonored and forgotten grave. Samuel Hollister had built a hotel building, costing sixteen thousand dollars. But Atchison waxed fat and Sumner is forgotten.

Charleston, Lafayette and Port Williams were Kansas towns founded in the 1850s. Charleston had a fair degree of prosperity and Lafayette in 1856 had a number of stores and a sawmill, the latter turning out "Kansas mahogany" as cottonwood lumber was called. The town disappeared about 1870.

Above St. Joseph were such ghost towns as Nodaway City, Jimtown, two miles above St. Joseph. Sonora, Elizabethtown, Boston, Forest City, Scott City, Kalamazoo, El Paso and Sacramento City were other ghost towns in that stretch of the river.

Moving on north, into Nebraska, St. Stephen was near the mouth of Muddy Creek, in the vicinity of the present Falls City. As early as 1849, Otoe City, six miles south of the present Nebraska City, was an important crossing for emigrants to Utah and California, and in 1857, Gideon Bennett established a steam ferry there.

A number of towns that were platted in Southeast

Nebraska in the mid-fifties at the time of the state's being thrown open to settlement, soon became ghost towns and the dwindling value of their town lots was made the subject of good natured chaffering. It was said that ten shares of the Hamilton townsite had been traded for a brass watch and a little black dog. Powhocco shares, on the other hand, were "quoted" at twenty for an old blind horse and two Peter Funk watches. Fairview was slipping badly, for thirty-six shares brought only a gilt watch chain and ten cents cash. Fredonia shares were twenty for a pewter watch and a pair of boots. Brownville, the only town in the group left today, was donating town lots, according to its rivals, "to any man who wore store clothes."

Cuming City, established in 1857, was an important town, with a newspaper, the Nebraska Pioneer, fifty-three dwelling houses, three stores, three hotels, several boarding houses and a number of saloons. Hiawatha, a town on the riverbank just east of Cuming City, was washed away.

The original town of La Platte was situated directly on the Missouri River between the Platte River and Papillon Creek. In 1856, the site was abandoned for higher ground. A new town, to the west, was platted and called Larimer, to honor General William Larimer, one of its founders. However, La Platte, which he also founded, was his main hope. Larimer had been a wealthy man in Pennsylvania, but had gone broke. He went to Council Bluffs and became a town promoter. In 1858 he was one of the principal founders of Denver.

Between Larimer and the Missouri River a new town named Platona was platted by Daniel Gantt, who built a hotel. It is now a ghost town, as is Triaqua, east of Platona. The present La Platte takes in part of the original Larimer. Other towns, now ghost towns, in that vicinity were Marietta, Groveland, Brooklyn, Wyoming, Osage, Cleveland, Liberty, Kanosha, Bluffdale, Rock Bluff, Williamsport, Woodland, Wheatland, Summit City, Pacific City, Oreapolis, Douglas and Bethlehem.

On the northern border of Mills County, Iowa, in 1853, there sprang up the town of St. Mary's, its nucleus a steamboat landing a few miles below Trader's Point. At one time St. Mary's had a population of two thousand and was considered a rival to Council Bluffs. It had a newspaper, the Gazette, of which C. Sexton was editor, the proprietor being P.A. Sarpy, who had been an important employee of one of the fur companies. By 1868 the river had taken the town and nothing remained.

Almost invariably, the river was the prime reason for these towns springing into existence. And when the river left them, or the commerce which the river carried, they passed out of existence. The dreams and ambitions which stirred the hearts of men and women who founded these towns and gave them animation long since have settled into dust. Their romances lie in oblivion along the riverbanks. Their bright, gay dreams, that once were the warp and the woof of Missouri River history, have vanished. Their history has been forgotten and even the fact that they or their towns ever existed to most persons is unknown. It might have been of such men and women and their works that the poet was thinking when he wrote;

So fleet the works of men
Back to the earth again,
Ancient and holy things
Fade like a dream;
And the hand of the master is dust.

Notes Toward a Bibliography

There is no single book adequately covering the whole story of the Missouri River, so many writers having been concerned with special themes, and one seeking to survey the field will be dismayed by the paucity of material readily available. Though a number of books have touched upon a single facet of its varied history, the river's real story has remained hidden away in old newspapers and files of historical societies. A great deal of reliance has here been placed on the publications of historical societies of states contiguous to the river, such as the Missouri Historical Society, St. Louis; the State Historical Society of Missouri, Columbia; the Kansas State Historical Society, Topeka; the Nebraska State Historical Society, Lincoln; the Iowa State Historical Society, Iowa City; the South Dakota State Historical Society, Pierre; the State Historical Society of North Dakota, Bismarck; and the Historical Society of Montana, Helena.

A primary source has been the county histories of all counties bordering the Missouri River; those heavy tomes sometimes called "mug books" because of their biographical features. They have information about the river towns and riverains not to be found elsewhere.

Old newspapers have yielded many nuggets; especially those published in St. Louis, Jefferson City, Boonville, Glasgow, Lexington, Liberty, St. Joseph, and Council Bluffs.

A card index file of old steamboats, approximately a thousand, was most kindly lent me by James Anderson, historian of the Native Sons of Kansas City, and has been a source of much information.

It virtually would be impossible to give local citations for the thousands of items that have been used wholly or in part, condensed, paraphrased, or fused.

The following list of books should be of help and interest to anyone desiring to read more about the Missouri River.

Bell, Ovid. Cote sans Dessein. Fulton, Mo., 1930. A history.

Brackenridge, Henry Marie. Views of Louisiana. Pittsburgh, 1814

Brower, Jacob Bradenburg. The Missouri River and Its Utmost Source. St. Paul, 1897. A curtailed narrative of geologic primitive and geographic distinctions descriptive of the evolution and discovery of the river and its headwaters.

Bruff, J. Goldsborough. Gold Rush: The Journals, Drawings, and Other Papers of, April 2, 1849-July 20, 1851. Edited by Georgia Willis Read and Ruth Gaines. New York, 1944.

Chappell, Philip Edward. A History of the Missouri River. Kansas City? 1911. Discovery of the river by the Jesuit explorers; Indian tribes along the river; early navigation and craft used; the rise and fall of steamboating.

Chittenden, Hiram Martin. List of Steamboat Wrecks on the Missouri River from the Beginning of Navigation to the Present Time. Government Printing Office, Washington, 1897.

――. History of Early Steamboat Navigation on the Missouri River; Life and Adventures of Captain Joseph LaBarge. New York, 1903.

――. The American Fur Trade of the Far West. (New edition) New York, 1935.

――. Life, Letters and Travels of Father Pierre-Jean De Smet, S.J., New York, 1905.

Deatherage, Charles P., Steamboating on the Missouri River in the Sixties. Kansas City, 1924.

DeVoto, Bernard. Across the Wide Missouri. Boston, 1947. A popular history, touching the upper Missouri's early days.

Dick, Everett Newfon. Vanguards of the Frontier. New York, 1941. A social history of the northern plains and Rocky Mountains form the earliest white contacts to the coming of the homemakers.

Dorrance, W.A. Where the Rivers Meet. 1939.

Drumm, Stella M., editor. Journal of a Fur-Trading Expedition on the Upper Missouri, 1812-1813 (Journal of John C. Luttig). St. Louis, 1920.

Floyd, Charles. The New Found Journal of. Worcester, 1894. From May 14 to August 17, 1804. Sergeant Floyd was with Lewis and Clark and died near the site of Sioux City.

Freeman, Lewis Ransome. Waterways of Westward Wandering. New York, 1927. Small-boat voyages.

Gardiner, Dorothy. West of the River. New York, 1941. The biography of the Missouri and the history of the vast country to the west of it.

Garraghan, Gilbert J. The Jesuits of the Middle United States. New York, 1938. The authentic story of the Society of Jesus in a part of the country touched by the Missouri River. Something of the fur men on the upper river and occasional glimpses of places and river towns where Jesuits carried
on their work.

Gass, Patrick. Journal of Lewis and Clark Expedition. Pittsburgh, 1807.

Gregg, Dr. Kate Leila. Westward With Dragoons. Tells of the building of Fort Osage.

Hanson, Joseph Mills. The Conquest of the Missouri. Chicago, 1909. Being the story of the life and exploits of Captain Grant Marsh.

Harris, Edward. Up the River with Audubon. Edited by John Francis McDermott. Norman, 1951.

Heckman, Captain William L. Steamboating. Kansas City, 1950. Lively reminiscences of sixty-five years on Missouri's rivers.

Hewitt, J.N.B., editor, Journal of Rudolph Friederich Kurz. Bulletin No. 15 of Bureau of American Ethnology. Washington, 1937.

Larpenteur, Charles. Forty Years a Fur Trader on the Upper Missouri. New York, 1898. Personal narrative of experiences between 1833 and 1872. Edited by Elliot Coues.

Lewis, Meriwether. History of the Expedition of Captains Lewis and Clark. 1814.

Margry, Pierre, editor. Discoveries and Establishments of the French Within the West (1614-1754). Typescript, Kansas City Public Library.

Maximilian, Prince zu Wied. Travels in the Interior of North America. Edited by Reuben Gold Thwaites. Cleveland, 1905.

Mondale, R.L. The Missouri Still Runs Wild. Kansas City, 1943.

Nasatir, Abraham Phineas. Before Lewis and Clark. Documents Illustrating the History of the Missouri River, 1785-1804. St. Louis, 1952.

Nebraska Historical Magazine. The Missouri River, Its Discovery, Its Region and Resources. Nebraska State Historical Society, Lincoln, 1927.

Neihardt, J.G. The River and I. New York, 1910.

James, Edwin. S.H. Long's Expedition, 1819-1820. Cleveland, 1905 (reprint).

Paden, Irene D. The Wake of the Prairie Schooner. New York, 1943.

Pancoast, Charles Edward. A Quaker Forty-Niner. Adventures on the American frontier. Philadelphia, 1930.

Pelzer, Louis. March of the Dragoons in the Mississippi Valley. 1917.

Pritchard, James A., the Overland Diary of, from Kentucky to California in 1849. Edited by Dale L. Morgan. Denver, 1959.

Sharp, Paul F. Whoop-Up Country: The Canadian-American

West, 1865-1885. Minneapolis, 1955. Particularly good for Fort Benton and surrounding area. Much scholarly research.

Spalding, C.C. Annals of the City of Kansas. Kansas City, 1858. Reprint, Kansas City 1950.

Stevens, W.B. One Hundred Years on the Missouri River. Missouri Valley Historical Society of Kansas City, 1921.

Van Osdel, A.L. Historical Landmarks. N.p. 1951. A list of early explorers and fur traders, with a narrative of their adventures in the wilds of the Northwest Territory.

Vestal, Stanley. The Missouri. 1945. A true conspectus, but the author too frequently go beyond sound of the steamboat's whistle.

Wyman, Walker Demarcuis. The Missouri River Towns in the Westward Movement. Iowa City, 1938.

———. Missouri River Steamboats. Nebraska History, April-June, 1946.

Wilhelm, Paul, Duke of Wurttemberg. First Journey to North America in the Years 1822 to 1824.

Stuttgart, 1835. Translated from the German by Dr. William G. Bek in the South Dakota Historical Collections, 1938.

Steamboats and Captains
On The Missouri River 1820–1870

A. B. Chambers ....
.................Capt Alexander Gillham
A. C. Goddin.................Capt Jack Ivers
A. G. Bird ....
A. M. Phillips.................................
A. S. Bennett ....
Admiral No. 1..................................
Admiral No. 2..................................
Agatha ....
Alert ....
Alex Kendall...................................
Alexander Hamilton
..............................Capt W. H. Hooper
Algoma ....Capt B. Yount
Alice No. 1 ....
Allegheny Mail....Capt Preston Brown
Alton ....
Amaranth.....Capt George A. Atchison
Amazon ....Capt Pierre Chouteau
Annawan...
Annie Lee ....
Antelope..
Anthony Wayne ....
Arabia ....Capt John S. Shaw
Archer.................Capt Henry J. Moore
Argus ....Capt Crooks
Arrow ....Capt James McCord
Asa Wilgus.........Capt Ashley Hopkins
Assiniboine ...Capt Bernard "Pratt, Jr."
Australia........................Capt McMullin
Balloon.................Master William Post
Banner State ....
Bay State ....
Belfast ....
Belle Creole ....
Belle of Jefferson ....
Belle of Peoria................................
Belle of St. Louis............................
Ben Bolt ....Capt Ambrose Reeder
Ben W. Lewis ....

Ben Johnson ....
Benton.................Capt Thomas W. Rea
Benton No.2 ....Capt John B. LaBarge
Bertrand.......................Capt James Yore
Big Horn No.4 ....
Big Horser ....
Billow No. 2 ....
Black Hills ....
Bluff City ....Capt John McCloy
Boreas No. 2 ....Capt Wall
Bowling Green ....Capt John J. Roe
Brazil...
Bridgewater ....
Brighton...
Brooklyn ....
Brunette ....
Brunswick ....
Butte ....
C. K. Peck ....
C. W. Mead ....
C. W. SombartCapt Henry McPherson
Calhoun ....
Cambria ....
Camden ....
Capital City.....................................
Capitola ....
Car of Commerce ....Capt Read
Caraway ....
Carrier ....Capt Henry McPherson
Carroll No. 1 ....Capt Weath
Carroll No. 2 ....
Cataract ....Capt Lou A. Welton
Chariton.................Master Mr. Perkins
Charles H. Green.............................
Charles P. Carroll ....
Chenowith.......................................
Cheyenne ....
Chieftan...............Capt John Shallcross
Chippewa ....Capt Crabtree
Cincinnati.......................Capt Embree

234

Frederick..

Frolic ....

Gate City ....

General Brady..

General Brooke...Capt Joseph LaBarge

General Charles H. Tompkins...............

General Custer ....

General Lane..

General Leavenworth .Master J. White

General Meade ....

General Neville ....Capt Crawford

General Terry..

General William B. Ashley
.........................Capt James Sweeney

Geneva No. 1 ....

Genoa..

General D. H. Buckner ....

George C. Wolf ....

George Spangler......................................

Georgetown ....

Gerald B. Allen ....Capt D. L. Keiser

Globe ....Capt Andrew Wineland

Gloster ....Master Mr. Williams

Gold Dust ....Capt John T. McCord

Golden State ....

Governor Allen..

Gus Fowler...

H. C. Coleman ....

Haidee..................Capt William Phelps

Haidee ....Capt Jacob Tice

Haidee.................Capt Joseph Bordeau

Halcyon...........................Capt Shepherd

Harry Clyde...

Headlight ....Capt William C. Postal

Henry Bry ....Capt JohnW. Luke

Henry K. Johnstone.........Capt Bristow

Henry Lewis.............Capt A. Emerson

Herald ....Capt Joseph Nanson

Hermann......................Capt Tom Baker

Hiawatha..

Hibernian ....

Highland Mary ....Capt Baldwin

Howard ....

Hungarian ....

Huntsville ....Capt William Miller

Iatan ....

Ida Reese No. 2
.................Capt Grant Prince Marsh

Illinois ....

Independence..........Capt. John Nelson

Isabel ....

J. F. Jay ....

J. P. Page ....

J. S. Pringle...

James E. Rankin ....

James Monroe...

James Mulligan ....

John Aull ....

John Golong..Master William B. Baker

John Hancock ....

John J. Hardin................Capt Douglass

John Nelson ....Capt John Shallcross

John R. Hugo ....

John Warner ....

Josephine ....

Judith ....

Julian No. 2 ....Capt John McCloy

Julie No. 1 ....Master J. M. Converse

Kansas.............Capt Henry McPherson

Kansaz ....

Kate Kinney..........Capt Joseph Kinney

Kate Swinney ....Capt Pierre Chouteau

Key West......Capt Grant Prince Marsh

Keystone..........Capt Thomas I Goddin

Kinney ....

Kit Carson ......Capt Nathaniel J. Eaton

Lake of the Woods .Capt Frank Dozier

Last Chance..

Leander..

Lebanon...

Lehigh..

Lewis F. Linn
.....Capt William C. "Dandy" Jewett

Lexington ....

Liberty.......................Capt J. B. Bonsett

Lightfoot............................Capt Henry

Lilly Maud ....

Little Livingstone ....

Little Mail..

Little Missouri ....Capt Bob Wright

Lloyd...
Louisa.......................CaptWill H. Wood
Louisville...
Low Water..
Lucy Lee...
Lynchburg..
M. S. Mephan...Capt Charles K. Baker
Magenta...................Capt Frank Dozier
Magnet.....................Capt W. McKnight
Maid of Orlean......................................
Maid of the Osage
........................Capt Nansen Bennett
Mandan ....Capt William Linn
Mandan......................Capt Harry Blees
Manhattan...........Master Mr. Dohlman
Marcella..
Margaret................Capt Joseph Kinney
Martha ....Capt Joseph LaBarge
Martha Aull ....Capt Jorgenson
Martha Jewett...
Mary ....Capt Fulkerson
Mary Blanc..
Mary Lowry...
Mary Thompkins...Capt Henry J. Beer
Maryland...
Mattie Belle ....
Mattie Lee ....
May Bryan...
Mendota ....
Mercer...
Messenger Boy ....
Meteor ....Capt Draffen
Midas ....
Minnesota..
Missouri...
Missouri Belle ..Capt William Littleton
Missouri Mail ....Capt Middleton
Missouri Packet.......................................
Monona ....Capt Nick Wall
Monongahela...
Monroe ....L. l. McLean
Monsoon...
Mountaineer ....Capt J. R. Spriggs
Muskingum...................Capt Mirabeau
Mustang ....Capt Patterson

Naomi ....Capt James McCord
Native ....
Ne Plus Ultra ....
Nellie Peck...Capt Grant Prince Marsh
New Haven...
Nile ....Capt Grant Prince Marsh
Nimrod ....Capt Dennis
Nodaway....................Capt John J. Roe
North Star ....
Oceana.................................Capt Miller
Octavia ....Capt Joseph LaBarge
Omega ....
Ontario...
Oregon.................................Capt Green
Osage ....
Osage Packet.......... Benjamin B. Bryan
Osage Vallley ....Capt Young
Otoe ....Capt James B. Hill
Otter......................Capt Abram Shinkle
Paragon...................Capt John McCloy
Patrick Henry ......Master D. C. Adams
Paul Jones ....Capt J. B. Doles
Pearl No.2...
Perry Belle...
Peter Balen ....
Petrel ....
Phil E. Chappell ....Master J. A. Ware
Phillos ....
Pin Oak..
Pirate ....
Pittsburg ....
Platte ....
Platte Valley.....Capt William C. Postal
Plattsmouth..
Plough Boy........................Capt Burnett
Plow Boy No.1.....................Capt Davis
Pocahontas No. 1Capt Henry J. Moore
Polar Star ....Capt Thomas H. Brierly
Pontiac ....
Post Boy...
Potosi ....
Prairie Bird ....
Princeton ....
R. W. Dugan...
R. Whitman...

R.M. Johnson ....Capt Colfax
Radnor ....Capt J. R. Douglas
Red Cloud ....
Reindeer ....
Republic...
Rhine ....Capt James McCord
Rob Roy ....
Robert Campbell ....
Robert Campbell No. 1
............................Capt William Edds
Roebuck...
Rosebud No.2 ....
Sacramento ....Capt Robert Beekers
Salada ....Capt F. T. Belt
Sam Gloon..............Capt John McCloy
San Caty ....Capt Frank Dozier
San Francisco .Capt Mortimer Kennett
Saranac No. 3 ....Capt Saltmarsh
Saranak ....
Selkirk..
Seventy-Six..
Shoal Water ....
Silver City ....
Silver Heels.....................Capt Barrows
Silver Wave ....
Skylark ....Capt Sousley
Sonora..
Sovereign...
Spread Eagle ....Capt Ben Johnson
"St, Louis Oak" ......Capt James Dozier
St. Ange ....Capt Thomas W. Scott
St. Anthony No. 2 .....Capt J. Gunsollis
St. Charles ....
St. Croix No. 1 ....Capt Hiram Bersie
St. Joseph ......Capt William "B," Baker
St. Louis ....Capt George Taylor
St. Louis Packet Capt. Alexander Scott
St. Luke ....Capt Joseph Kinney
St. Mary ....Capt Joseph LaBarge
St. Nicholas..................Capt Ben Glime
St. Paul ....Capt J. L. Bissell
St. Peters........................Capt Chouteau
Star of the West...........Capt Parkinson
Stella Blanch ....
Stonewall ....Capt J. P. McKinney

Sultan ....Capt John McCloy
Susie Silver...............Capt David Silver
T. T. Hilman ....
Talisman................Master J. W. Pollock
Tallyrand ....
Tamerlane ....Capt Miller
Tempest No. 2...
Thames ....Capt Dennis
Thomas E. Tutt.........Capt P. M. Dozier
Thomas Jefferson ....Capt. H. J. Offut
Timour No. 1 ....
Tioga ....
Tobacco Plant..
Tom Rogers ....
Transient..
Trenton...
Tributary..
Tropic ....
Tuscumbia ....
Twilight ....
Tyler ....Capt John Gunsaullis
Umpire..
Union ....Capt W. Bennett
Union....................Master Mr. Symmes
Vienna ....
Violet ....
W. B. Dance ....Capt George Boyd
W. H. Russell ....Capt Joseph Kinney
W. J. Behan ....
W. J. Lewis ....Capt E. T. Herndon
W. J. Lewis No. 2.......................................
Wakenda..
Walter Scott..............Capt W. B. Culver
WapelloCapt Nathaniel Jackson Eaton
War Eagle...............................Capt Wall
Warden Pope ....
Warrior .....Capt Joseph Throckmorton
Warsaw ....
Washington
..............Capt. Henry Miller Shreve
Watosa ....
Wave ....Capt William Waldo
Waverly ....Capt John "P," Keiser
Waverly ....Capt Thomas W. Rea
Welcome ....Capt Thomas Townsend

Wenona ....Capt Robert M. Barclay
West Wind ....Capt Ray
Western Engineer ....
Whirlwind ....Capt Dodge
White Cloud ....
White Eagle...
Wild Wagoner ....Capt A. C. Goddin
William Baird...
William D. Duncan...........Capt Crooks
William Paris ....
Wilmington.................Master C. F. Gay
Wyandotte...................Capt James Yore
Wyoming ....Capt Coulson
Yellowstone ....Capt B. Young
Yuba ....
Yucatan.............................Capt S. Banks
Zebulon M. Pike ....Capt Jacob Reed

Index